Spenserian satire

Manchester University Press

The Manchester Spenser

The Manchester Spenser is a monograph and text series devoted to historical and textual approaches to Edmund Spenser – to his life, times, places, works and contemporaries.

A growing body of work in Spenser and Renaissance studies, fresh with confidence and curiosity and based on solid historical research, is being written in response to a general sense that our ability to interpret texts is becoming limited without the excavation of further knowledge. So the importance of research in nearby disciplines is quickly being recognised, and interest renewed: history, archaeology, religious or theological history, book history, translation, lexicography, commentary and glossary – these require treatment for and by students of Spenser.

The Manchester Spenser, to feed, foster and build on these refreshed attitudes, aims to publish reference tools, critical, historical, biographical and archaeological monographs on or related to Spenser, from several disciplines, and to publish editions of primary sources and classroom texts of a more wide-ranging scope.

The Manchester Spenser consists of work with stamina, high standards of scholarship and research, adroit handling of evidence, rigour of argument, exposition and documentation.

The series will encourage and assist research into, and develop the readership of, one of the richest and most complex writers of the early modern period.

General Editor   J.B. Lethbridge
Assistant General Editor   Joshua Reid
Editorial Board Helen Cooper, Thomas Herron,
James C. Nohrnberg & Brian Vickers

Also available
Literary Ralegh and visual Ralegh   Christopher M. Armitage (ed.)
A Concordance to the Rhymes of The Faerie Queene   Richard Danson Brown
& J.B. Lethbridge
A Supplement of the Faery Queene: By Ralph Knevet   Christopher Burlinson
& Andrew Zurcher (eds)
Pastoral poetry of the English Renaissance: An anthology   Sukanta Chaudhuri (ed.)
*Spenserian allegory and Elizabethan biblical exegesis:
A context for* The Faerie Queene   Margaret Christian
*Monsters and the poetic imagination in Edmund Spenser's 'The Faerie Queene':
Most ugly shapes and horrible aspects'*   Maik Goth
Celebrating Mutabilitie: Essays on Edmund Spenser's Mutabilitie Cantos   Jane Grogan (ed.)
Castles and Colonists: An archaeology of Elizabethan Ireland   Eric Klingelhofer
Shakespeare and Spenser: Attractive opposites   J.B. Lethbridge (ed.)
A Fig for Fortune: By Anthony Copley   Susannah Brietz Monta
Spenser and Virgil: The pastoral poems   Syrithe Pugh
*Renaissance erotic romance: Philhellene Protestantism, renaissance translation
and English literary politics*   Victor Skretkowicz
God's only daughter: Spenser's Una as the invisible Church   Kathryn Walls

Spenserian satire

A tradition of indirection

RACHEL E. HILE

Manchester University Press

Copyright © Rachel E. Hile 2017

The right of Rachel E. Hile to be identified as the author of this work has been asserted by her in accordance with the Copyright, Designs and Patents Act 1988.

An electronic version of this book is also available under a Creative Commons (CC-BY-NC-ND) licence, which permits non-commercial use, distribution and reproduction provided the author and Manchester University Press are fully cited and no modifications or adaptations are made. Details of the licence can be viewed at https://creativecommons.org/licenses/by-nc-nd/2.0/uk/

Published by Manchester University Press
Altrincham Street, Manchester M1 7JA, UK
www.manchesteruniversitypress.co.uk

British Library Cataloguing-in-Publication Data is available

ISBN 978 0 7190 8808 7 *hardback*
ISBN 978 1 5261 3951 1 *paperback*

First published by Manchester University Press in hardback 2017

This edition first published 2019

The publisher has no responsibility for the persistence or accuracy of URLs for any external or third-party internet websites referred to in this book, and does not guarantee that any content on such websites is, or will remain, accurate or appropriate.

Contents

	Acknowledgments	*page* vii
	Introduction	1
1	Indirect satire: theory and Spenserian practice	11
2	Spenser's satire of indirection: affiliation, allusion, allegory	38
3	Spenser and the English literary system in the 1590s	64
4	Spenserian "entry codes" to indirect satire	87
5	Thomas Middleton's satires before and after the Bishops' Ban	119
6	After the Bishops' Ban: imitation of Spenserian satire	145
	Conclusion	173
	Bibliography	177
	Index	196

Acknowledgments

I am grateful to know so many smart people who took the time to think and talk with me about the ideas presented in this book. I owe so many improvements in this manuscript to feedback from friends and colleagues including Erin Ashworth-King, David Bergeron, Felicia Bonaparte, Bruce Danner, Joel Davis, Kathryn DeZur, Carl Drummond, Andrew Escobedo, Sam Fallon, Jean Goodrich, Sinikka Grant, Richard Hardin, Paul Hecht, Sean Henry, Thomas Herron, Denna Iammarino, William Kerwin, Roger Kuin, Ann Livschiz, Scott Lucas, Catherine Martin, William Oram, Anne Lake Prescott, Beth Quitslund, Mark Rankin, Ernest Rufleth, Yulia Ryzhik, William Smith III, John Staines, Theodore Steinberg, Robert Stillman, Andrew Strycharski, Donald Stump, Jennifer Vaught, and David Wilson-Okamura.

I am fortunate to work at an institution that values and supports research in the humanities. I thank Indiana University-Purdue University Fort Wayne (IPFW) for awarding me a summer research grant in 2012 and a sabbatical leave in spring 2013. Priceless support and help came from the librarians at the Walter E. Helmke Library at IPFW, whose commitment to and skill in connecting people with the information that they want overwhelms me with gratitude frequently. Many thanks to Julian Lethbridge and Joshua Reid, series editors for The Manchester Spenser, for their good counsel.

I am grateful to the friends and family members who make my life better, too many to list, but special thanks to Ralph and Mary Anne Hile, Melissa Hile, Joey Bassett, Helen Bassett, and Steve Wells. My husband, Steve Wells, through his support and encouragement, was the doula for this book.

For my teachers

I have dedicated this book to my English teachers, and some deserve special appreciation. Norma Haraughty and Frank Robertson, my sixth-grade and twelfth-grade teachers, nurtured my love of language and literature with their own enthusiasm and good humor. The late Joel J. Gold was a good teacher to me in college and in graduate school, and I know I helped him by serving as the source of one of his many amusing anecdotes (the one about the greedy eyes of a graduate student offered free books).

To David M. Bergeron, who chaired my comprehensive exam committee, and to Richard F. Hardin, who chaired my dissertation committee, I owe incalculable debts for the help and guidance they gave me in developing as a reader, a scholar, a thinker, and a writer. In David's Shakespeare class, I learned the joy of textual scholarship and, along with Michelle Stie and Susan Dunn-Hensley, how to really study for a terrifying exam. He also taught me much about the nuts and bolts of writing and, with his husband Geraldo de Sousa, the beauty of a lifetime of scholarly generosity and community. To Dick Hardin I owe the ability to locate and extirpate unsupported generalizations and extensive in-text material that should be radically shortened and moved to a footnote. I am grateful to Dick for many of the best pieces of advice I have ever received, and to him and his wife Virginia for countless instances of hospitality to me and my family, both when I was a graduate student and up to the present.

I am so fortunate to be in a field with such a caring and generous spirit of community, and my friends among the Spenser and Sidney scholarly circle have become, and will continue to be, my English teachers. I am especially grateful to Mary Ellen Lamb, Roger Kuin, Anne Lake Prescott, and other regulars at the Kalamazoo Medieval Congress.

Introduction

We know that all texts are indeterminate, incomplete ... but some are *extra*-indeterminate, written by design to be *extra*-incomplete, to require, more than other texts, that the reader transfer meaning from other texts and from other semiotic fields altogether in order to correctly interpret the meaning. This book focuses on one such type of text, what I call "indirect satire," by which I mean satirical writing that the reader cannot understand *as satire* without this intersemiotic transfer of meaning into the textual interpretation. Sometimes, in the densely allusive literary culture of the early modern period, intertextual transfer suffices to "get" the joke, and much of this book will focus on indirect satirical writing that uses intertextuality, especially with Spenser's works, to create its satirical meanings. However, intersemiosis is a broader term than intertextuality, and another project of this book is to explore literary fame and ideas of "the Author" as a semiotic system used by the satirical poets discussed in this book in order to position themselves within the literary field and to clue the reader to search for indirect satirical meanings. By looking at textual indeterminacy in this way, I am thinking about the *process* of interpretation, rather than the *products* of interpretation, in order to shift the focus away from efforts to "fix," through interpretive certainty, texts that were written with the goal of resisting all such certainty in order to protect the author from punishment or censorship.

Speaking of *The Faerie Queene*, T.K. Dunseath wrote in 1968, "Unless the study of historical allegory can further the larger understanding of Spenser's poem, its single pursuit becomes self-serving, a pointless exercise in scholarly ingenuity" (Dunseath, *Spenser's Allegory*, 6). Surely he was reacting, entirely consistently with New Critical scholarly fashion, against the worst excesses of what came to be known—once the New Historicism had been born—as the "old historicism," the often entirely too ingenious searching after point-for-point correspondences between poem and history. The approach characterized literary scholarship of the early twentieth century but was especially pronounced in studies of satirical and allegorical works, where scholarship often ended with identification rather than interpretation. In Spenser studies, the endless wrangling of early twentieth-century scholars over the "true" identities of *Mother Hubberds Tale*'s Fox and Ape, or of *Muiopotmos*'s Clarion and Aragnoll, at the remove of almost a century, seems … academic, perhaps even unimportant.[1] To be fair, though, more recent attempts to connect Spenser's satirical poetry to his historical moment suffer from the same indeterminacy, leading to interpretive proliferation: Is Radigund a mirror for Queen Elizabeth or an allegorical representation of Mary, Queen of Scots?[2] In *Mother Hubberds Tale*, does Spenser criticize the English or the Irish political situation?[3] And so on.

Different waves of critical fashion have responded to this textual indeterminacy differently. The Old Historicists erred on the side of ignoring it, asserting a certainty regarding identifications that the sheer number of competing identifications rules out. The New Critics avoided the question, focusing their attention on the text; concomitantly, the privileging of text over context meant a critical devaluation of clearly topical satires as holding little interest for present-day readers. The New Historicists provide more nuanced readings of connections between text and historical context, and certainly more cautious identifications.

In the present study, I occasionally attempt to provide identifications of various satiremes (i.e., the smallest meaningful unit of a satire), and there are, assuredly, plenty of close readings of texts. However, I focus here primarily on reading satirical texts of the late sixteenth and early seventeenth centuries in relation to one another, with specific attention to the role that Edmund Spenser plays in that literary subsystem. I aim to argue a number of points, which will be of interest to varying audiences. For Spenser scholars, who recognize Spenser's supremacy in "serious poetry" of the period and have carefully studied his influence on epic, pastoral, and lyric poetry, my analysis of Spenser's reputation as a satirical poet will contribute to our understanding of Spenser as "the poet's poet." For scholars of satire, I offer a fuller discussion and theorization of the type of satire that Spenser wrote, what I call "indirect satire,"

---

1 See Danner (*Edmund Spenser's War*, 190–91), for a summary of some early twentieth-century identifications of the characters in *Mother Hubberds Tale*; for a sampling of some identifications proposed for *Muiopotmos*, see Chapter 4 below.
2 See, respectively, Villeponteaux ("Not as women," 218) and Stump ("Two deaths," 99).
3 See, respectively, Herron ("Reforming the fox") and Danner (*Edmund Spenser's War*, chapter 5).

than has been provided elsewhere. Spenser's satire does not fit well into the rather blunt categories of Juvenalian, Horatian, Menippean that have been used to taxonomize satirical writing from the classical era up to the eighteenth century, but including him with the complaint tradition is also imprecise.[4] A theory of indirect satire benefits not just Spenser studies but satire studies as well. Finally, for scholars of English Renaissance satire in particular, who have tended to focus on the formal verse satires of the 1590s to the exclusion of attention to more indirect forms such as Spenser's, this book is a corrective, an invitation to recognize the merits of, and acknowledge the wider influence of, a style of satire that has received little attention.

The world that Milton made: a speculation on Spenserian satire

So what happened to indirect satire, the form of satire in which Spenser was so influential? I believe that, in England, this satirical tradition simply withered away when the increasing freedom of the press rendered it less useful, less necessary. We can presumably agree on the innumerable intellectual, moral, and political benefits that follow from freedom of expression. To the extent that we give credit for the widespread enjoyment of this freedom to John Milton, whose arguments in *Areopagitica* (1644) contributed to the loosening of restrictions on the press in the late seventeenth and early eighteenth centuries, we also owe him gratitude for the flourishing of satirical writing in eighteenth-century England. However, this greater freedom, which allowed satirists to write with fewer constraints and less fear, meant the decline of the tradition of indirect satirical writing, a type of satire exemplified by Edmund Spenser and imitated or alluded to by numerous other writers in the late sixteenth and early seventeenth centuries. Greater freedom of the press made a dead end of England's indirect satirical tradition, which developed out of the medieval complaint and reached its apex with Spenser and the Spenserian satire of his contemporaries, and thus we can, if we wish, blame John Milton for the scholarly neglect of the Spenserian tradition in satire.

Whether or not you join me in blaming Milton, I aim in this book to write Spenser back in to the history of satire, considering the ways that he and others who followed his lead responded to the censorship

4 Richard Danson Brown, focusing on the "newness" of Spenser's poetic project, describes the poems of the *Complaints* volume as "renovation of traditional complaint" (*The New Poet*, 11). Whereas Brown looks at the ways that Spenser diverges from traditional complaint, I here analyze some of the same works as outliers to the tradition of satire, and thus, from different directions, we both find Spenser forging his own path.

conditions of their day by creating satires more indirect than the harsher English genealogy of satire that paid homage to the Roman Juvenal, such as the verse satires fashionable in the 1590s and the more urbane but no less caustic satirical writings of the eighteenth century. Alvin Kernan famously considered the "satiric personality" recognizable in any number of early modern English satirical works, the personality vividly expressed in the unseemly narrative voices of the formal verse satires of the 1590s (Kernan, *Cankered Muse*). Kernan's privileging of the rough "satyr" approach to satire represents a fairly common critical approach, which has led to neglect of Edmund Spenser's contributions to the mode. John Peter's 1956 dismissal of Spenser's satirical work seems to have set the tone: "Spenser ... whatever his interest in another context, is hardly a key-figure in the development of Satire. His allegorical method is distinctly medieval ... , more easily related to the allegorical method used elsewhere in his own poems than to any trend or tradition that we examine here. Beyond Drayton's *The Owle*, moreover ... it seems to have had very little contemporary influence" (Peter, *Complaint and Satire*, 132–33). This despite Hoyt Hudson's painstaking article, published more than twenty years earlier, detailing the Spenserian debts of five other beast fables in addition to *The Owle*. In the same year as Peter's book, Ellen Douglass Leyburn, despite her sympathy for the allegorical mode of satire, nevertheless damned Spenser's best-known satire, not for being allegorical but for failing allegorically: "*Mother Hubberds Tale* is passionate satire, but it fails as a work of art because the satire is not allegorically realized" (Leyburn, *Satiric Allegory*, 136). In general, the prescriptivism of mid-twentieth-century approaches to satire left Spenser forgotten or undervalued because his contributions to the mode fit poorly with various ideas about how satire *should* work.

Unfortunately, not only early modern English scholars but theorists of satire as well have tended to focus on the harsher varieties of satire, and this leads to blind spots in the critical endeavor: if a theory of satire seems a better fit with John Marston than with Spenser—as do Robert C. Elliott's idea of satire as stemming from magic rituals of exclusion and Fredric Bogel's more recent and comprehensive view of satire as a broadly social ritual of exclusion (Elliott, *Power of Satire*; Bogel, *Difference Satire Makes*)—then the very definition will make Spenser seem less important as a satirist, and thus those interested in Spenser will privilege his other works and those interested in satire will examine other writers, and never the twain shall meet. Broad theories of satire that aim to account for the "satiric impulse" or "satire through the ages" will of necessity ignore the outliers, but, in the case of Elizabethan Spenserian satire, the works lie outside of the historical mainstream largely because of the political situation in which the authors wrote—it seems unfair to blame them for not meeting some imaginary ideal of "satirical-ness" when hands and lives were on the line (as with John Stubbs and John Penry, respectively, with Stubbs losing a hand in 1579 for authoring *The Discovery of a Gaping Gulf* and Penry his life in 1593 for his role in printing the Martin Marprelate tracts). Annabel Patterson describes political censorship in Elizabethan England as "so pervasive that it rose to the forefront ... as the central problem of consciousness and communication"; she believes that, far from being misunderstood or obfuscated, "the prevailing codes of communication, the implicit social contract between authors and authorities, [was] intelligible to all parties at the time, as being a fully deliberate and conscious arrangement" (Patterson, *Censorship and Interpretation*, 17). Cyndia Clegg, aiming to persuade readers that the extent of *literary* censorship in Elizabethan England was less than scholars have traditionally thought, works against her own argument by concluding her book with the observation that "literature became the object of scrutiny when poets exceeded their liberty or when the conditions of reading drew a literary text into the political domain," suggesting a depoliticized understanding of what literature *is* that is at odds with the historical record (Clegg, *Press Censorship Elizabethan*, 224). The subtext seems to be that literary authors were safe as long as they made no attempts to make anything happen in the real world with their scribblings—poets' "liberty to speak," radical in Skelton's *Speke Parott* and a touchstone for poets for the next century, in this view extends to the point of impact or influence, and then dies.

The censorship of Stubbs's *The Discovery of a Gaping Gulf*, an aggressive Puritan warning against Queen Elizabeth's possible marriage with the Duc d'Alençon, coincided with Spenser's first independent publication and serves as an important context for thinking about how the young man approached the issue of a poet's "liberty to speak." In November 1579, Stubbs had his right hand chopped off as punishment for writing *Discovery of a Gaping Gulf*; a distributor, William Page, lost his hand as well, but printer-publisher Hugh Singleton received a pardon.[5] In the following month, Singleton brought out Spenser's *Shepheardes Calender*. Numerous scholars have examined the implications of this publishing relationship with reference to what it tells us about Spenser's politics

---

5 See Clegg (*Press Censorship Elizabethan*, chapter 6) for details of the incident. For details of the life and career of Hugh Singleton, see Byrom, "Edmund Spenser's first publisher."

and religion;[6] I mention it here to support my contention that Spenser, throughout his career, had a sensitive awareness of the *realpolitik* of the dissent system in England. His writing shows him to have been thoughtful and deliberate—perhaps even cautious—leading to his desire to maintain the equilibrium of the system by voicing criticisms indirectly. He was no Stubbs, which benefited him when he did disturb the system with his 1591 *Complaints* volume, because although the authorities "punished" the book by calling it in, the author's career continued to flourish, and the £50 annuity awarded to Spenser in recognition of the 1590 installment of *The Faerie Queene* continued to be paid until his death.[7]

Scholars have found satire, at least episodically, in *The Shepheardes Calender*, in *The Faerie Queene*, and in the poems of the *Complaints* volume, and Spenser's ideas, shared with many contemporaries, about the moral leadership role of the true poet confirm the sense that Spenser viewed himself as more a teacher than an entertainer. He managed to express a number of criticisms of those in power, but indirectly enough to make the criticisms deniable if necessary, and in this he followed the practice of earlier English poets such as John Skelton and Thomas Churchyard. Scott Lucas describes the strategy as the attempt "to seek rhetorical forms that could at once maximize the communicative function of their works while minimizing the chance that hostile readers could use their own words against them as evidence of offensive intent" (Lucas, "Diggon Davie," 152). This need to balance communication with obfuscation complicates analysis, especially at the remove of four hundred years, but finding traces of this effort again and again in Spenser, and in poets who imitated or alluded to his satirical works during and after his life, suggests the need to create a more detailed and rigorous theory of indirect satire.

---

6 Beginning with Byrom, of course, but also see more recent comments (with more nuance regarding Singleton's Puritanism) such as Norbrook (*Poetry and Politics*, 63) and King (*Spenser's Poetry*, 234–36).

7 *Complaints* was entered in the Stationers' Register December 29, 1590; the annuity was awarded to Spenser in February 1591 (new style), and the letter from Sir Thomas Tresham that gives news of the recall of copies of *Complaints* was dated March 19, 1591 (new style). For a discussion of the annuity with reference to the publication of *Complaints*, see Brink ("Who fashioned Edmund Spenser?") and Hile ("Edmund Spenser"); for the timing of the publication and censorship of *Complaints*, see Peterson ("Laurel crown"); for the ongoing payment of the annuity, see Berry and Timings ("Spenser's pension"). In a recent unpublished paper, Jean R. Brink has argued that Spenser sold his pension to Thomas Walker (Brink, "Spenser's death revisited," 49th International Congress on Medieval Studies, Kalamazoo, MI, May 8–11, 2014). Whether Berry and Timings or Brink is correct does not affect my point here, which centers on Spenser's staying sufficiently in the good graces of the court that his pension was not affected by the uproar over the *Complaints* volume.

Critics working on satire in the past two decades have deplored the limited influence of recent literary theory on studies of satire, with Dustin Griffin blaming the complexity and diversity of satire, which make categorization and generalization difficult, and Fredric Bogel blaming the resistance to theory among scholars of eighteenth-century literature (Griffin, *Satire*, 31; Bogel, *Difference Satire Makes*, 5). The attempts by these and other scholars to rectify this situation through more careful attention to theoretical understandings of satire are all to the good, but because these more recent satire theorists have largely focused on the eighteenth century, their findings are of limited applicability in understanding the characteristic approach to satire of poets like Spenser and his admirers and imitators in the late sixteenth and early seventeenth centuries. Those theorists who have addressed allegorical satire have tended to do so cursorily and often unsatisfactorily: Dustin Griffin lumps together allegorical satire with the grab-bag of Menippean satire; Kirk Combe categorizes it as belonging to the complaint tradition of satire, but his undisguised preference for the "satire" that he contrasts with his strawman "complaint" limits the usefulness of his observations on the "sniveling grievances and blurry hopes for amelioration" that he sees as characteristic of the complaint; George A. Test follows Ellen Douglass Leyburn in collapsing the distinction between satire and allegory by stating that both work by "indirection," a conclusion that, because of its generality, is difficult both to argue against and to use productively (Griffin, *Satire*, 109; Combe, "New voice," 77; Leyburn, *Satiric Allegory*, 7; Test, *Satire*, 187).

I do not believe that all satire necessarily operates through indirection; however, indirect methods of satirical signification characterize Spenser's practice and are thus the focus of this study. Before looking at specific examples of satirical writing in Spenser and his imitators, I devote the first chapter to an analysis of indirect meaning-making in satire, discussing how allusion, symbol, and analogy can work to create allegorical satirical meanings that invite the reader to project insights from the text to the real world. Chapter 1 explores the literary, natural-historical, symbolic, and allegorical meanings that Spenser's culture attached to foxes in order to give a sense of the complexity of Spenser's use of animal imagery to create indirect satire in his most famous satirical character, the Fox of *Mother Hubberds Tale*. This book does not offer an exhaustive analysis of Spenser's entire corpus of work, instead examining a few key texts before shifting the focus to Spenser's influence on and meaning for younger poets who imitated him in their own satirical works. Chapter 1, however, closes with a sketch of Spenser's career as a satirist, aiming to create a sense of story and to connect the story of Spenser-as-satirist with better-known discussions of Spenser's career trajectory from such scholars as Richard Helgerson and Patrick Cheney.

Chapter 2 begins by discussing previous scholarly work on Spenserian satires—with reference to the ideas on indirect satire outlined in Chapter 1—before moving to an application of these ideas to two Spenserian contexts. First, I discuss Spenser's self-designation as "the New Poet" in *The Shepheardes Calender* as an allusion that signals satirical intent. Whereas the "Old Poet" referenced is clearly Chaucer, the phrase "new poet" itself serves as an allusion, setting up a satiric genealogy connecting Spenser to John Skelton and, through him, to Catullus (a poet who, though "new" to Cicero, was an "old" poet when the young Virgil briefly imitated him before rejecting his style to form his own). In the second half of the chapter, I consider Spenser's use of allegorical satire and allegory *as* satire in *Daphnaïda*, analyzing the ways that Spenser signals readers to interpret the poem satirically through playful use of allegory and metaphor.

With Chapter 3, I move the discussion from Spenser to a wider circle of influence, starting with two somewhat reductive views from contemporaries of what Spenser "meant" in the literary system of the late sixteenth and early seventeenth centuries. Two friends, Joseph Hall and William Bedell, wrote works that suggest an image of Spenser as an uncomplicated, straightforwardly decorous poet. Hall repeatedly alludes to well-known Spenserian images, which he imports into his own satires in *Virgidemiarum Six Bookes* in order to contrast them with his own disgusting imagery, suggesting an impatience with Spenser's well-known delicacy and decorum. The less truculent Bedell implies a similarly uncomplicated view of Spenser in his poorly executed Spenserian poem, *The Shepherd's Tale of the Pouder-Plott*, which takes as inspiration the Spenserian pastoral satire of *The Shepheardes Calender* and produces instead pastoral panegyric for King James I. In these two views of what "Spenser" meant to the writers of his time, we see the side of Spenser that Karl Marx later immortalized as "Elizabeth's arse-kissing poet."

But other writers found in Spenser, and particularly in his indirect satirical tools of allusion and allegory, inspiration for creating their own puzzlingly indirect works, and Chapter 4 provides two case studies. I explore the intertextual relationships between Thomas Nashe's *Choise of Valentines* and Spenser's "March" and between Tailboys Dymoke's *Caltha Poetarum* and Spenser's *Muiopotmos*, arguing that these poets use allusions to and intertextuality with Spenser to signal that the reader ought to read for allegorical satire. In Nashe's case, I believe that he creates his

Choise of Valentines in part to take satirical aim at Spenser himself, or, rather, the oversimplified version of "the decorous Spenser" discussed in Chapter 3, to suggest the foolishness of subscribing to idealizing views of love while also offering some sly insults to Frances Walsingham and Queen Elizabeth. The offense to the Queen is clearer, though still indirect, in *Caltha Poetarum*, and the second half of Chapter 4 uses that work to consider the possibility that some contemporary viewers found satire on Queen Elizabeth in Spenser's *Muiopotmos*. The chapter closes with a coda that aims to bring together the two halves of the chapter through a brief discussion of Shakespeare's *Venus and Adonis*.

Where Chapter 3 examines connections between literary works and their writers' ideas about "Spenser" as an author, and Chapter 4 puts five literary texts into conversation with one another, Chapter 5 considers two early works of Thomas Middleton with reference to the social and political context of the turn of the seventeenth century, with special attention to how the Bishops' Ban of 1599, which banned several books and restricted the future publication of satirical works, affected the literary subfield of satire in England. Following the 1591 calling-in of Spenser's *Complaints* volume, which included the satirical animal fable *Mother Hubberds Tale*, authors largely avoided publishing anything like an animal fable. I find, though, that the young Thomas Middleton wanted to signal his allegiance with the values and ideas espoused by Spenser, and that he does this indirectly in his 1599 *Micro-Cynicon* through allusions and analogies that render his formal verse satires circuitously Spenserian; his efforts to avoid offending were unsuccessful, and *Micro-Cynicon* was burned by order of the Bishops' Ban. Five years later, Middleton published a much more obviously Spenserian work that, with its nostalgia for Queen Elizabeth's reign and use of talking insects and birds, suggests more fully the ongoing importance of Spenser as an inspiration to the young poet Middleton before he became the dramatist Middleton. The chapter closes by briefly contrasting the pervasive Spenserianism of the young Middleton with John Donne's perhaps faddish use of animal fable in his *Metempsychosis; Poêma Satyricon*.

The final chapter looks at two moments in the early seventeenth century: Michael Drayton's response to the change of monarchs in two poems, *To the Maiestie of King James* from 1603 and *The Owle* from 1604, and George Wither's self-fashioning as a Spenserian satirist in a series of four texts a decade later, from *Abuses, Stript and Whipt* (1613) to *The Shepheards Hunting* (1615). In both cases, I find the authors signaling their allegiances to Spenser indirectly, with Drayton creating in *The Owle* an animal satire that references Spenser by alluding to his poetic forebears and Wither including pervasive animal and beast fable imagery in his formal verse satires in *Abuses, Stript and Whipt*. Significantly, though, the imprisonment that Wither endured as punishment for publishing *Abuses, Stript and Whipt* led to such an increase in his reputation as a courageous poet that he felt confident enough, in *The Shepheards Hunting*, to allegorize his own life and situation in ways that depict him as the new Spenserian satirist.

This book does not offer an unbroken and comprehensive narrative; rather, these are "explorations" or case studies, but nevertheless, there *is* a story here. Building on Annabel Patterson's characterization of political censorship in Elizabethan England as "the central problem of consciousness and communication" (*Censorship and Interpretation*, 17), this book aims to suggest the story of a code, the indirect satirical code that took many forms, only one of which was the Spenserian variety examined here. Indirection in satire is fun—the ingenuity required to crack the code offers pleasure to writer and reader alike—but it was also, in the period under consideration here, deadly serious, because a misstep could lead to censorship or imprisonment. Thinking about Spenser as both a real author grappling with these issues himself *and* as an idea, touchstone, or inspiration for other authors later trying to negotiate the same conflicts will, I hope, suggest to other scholars the potential fruitfulness of thinking more deeply and thoroughly about the forms that indirect satire can take.

1

Indirect satire: theory and Spenserian practice

In Edmund Spenser's *Prosopopoia; or, Mother Hubberds Tale*, a tonal shift characterizes the final episode, in which the villainous Fox and Ape, having wreaked havoc in the three estates as husbandmen, clerics, and courtiers, go even farther by usurping royal power. The self-conscious Chaucerianism of the first episodes—summarized by Kent van den Berg as "the recreative fiction that animals are like men"—gives way to a more fully developed, and more clearly satirical, fictional world in which "men are like animals" ("Counterfeit," 92). Fable shifts to allegory when the generic landscape of the first three episodes—a vaguely England-like place that has sheep, priests, a court, and so forth—becomes a more sharply focused fictional world, an allegorical world that invites the reader to make connections to the real world and real people. This changed relationship between the fictional world of *Mother Hubberds Tale* and the real England of its readers contributes to the shift from the feeling of medieval complaint to the indirect satire that is the subject of this book.

In this chapter, I aim to begin the process of thinking analytically about indirect satire, an understudied and undertheorized form of satirical writing. Numerous scholars have described Spenser's satirical methodology in ways that emphasize his efforts to balance goals of criticism with a strong impulse toward self-preservation: Lauren Silberman comments on the slipperiness of potential topical identifications in *Mother Hubberds Tale*: "As the poet holds up mirrors more than one to himself and his objects .... Spenser makes it virtually impossible to isolate a discrete political attack on an identifiable object" ("Aesopian," 237). Annabel Patterson, analyzing the repeated references to passports in the same poem, extends the concept metaphorically (by way of Sidney's "great passport of Poetry") to satirical poetry, which "becomes the safe-conduct by which criticism of church and state passes through the world with impunity" ("Still reading," 444). Speaking of *The Shepheardes Calender* as part of the broader tradition of sixteenth-century protest literature, Scott Lucas argues that authors of "potentially dangerous material" sought "rhetorical forms that could at once maximize the communicative function of their works while minimizing the chance that hostile readers could use their own words against them as evidence of offensive intent," a more direct expression of the metaphorically expressed ideas quoted from Patterson and Silberman (Lucas, "Diggon Davie," 152).

Thus, the *why* of Spenser's satirical methodology seems clear. I wish to add to the conversation an analysis of *what* indirect satire is and *how* authors such as Spenser and his imitators create literary works that convey criticisms of particular persons or institutions only through hints or allusions that prompt the crystallization of satirical meanings within the mind of the reader. In contrast to direct satire, which more or less clearly identifies its targets of criticism, both scholars and readers have a harder time identifying and interpreting indirect satire, because of the satirist's efforts to provide a smokescreen of deniability about criticisms launched at those with the power to punish. Thus, it is important to carve out space from the genres of fable, complaint, and pastoral for the indirect satirical poems written by Spenser and imitated by many others at the end of the sixteenth century.

Indirect satire, distinct from the less focused criticisms of humanity or society found in fables or complaint, which I will refer to as "general satire," creates a fictional world that references the real world—that is, an allegorical world—in order to criticize the real world. The author uses allusion, symbol, and analogy selectively to point the reader to make connections on the appropriate axes between the allegorical and real worlds. If we imagine the real world as one plane and the fictional allegorical world as a parallel plane, these indirect references serve to connect points on the real plane with points on the allegorical plane: more connecting lines make the reader's job of interpretation easier but increase the possibility of punitive or censoring retribution; fewer of these indirect references, of course, have the opposite effects, leading to the vanishing point of general satire found in fable, complaint, or pastoral, the genres that indirect satire often purported to be in the late sixteenth century.

Why call it "indirect satire" if allegory is a key to its creation of meaning? Why not call it "allegorical satire"? I focus on indirection because allegory is a pervasive mode of satirical meaning-making (and indeed, pervasive in literary meaning-making in general): the general satire one might find in a fable or pastoral derives from the allegorical connection between, say, the barnyard of the fable or the Arcadia of the pastoral and the real world of writer and reader. Even satires as direct in their attacks on targets as the Martin Marprelate tracts use allegory to create some meanings simply to be clever: what is the creation of the brothers Martin Junior and Martin Senior but an allegory representing the idea that repression of dissent will breed more dissent? Although I will focus repeatedly in this book on the way that "allegorical intuition"—which sometimes hits a reader in a flash midway through a poem with the sense that the work references the real world in some way—serves as a signal to seek and decipher satirical meanings, I interest myself here in the approach to and specificity of the writer's targets, with indirect satire toeing an uneasy line between general satire and direct satire.

The reader may intuit this sense that the author intends meaning beyond the text when the author's use of apparently benign modes such as complaint, fable, and pastoral is characterized by details that suggest that the fictional world of the work allegorizes the real world. Satire appears, in either large or small doses, in a number of Spenser's works, and the fruitfulness of his invention and his talent leads to a variety of forms, but Spenser's signature in satire is indirection, as we see him create countless ways of expressing criticism, contempt, disgust, without quite coming right out and saying it. Before moving into a more theoretical discussion of indirect satire, I will illustrate my points about the techniques of indirect satire by attention to Spenser's most famous satirical character, the Fox, with reference to the precursors of the figure.

The literary ancestry of Spenser's Fox

Of the two main characters in *Mother Hubberds Tale*, Spenser repeatedly emphasizes the greater guilt of the Fox: the first reference to the characters tells us that the Fox "misguided" the Ape, and the last reference calls him "first Author of that treacherie" (Spenser, *Mother Hubberds*, lines 38, 1379). In between, Spenser develops a portrait of a bloodthirsty, greedy, corrupt creature who aims for ever-increasing power, most importantly through his role as chief advisor to the Ape in his role as the false king. Whereas sixteenth-century allegorical satire often leads to readerly and critical dissension, with multiple competing hypotheses regarding attribution (including multiple scholarly disagreements about whom Spenser satirizes through the Ape), reading the Fox has been, from the beginning, uncomplicated: the Fox allegorically represents William Cecil, Lord Burghley, Queen Elizabeth's chief advisor. We know that Elizabethans interpreted Spenser's Fox as referring to Burghley because of Richard

Peterson's discovery of a letter from Thomas Tresham regarding the "calling-in" of the *Complaints* volume and by Bruce Danner's careful cataloguing of numerous sixteenth- and seventeenth-century readers' identification of the fox in *Mother Hubberds Tale* with Burghley (Petti, "Beasts"; Peterson, "Laurel crown"; Danner, *Edmund Spenser's War*, chapter 5). So Spenser succeeded in communicating with his audience, though perhaps too well, given that *Mother Hubberds Tale*, after being called in by March 1591, was not published again until 1612, after the deaths of not only Lord Burghley himself but also his equally powerful son, Robert Cecil, Earl of Salisbury. Although this indirect satire may thus have been a bit too direct, the relatively clear interpretive response of its earliest readers to the Fox makes this an excellent object for analysis of Spenser's characteristic satirical methods.

Other foxes in Aesopian fables such as Chaucer's *Nun's Priest's Tale*, *Reynard the Fox*, mid-sixteenth-century anti-Catholic polemic, and Spenser's own "Maye" from *The Shepheardes Calender* illustrate the two "types" of prosopopoietic foxes in early modern literature—fox as corrupt courtier and fox as corrupt pastor. Both types of fictional fox import meaning intersemiotically from medieval and early modern fox symbolism and natural-historical ideas about foxes (a concept that Sean Henry explores with reference to the crocodile in *Mother Hubberds Tale* in "How doth the little Crocodile"). The varying connections between the fictional world and reality in these different texts demonstrate the continuum between fable and satiric fable, and the same continua can be imagined, of course, between complaint and satirical complaint, pastoral and satirical pastoral, or any other genre or mode that an indirect satirist might coopt for satirical purposes.

Fable functions allegorically, of course, with the explicitly stated moral guaranteeing that all readers will be able to make the desired connection between the forest or barnyard and the real world. In the terms of cognitive blending theory, best known to literary scholars through its influence on cognitive metaphor theory, we can speak of the barnyard or forest as one of the "input spaces" (see Fauconnier and Turner, *The Way We Think*, chapter 3). In Chaucer's *Nun's Priest's Tale* and the anonymous *Reynard the Fox*, "the court" serves as another of the input spaces, but they function differently, with Chaucer juxtaposing court and barnyard language and imagery in order to create the mock-heroic sense of deflation and the *Reynard* poet progressively metamorphosing the setting from a fully animal world to a hybrid world in which Reynard seems "really" to be royalty. Although *Reynard* offers a clearer picture of real-world courtly abuses, neither poem attacks a specific target, and thus both are, at most, general satire.

Chauntecleer, Pertelote, and Russell the Fox inhabit a fable-world barnyard, not a pointedly allegorical version of the real world. Chaucer's references to the court create a blended space in the reader's mind, but in a way that pushes the scene firmly back to the barnyard, rather than pointing insistently to the real world. Quick juxtapositions of barnyard and court crystallize in readers' minds the sense that Chauntecleer is not a hero or prince but a mock-version of same. Immediately after a detail that emphasizes the animality of the characters, when Chauntecleer clucks to call his hens to him "For he hadde founde a corn, lay in the yerd" (Chaucer, *Nun's Priest*, line 3175), Chaucer describes him as royal ("real"), as looking like a "grym leoun," and as walking on his toes because he disdains to set his whole foot on the ground (lines 3176, 3179–81). Immediately thereafter, "he chukketh whan he hath a corn yfounde," and then the narrator describes him as "roial, as a prince is in his halle" (lines 3182, 3184). The incongruous blend of barnyard and court doesn't prompt the reader to seek real-world targets to connect with Chauntecleer's pride; instead, it delineates his character in a way that motivates his susceptibility to the flattery of the fox, Russell. Both Chauntecleer and Russell are susceptible to flattery because they prize themselves too highly, as though they really are courtiers, but both remain for readers simply animals. The explicit moral to courtly readers ("Allas, ye lordes, many a fals flatour / Is in youre courtes / ... / Beth war, ye lordes, of hir trecherye," Chaucer, *Nun's Priest*, lines 3325–26, 3330) invites readers to apply the lessons of the fable to real life. Yet this moral, applied from the barnyard to the real world, clarifies the distance between the two worlds.

In *Reynard the Fox* (translated into English by William Caxton in 1481 and reprinted several times over the following century before the time of Spenser's career), like *The Nun's Priest's Tale*, the work begins in a fable-world, with animals behaving like animals: the initial complaints of the animals against Reynard, like Chauntecleer's corn in the yard, remind us of animal behaviors and preoccupations, not those of humans. Isegryme the Wolf complains that Reynard "hath bepissed my children where as they lay, in suche wyse that they therof be waxen blinde" (*Raynarde the Foxe*, A5v). Curteyse the Hound accuses Reynard of stealing a pudding from him. And although Reynard's home, Malepardus, is called a "castel" (*Raynarde the Foxe*, passim), the description calls to mind a fox-hole: "for Malepardus was ful of holes, here one hole & there an other, and yonder an other, narow, croked, & longe, with many wayes to go out, whiche he opened & shette when it pleaseth hym, and when he had nede" (*Raynarde the Foxe*, B5v).¹

As the plot progresses, however, the characters begin to seem more human, and the fable-world contains enough of the institutions of the real world (a king, legal system, castles, duels, and so forth) to take on the character of a hybrid world, fully animal and fully human, in which Reynard's crimes begin to seem less like those of a fox and more like those of a sociopath. He expertly plays the typical desires of the animals who try to bring him to justice (Bruin the Bear wants honey, Tybert the Cat wants mice) against the fable-humans' desires to acquire and defend property in order to punish his animal summoners, allowing him to avoid his day in court. Reynard's character changes over the course of the work, so that by the end, the animal who had "bepissed" the eyes of the wolf cubs becomes a nobleman who "with his frendes and lynage departed nobly fro the kynge; and wente unto his castell Malepardus" (*Raynarde the Foxe*, S8r). The work by the end clearly references the real world of medieval Europe:

> There is in ye worlde moche sede lefte of ye Fox ... though they haue no reed berdes, yet there ben found moo Foxes now than euer were here tofore ... These reigne now moche in euery countre ... in ye popes court ye emperours, the kynges, dukes or any other lordes. (*Raynarde the Foxe*, T1r–T1v)

Yet the author cautions the reader not to read too closely: "There is no good man blamed therein[;] it is spoken generally. Let euerye man take his owne parte as it belongeth & behoueth, and he that fyndeth hym giltye in any dele or part therof, lette hym amende hymselfe" (*Raynarde the Foxe*, T4r).

In other words, the narrator avers that this is general satire, not indirect satire. *Reynard the Fox* allegorizes the real world more clearly than does *The Nun's Priest's Tale*, but still not specifically, and so I find no evidence of indirect satire in the English version.² The names of the animals are unremarkable and thus do not suggest allusions to real people. The most unusual word in the work, Malepardus ("Maleperduys" in Caxton's 1481 edition), the name of Reynard's fox-hole/castle, turns out to be a corrupted

---

1 Compare with Edward Topsell's description of foxes' dens: "for the abode of Foxes in the day time is in the caues and holes of the earth, and come not abroad til the night. These dens haue many caues in them, and passages in and out, that when the Tertars shall set vpon him in the earth, he may go forth some other way" (Topsell, *Historie*, 223).
2 The Reynard tales originated in the twelfth century with the Latin *Ysengrimus*, and French, Dutch, German, and English versions and translations circulated in Europe during the late medieval period. Scholars have found topical satirical content, with various targets, in the medieval Continental versions; see Varty, *Reynard the Fox*, especially chapters by Jill Mann, Jean Subrenat, and Jean-Marc Pastré.

version of the French word for St. John's wort: "This plant is called *Millepertuis* (or thousand holes) because the leaues of it are all full of so small holes, that one can scarce see them, but onely betwixt their sight and the sun" (de la Primaudaye, *French Academie*, 335). Obviously a name that means "thousand holes" serves as a fitting moniker for Reynard's confusing den with many paths and exits, not an allusion to signal a real-world satirical target. Without verbal allusions or plot segments that parallel real-world occurrences in order to connect fiction to reality in a way that creates a clear, sharp critique of some particular person or institution, the fifteenth- and sixteenth-century English versions of *Reynard the Fox*, in their application to the real world, remain general satire.

Both *The Nun's Priest's Tale* and *Reynard the Fox* exemplify the Aesopian tradition of fable, which Annabel Patterson describes as a "complex medium of political analysis" that in the late sixteenth century became in England "a flexible and constantly renewable system of metaphorical substitutions for actual events, persons, or political concepts that can, but need not, be recognized as such" (Patterson, *Fables*, 75, 52). The fable form itself, Patterson argues, codes political ideas in animal stories (just as the pastoral and the complaint are known for calling attention to the evils of the world), but this does not always rise to the level of a clear particular attack. Nevertheless, in the Reynard stories, the figure of the fox serves to satirize a specifically courtly set of abuses, even if no particular persons seem to be targeted.

In addition to this political, courtly type of fox satire, Spenser also draws on a distinct tradition of prosopopoietic foxes that derives from what Katherine C. Little refers to as "ecclesiastical pastoral" (*Transforming Work*, 3–5), in which foxes allegorize one type of corrupt pastor. Little argues for a medieval influence on early modern pastoral through the ecclesiastical pastoral that allegorizes priests as shepherds, as distinct from the classical pastoral tradition that has received the bulk of scholarly attention for its influence on early modern pastoral. Similarly, with regard to the literary ancestors of Spenser's Fox, we can distinguish the foxes that form part of the Aesopian tradition, which tends to comment on political situations, from foxes that derive from sixteenth-century ecclesiastical pastoral and thus comment on concerns about the clergy.

Little's definition of ecclesiastical pastoral as "allegorical pastoral ... in which the reader is meant to understand the shepherds as priests and the 'shepherding' they discuss as referring to clerical duties and/or religious beliefs and practices" can illuminate the way that this type of pastoral shades into satire through extension of the allegory (Little, *Transforming*

Work, 3). The evil figure who thwarts the good shepherd is not a bad shepherd but rather a fox or a wolf; a usefully heavy-handed example of this appears in the mid-sixteenth-century polemics of William Turner, who wrote *The Hunting and Finding Out of the Romish Fox* … (1543), *The Rescuing of the Romish Fox* … (1545), and *The Hunting of the Romish Wolf* (1555; republished with a new preface and title during the 1560s as *The Hunting of the Fox and the Wolfe, because they make havocke of the sheepe of Christ Jesus*). Harold Stein summarizes the overall symbolism of Turner's works thus:

> Thus to Turner a fox is a person who seems to be or pretends to be a member of the Church of England, though at heart he has Romish beliefs, while a wolf is a Romanist in both belief and outward profession. Edwardian foxes become Marian wolves, and, as we now know, Marian wolves similarly become Elizabethan foxes. (Stein, "Spenser and Turner," 349–50)[3]

Numerous scholars have noted the applicability of this animal symbolism to Spenser's "Maye" and "September" eclogues, citing as evidence the facts that, in "Maye," Spenser changed the wolf of his Aesopian source (Caxton's ninth fable of book 2) into a fox and that, in "September," Hobbinol's naïve response to Diggon Davy's comment on (allegorical) wolves that there are no (literal) wolves in England follows a passage in Turner's *The Hunting of the Romish Wolf* (Hume, *Edmund Spenser*, 21–23; Stein, "Spenser and Turner," 350–51; Norbrook, *Poetry and Politics*, 66–67).

Additionally, at least some readers of Spenser's *Mother Hubberds Tale* in 1591 would come to the text with the knowledge that William Cecil, Lord Burghley, was nicknamed "the fox" by his enemies. Anthony Petti cites numerous examples of references to Burghley as a fox, though Petti is sometimes unclear about whether such references pre- or post-date Spenser's poem. Within the circle of the court, Robert Devereux, Second Earl of Essex, commonly referred to Burghley as "the old fox"; Petti also finds fox imagery applied to Burghley by a (relative) outsider in a mid-1570s letter written by a Catholic that included a key to the letter's animal-themed cipher beginning: "The names of our enemies. The hare, the ladie Elizabeth that calleth herself queene; the foxe, Cicill" (qtd. in Petti, "Beasts," 79). Although Thomas Herron has complicated our understanding of the topical references in Spenser's satire by reminding us of the need to consider Irish readings and identifications of the Fox and other characters, for the English audience analyzed here, fox imagery

---

3 Janice Devereux notes that in addition to William Turner, Luke Shepherd and John Bale also referred to their enemy, the Catholic Stephen Gardiner, Bishop of Winchester, as a fox in the mid-sixteenth century (Devereux, *An Edition*, 121n182).

strongly represents Lord Burghley (Herron, "Reforming the fox").

Spenser reinforces the reader's awareness of the Burghleyan fox connection in *Mother Hubberds Tale* by making an even clearer attack on Burghley in *The Ruines of Time*, the poem that opens the *Complaints* collection. Elegizing Robert Dudley, Earl of Leicester, Spenser writes: "He now is gone, the whiles the Foxe is crept / Into the hole, the which the Badger swept" (*Ruines*, lines 216–17). The belief that foxes usurped the dens of badgers, claiming a badger's clean ("swept") den by marking it with urine and excrement, was part of English understanding of the natural history of real foxes (see, e.g., Topsell, *Historie*, 34, 223). Calling to the reader's mind Burghley (whose political ascendancy following Leicester's death makes him the obvious referent for the fox) while also reminding Elizabethans of the disgust attached to the actual animal makes this a stinging insult. Bruce Danner argues that *Ruines of Time* creates more offense than *Mother Hubberds Tale*, because "the *Ruines* criticizes Cecil without the mediating fiction of an allegorical beast fable.... Such remarks constitute a level of specificity beyond even the suggestive, but allegorically inflected allusions to Burghley and Robert Cecil in *Mother Hubberds Tale*" (Danner, *Edmund Spenser's War*, 92–93).

All of these symbolic foxes—the Aesopian/Reynardian political fox, the ecclesiastical pastoral fox, the Burghleyan fox—inform Spenser's character of the Fox in *Mother Hubberds Tale*. Lauren Silberman observes that Spenser does not characterize the Fox and Ape as static figures; instead, "the way in which they are presented shifts along the continuum from naturalistic to anthropomorphic—from the pole of 'mouse' to the pole of 'Mickey,' if you will" (Silberman, "Aesopian," 228). In part, as regards the Fox, these shifts in characterization occur when Spenser moves to another symbolic context for the meaning he wishes to convey through this figure. The first two episodes play with the conventions of pastoral ecclesiastical satire: as literal shepherds of actual sheep (the Ape disguised as a "shepheard swaine" and "the false Foxe [as] his dog" [Spenser, *Mother Hubberds Tale*, lines 303–4]), they devour their charges mercilessly, just as allegorical wolf- and fox-pastors do in ecclesiastical pastorals such as those by Turner and those in *The Shepheardes Calender*. As always, the Fox serves as the instigator and is thus more guilty than the Ape:

> [E]ver as they bred,
> They slue them, and upon their fleshes fed:
> For that disguised Dog lov'd blood to spill,
> And drew the wicked Shepheard to his will.
> (Spenser, *Mother Hubberds Tale*, lines 317–20)

In the next episode, however, when they infiltrate the clergy, with the Fox as priest and the Ape as his parish clerk, they shift, to use Silberman's analogy, from "mouse" to "Mickey," because their crimes as clergy are not the allegorical devouring of sheep, which they have already done literally in the first episode, but everyday corruptions: they "ill / Did order their affaires" and were accused by their parishioners of unnamed "crimes and heresies" (lines 559–60, 564). Both episodes draw on native English traditions of polemic and complaint, with the first episode perhaps more indebted to the polemics of rural laborers and poverty that draw on the *Piers Plowman* tradition, as analyzed by Mike Rodman Jones (*Radical Pastoral*). They are linked by their preoccupation with ordinary people, as opposed to courtiers, and by the clever twist of having the Fox and Ape perform their crimes of bloodthirsty rapine as *actual* shepherds, immediately before their turn as clergy members.

The rural ecclesiastical satire of the first two episodes then shifts to court satire for the final two episodes: the Ape as courtier, with the Fox as "his man Reynold" who "Supports his credite and his countenaunce" (lines 667, 668), and the Ape as usurper-king, on the condition that he will swear to be "ruled ... / In all affaires" by the Fox (lines 1051–52). Where the first two episodes, in line with the fox symbolism of ecclesiastical pastoral satire, characterized the Fox with reference to his bloodthirstiness (first episode) and lack of care for parishioners (second episode), the literary context now changes to the courtly satire reminiscent of the Reynard tales, especially in the third episode, and political satire akin to the Aesopian tradition in the fourth episode, which is generally recognized as having the most direct topical applications but also the most careful efforts at creating "Aesopian political deniability" (Silberman, "Aesopian," 242). As van den Berg summarizes the fourth episode: "on the one hand, it retreats from the human world to the animal kingdom; on the other, it engages the human world more directly through sustained topical allusions to actual persons and specific abuses" ("Counterfeit," 92). We see this continued concern with the lines between human and animal in the Ape and Fox's argument over which should act as the king, when the Fox says:

> where ye claime your selfe for outward shape
> Most like a man, Man is not like an Ape
> In his chiefe parts, that is, in wit and spirite;
> But I therein most like to him doo merite
> For my slie wyles and subtill craftinesse,
> The title of the Kingdome to possesse.
>
> (lines 1041–46)

The courtly and royal contexts of these final two episodes are too obvious to require proof, and I believe that the Fox's character becomes inflected here with a slightly different meaning because of the connection to courtly, political beast satire associated with the Reynardian and Aesopian tales.

Significantly, it is also in these final episodes that the connections linking the Fox with William Cecil, Lord Burghley, come into play. In *Mother Hubberds Tale*, although the Fox shows his corruption throughout the poem, he becomes most similar to Lord Burghley in the fourth episode, in which the Ape impersonates the king and the Fox serves as his second-in-command. Here Spenser moves beyond allusion (to earlier literary foxes and perhaps to fox references to Burghley) and symbolism (from the disgust attached to foxes from popular natural histories as exemplified by Edward Topsell) to create satirical meanings by means of analogous situations. The narration of the Fox's crimes allegorizes the litany of complaints leveled against Burghley: he is greedy (nothing "that might him profit bring, / But he the same did to his purpose wring" [lines 1141–42]); he wields disproportionate influence with the monarch ("Nought suffered he the Ape to give or graunt, / But through his hand must passe the Fiaunt" [lines 1143–44]); he does not support learning and the arts ("For men of learning little he esteemed; / His wisedome he above their learning deemed" [lines 1191–92]); and his ostentatious building projects show his pride and selfishness ("But his owne treasure he encreased more / And lifted up his loftie towres thereby" [lines 1171–72]).[4] Bruce Danner notes that the Fox's building program is out of place: it "plays no previous or subsequent role in the poem," and so, he suggests, "Its function ... seems calculated to draw attention beyond the formal boundaries of the narrative to the arena of contemporary reference" (Danner, *Edmund Spenser's War*, 164).

Early readers recognized mockery of Robert Cecil's hunchback in the reference to the Fox's cubs, whose "backs nigh broken were" from the weight of all the honors and offices he heaped upon them (line 1158), a passage Catholic polemicist Richard Verstegan alludes to by mentioning "the false fox and his crooked cubs" in his attack on Burghley (Verstegan, *A Declaration*, 68). Danner has carefully catalogued the numerous contemporary identifications of the Fox with Burghley, noting that these consistent identifications constitute "nothing less than the most thoroughly documented topical allusion of Spenser's career" (Danner,

---

4 See Danner, *Edmund Spenser's War*, chapter 5, for a thorough analysis of the historical context of Burghley's building projects.

Edmund Spenser's War, 163). Although we can thus with some certainty identify the Fox as Burghley, we nevertheless do not know the source of Spenser's animus against him; Andrew Hadfield outlines a number of possibilities before concluding that "we shall probably never know for certain why Spenser singled out Burghley as the representative of all that was wrong with court life" (Hadfield, *A Life*, 275). Certainly the volume as a whole indicates Spenser's confidence and willingness to provoke controversy, as Hadfield notes.

The social dynamics of satire

Whereas the many criticisms of the Fox quoted in the previous section certainly applied to Burghley, the Fox's building projects, in their specificity and lack of connection to the plot—similar to the reference to his "cubs" that marks him as a parent—lead the reader to look outside the text for meaning, that is, to think allegorically by looking for parallels in the real world to explain something unusual or out of place in the fictional world. This, I argue, is what makes indirect satire, as practiced by Spenser and others who imitated him, distinctive: the greater cognitive demands it makes of the reader. When the writer places in the text only *clues* to satirical meaning—allusions, symbols, and analogies that prompt the reader to use prior knowledge, outside knowledge, to read allegorically to make sense of the text—the reader must interpret the clues to arrive at the satirical meaning. The author thus increases personal safety, but at cost to comprehensibility: some satirical meanings may go unnoticed, and others may be found that the author never intended. This affects the reception of the text both at the time of composition and in later centuries, as critics struggle to interpret correctly satirical messages that depend upon the knowledge and attitudes of the original target audience.

In making a distinction between "general," "indirect," and "direct" satire, my goal is not to return to the somewhat rigid taxonomizing impulses that characterized the study of Renaissance satire in the mid-twentieth century. We can see new-critical interests at work in, for example, Alvin Kernan's ideas about the importance of the satiric persona, Mary Claire Randolph's two-part taxonomy of formal verse satire as attacking a vice and endorsing the corresponding virtue, or John Peter's dichotomized association of complaint with the medieval period and satire with the Renaissance (Kernan, *Cankered Muse*; Randolph, "The structural design"; Peter, *Complaint and Satire*). In all of these examples, interest focuses on the *text*, with attention to the persona of the speaker as found in the *text*. Discussions of prose vs. verse satire, "Juvenalian" vs. "Horatian" vs. "Menippean" have continued to develop the new-critical taxonomic impulse by focusing on form and tone.

Instead of adding a new type of taxonomy, I want to bring to the study of Renaissance literature more recent satire theorists' approaches, which, taken together, constitute what we might call a "social turn" in satire studies, expressed most succinctly in W. Scott Blanchard's definition of satire as a "genre for the expression of social dissensus" ("Renaissance prose satire," 118). The decision to write general or indirect or direct satire—and these should be conceptualized as a continuum, not a set of discrete quantum levels—arises in part from concerns related to the social sphere:

1. The actual specificity of the real-world target: Does the author genuinely want to criticize a large group of people, such as "courtiers," or one specific courtier, such as the Earl of Oxford?
2. The potential social costs of directly attacking the target, ranging from social awkwardness to difficulty getting published to imprisonment or execution.
3. The ability of the anticipated audience to piece together satirical meanings from indirect clues: the audience will be more able to make these cognitive leaps if author and audience share extensive background knowledge.

This way of thinking about satire as a social practice draws from and adds nuance to the work of numerous critics who have considered the social dimension of satire. Fredric Bogel describes satire's social function as exclusion: creating and policing boundaries between the in-group and the outsider (Bogel, *Difference Satire Makes*). George A. Test explains the multiplicity of satirical forms as deriving from the limitless possibilities created by theorizing satire as exhibiting greater or lesser degrees of four traits that work together to create satire: aggression, judgment, laughter, and play (Test, *Satire*)—characteristics not so much formal or historical as *social*: aggression *toward*, judgment *on*, laughter *at*, play *with*. Test's illustrations of these social relations in various examples of satire tend to emphasize the connections between author and subject, leaving the reader in a somewhat more passive role. Dustin Griffin balances this view by arguing that inquiry, specifically the shared inquiry into a subject by writer and reader, characterizes satire at its most morally complex and interesting (Griffin, *Satire*). To the extent that interpreting indirect satire depends upon reading allegorically to connect the text to the pretext or context, I draw also from Maureen Quilligan's careful analysis of the role of the reader in making sense of allegorical writing (*The Language of Allegory*, chapter 4).

The distinction I make between direct and indirect satire continues this emphasis on the social experience of reading or writing satire, specifically with respect to the making of meaning. Many of the theoretical comments on satire refer to and analyze what I am calling "direct satire," which we now call simply "satire," because greater freedom of expression in Western democracies since the late seventeenth century has diminished authors' need for a toolbox of indirect satirical methods. Indirect satire flourishes under repressive conditions, complicating comments such as Ralph Rosen's discussion of ancient satire, in which he asserts "the antagonism itself is always explicit, for it is in the poet's interest to clarify who is the blamer and who the target" (*Making Mockery*, 19). This tendency to consider only direct satire in analyses of "satire" also plays a role in the idea that satire must be funny; Rosen again: "it must be said, at the risk of stating the obvious, that I understand satire as a species of comedy, or more generally 'the comic' … it exists in order to make an audience laugh" (19). Of course satire can be funny, but satire is not the same as comedy any more than satire is the same as pastoral. Using George Test's taxonomy, we could say that Rosen is describing a type of satire strong on aggression and laughter, whereas indirect satire is stronger on Test's judgment and play. Thinking of satire as aggressive and laughter-provoking works well for examples of early modern English direct satire such as the tracts of the pseudonymous Martin Marprelate, which attacked particular English bishops by name, referred to specific foibles and embarrassing incidents, and mocked both; Thomas Nashe's satirical abuse of Gabriel Harvey and his brothers; the Catholic apologist Richard Verstegan's attacks on William Cecil, Lord Burghley; and the sort of personal libels collected by Alastair Bellany and Andrew McRae on their "Early Stuart Libels" website.

These four examples of direct, naming-names satire in the late Elizabethan and early Stuart period provide a useful primer on the dangers of direct satire at this time of heavy censorship:[5] The Marprelate tracts, unregistered with the Stationers' Company and printed on a secret press, led to a manhunt, a public-relations war, and the execution of John Penry (Black, "Introduction"). The Bishops' Ban of 1599, which primarily

---

5 For general studies of press censorship during this period, see Clegg, *Press Censorship Elizabethan*; Clegg, *Press Censorship Jacobean*; Dutton, *Licensing, Censorship*; and Patterson, *Censorship and Interpretation*.

singled out specific, named works, made a blanket condemnation of the whole Nashe–Harvey controversy by decreeing "That all nasshes bookes and D Harvyes bookes be taken wheresoever they maye be found and that none of theire bookes bee ever printed hereafter" (qtd. in McCabe, "Elizabethan satire," 188). Verstegan's books were printed on the Continent and smuggled into England, and the libels collected by Bellany and McRae remained unpublished and circulated in manuscript. In sum, then, three of these four examples constitute what McRae terms "unauthorized texts" (McRae, *Literature, Satire*, 1), and the authorized texts of the Nashe–Harvey squabble later became censored texts.

We can easily understand the rage of the Elizabethan bishops at the ridicule dished out by the witty and irreverent Martin family (the pseudonymous Martin Marprelate turned out to have two sons, Martin Junior and Martin Senior), though we might consider the bishops' murderous response somewhat lacking in moderation. No one needs to write an article explaining why the Elizabethan bishops took offense at the Marprelate tracts; I will provide a single example, a syllogism from the *Epistle*, remarkable for the sheer number of bishops that it insults directly: "Those that are petty popes and petty antichrists ought not to be maintained in any Christian commonwealth. But every lord bishop in England, as, for ilsample, John of Cant., John of London, John Exeter, John Rochester, Thomas of Winchester, the bishops of Lincoln, of Worcester, of Peterborough, and to be brief, all the bishops in England, Wales, and Ireland, are petty popes and petty antichrists. Therefore no lord bishop … is to be tolerated in any Christian commonwealth" (Marprelate, *The Epistle*, 9). It requires no great critical acumen to recognize why a bishop in the Church of England at the end of the sixteenth century would prefer not to be named as a petty pope and Antichrist. In direct satires such as these, plenty of interpretive issues and problems remain, of course, but the reader does not wonder whom the author is criticizing, even at a remove of more than four hundred years.

Other censorship episodes, however, offer less clarity. In the case of the 1591 "calling in" of Spenser's *Complaints* volume, scholars treated the censorship as an unconfirmed rumor until 1997, when Richard Peterson published a newly found letter from Sir Thomas Tresham written in March 1591 (new style) during the actual recall of the book. Although everyone could agree about *why* Lord Burghley would want the book censored, the lack of proof that the book had indeed been suppressed led to scholarly caution and uncertainty. Harold Stein, for example, speculated from the lack of an official proclamation regarding the calling in that the authorities used "semi-official pressure" to get Spenser's publisher, William Ponsonby, to impound the unsold copies himself (Stein, *Studies*, 85). Cyndia Clegg, presumably partly because she bases her argument on the belief that critics have overstated the extent of literary censorship in the Elizabethan period, treats the censorship of *Complaints* as a minor event, despite Peterson's proof by the time of Clegg's publication that the book was called in. Clegg dismisses the seriousness of the event by commenting that "whatever concern Spenser's tale elicited, it was mitigated shortly after" (Clegg, *Press Censorship Elizabethan*, 223).

Likewise, scholars have not been able to determine with certainty against what offense or offenses the Bishops' Ban reacted, leading to interpretive proliferation over the past decades. Those arguing for moral motivations for the ban include John Peter (*Complaint and Satire*, 149), Bruce R. Smith (*Homosexual Desire*, 164), and Lynda E. Boose ("Bishop's Ban," 196). Arguments for political causes for the ban appear in works by Richard McCabe ("Elizabethan satire"), Annabel Patterson (*Censorship and Interpretation*, 47), and Cyndia Clegg (*Press Censorship Elizabethan*, 198–217). Given the generic diversity of the texts included in the ban, recent critics have looked for overarching themes that can help to explain the collective offensiveness of the named works. According to Douglas Bruster, the named works' "embodied writing" offended because they "took liberties with bodies considered either above mention or above certain kinds of mention" ("Structural transformation," 50, 53). William Jones also avoids genre-based interpretations by arguing that the ban attempted to address a concern about ideology, specifically the Juvenalian mode as "a tangible threat to the ideological stability of the English nation" ("Bishops' Ban," 332). If we think in social rather than taxonomic terms, it becomes less important to find a common thread connecting all of these named works. The books were banned not because they outraged the public, and not because they outraged one bishop who created the entire list. Rather, we likely see here a collection of personal prejudices, but because they are the personal prejudices of a *group* of bishops, rather than a single bishop, we cannot find one common offense that each work offers.

Both of these examples—uncertainty regarding the circumstances surrounding the censorship of Spenser's *Complaints* and uncertainty about what inspired the confirmed censorship of the Bishops' Ban—arise from the slipperiness of indirect satire. It makes sense that the Elizabethan authorities in charge of these suppressions would prefer to be as vague as possible regarding their decisions: after all, by its nature, indirect satire is not readily comprehensible to every reader, so the suppressors would not find it in their interest to help naïve readers to become knowing readers.

Meaning-making in indirect satire: allusion, symbol, analogy, and the "allegorical intuition"

In the previous section I noted that social considerations play a significant role in an author's decision to write indirect satire instead of more general or more direct satirical works and discussed the specificity of the target and the potential social costs of writing more direct satire. This section will analyze the greater interpretive burden that indirect satire puts on the reader. For any instance of indirect literary meaning-making to succeed, the writer and the reader must share a common store of knowledge, or else the reader will not be able to make the appropriate connections in order to perceive the intended meanings. Brenda Machosky, in a discussion of allegory, claims that "all acts of interpretation are metaphoric in principle, substituting meaning for the literary text. (Hence Northrop Frye's famous comment in *The Anatomy of Criticism* that 'all commentary is allegorical interpretation' [89].)" (*Structures of Appearing*, 191).

Machosky conflates metaphor and allegory in this quotation, but teasing the two apart is important because of its implications for seeing the process of understanding indirect satire as *allegorical* interpretation, not metaphoric. Cognitive metaphor theorists define metaphor as the mapping of ideas and images from one conceptual domain (the "source domain") on to another (the "target domain"), so that the unknown or less known can be understood through comparison with a more familiar domain of meaning (Lakoff and Johnson, *Metaphors*). Whereas I.A. Richards's highly influential discussions of metaphor tend to oversimplify the process of communication and meaning-making (for example, in the suggestion that the "tenor" or message is uncomplicatedly transported by the "vehicle," creating a conceptual barrier between meaning and expression that underestimates the complexity of the processes of both writing and reading), contemporary cognitive metaphor theorists postulate more fluid boundaries between the source and target domains, such that meaning flows, at least potentially, in both directions.

In several articles extending the work of cognitive metaphor theorists to allegory, Peter Crisp argues that we can distinguish allegory from extended metaphor because allegory includes no direct references to the target domain (i.e., the meaning or world "out there" that allegorical figures and events represent); according to Crisp, whereas an extended metaphor will bring together linguistic details reminiscent of both the source and the target domains, allegory creates a self-contained world: all source domain, with perhaps an allusion to the target domain in the form of personifications ("Allegory, blending"). I find Crisp's argument for the distinction between extended metaphor and allegory compelling, even though I disagree with him about the cognition involved in making sense of allegory. The human mind's ability to make sense of allegory—to correctly identify, say, the real-world satirical target of a short poem that does not mention the person by name—depends, according to Mark Turner, on three "principles of mind," story, projection, and parable, that allow us to make sense not only of literature but also of reality, with "story" organizing our thinking, "projection" describing how "one story helps us make sense of another," and "parable" being "the projection of one story onto another" (Turner, *Literary Mind*, v).

Turner's "parable" uncontroversially names what we mean when we speak of allegorical interpretation, but, especially when a satirist aims at self-protection by writing allegorically, how does the reader know what to project? What hints create the allegorical intuition that prompts further reflection, leading to appropriate projection? Crisp repeatedly notes that allegory makes no "direct" reference to the target domain, but he leaves unexplored the ways that allegory makes *indirect* reference to the target domain, and this indirection in the creation of meaning is what makes indirect satire possible. I will discuss three ways that an author can *indirectly* refer to the target domain, providing clues to spur allegorical interpretation: allusion, symbol, and analogy.

By "allusion," I refer to a primarily verbal or naming reference that points the reader outside the text. Theorists of allusion have focused, not surprisingly, on literary allusion, but I extend their work here to historical allusion, given that such allusions are of primary interest when considering indirect satire; we can extend these theorists' comments about the relationship that develops between two (literary) texts to the relationship that develops in the reader's mind between the text and the historical situation to which it alludes. Ziva Ben-Porat, for example, asserts that "the literary allusion is a device for the simultaneous activation of two texts," leading to "the formation of intertextual patterns whose nature cannot be predetermined" (Ben-Porat, "Poetics," 107–8). For Ben-Porat, then, the desired "end product" of allusion—those "intertextual patterns"—exists not in either text but in the reader's mind. Allan Pasco uses the botanical metaphor of grafting, in which "the grafted cutting becomes an integral part of the new stock," to define allusion as existing in this between-texts space: "Neither the reference nor the referent, it consists in the image produced by the metaphoric combination that occurs in the reader's mind" (Pasco, *Allusion*, 12). Thus, the reader plays a key role in piecing together the full meaning of an allusion. In Spenserian satire, we find satirical allusions most notably in *The Shepheardes Calender,* where anagrams or nicknames (e.g., Morrell for Aylmer) serve to clue the reader to the allegorization of historical personages.

When I refer to "symbol" as a way of pointing the reader of an indirect satire outside the text to prompt allegorical interpretation, I speak of the complex of an object or image and the set of visual and conceptual meanings that attach to it within a particular culture. (Note that I believe Coleridge's distinction between symbol and allegory, in which symbol is natural and allegory is arbitrary, has clouded discussion for too long, so I will simply state that I use both terms here to refer to processes of meaning-making that depend on social construction and communal understandings shared by members of a culture.) In *The Faerie Queene* (2.4.4), the forelock of the figure eventually identified (allusively, several stanzas later) as Occasion served within the culture as a symbol of Occasion or Opportunity, generally represented in contemporary emblem books as positive opportunities. Spenser alters this symbolic meaning by combining it with the negative associations that his culture attached to ugliness and age, so that the hag becomes an appropriate personification of the occasion to wrath. I view personification, then, not as a separate figure of indirection in satirical or allegorical meaning but as a way of pointing to the target domain that relies on a combination of allusion and symbol; Spenser is well known for ekphrastically developing the symbolic signification of a personification before he clarifies the figure's identity by allusion to the abstract quality that it represents.

What I am calling "analogy" or "analogous situations" in this book represent the most indirect of the indirect methods of signaling satirical meaning. Whereas all satirical meaning-making in allegorical satire depends upon Turner's principle of mind "parable," with analogy, the reader's only clue or connection to the real-world target space of the satire's critique comes from the plot or narrative's similarity to some real-world situation that the reader already knows about. Spenser uses analogy extensively in the satirical episodes in *Faerie Queene*, especially Book 5's trial of Duessa, the Burbon episode, and the Belge episode. But in these cases, Spenser supplements the use of analogy with allusion and symbol. When there is high potential for censorship or punishment, however, creating indirect satire strictly through analogous narratives offers the greatest amount of deniability, and we see Spenser relying on this method in the fourth episode of *Mother Hubberds Tale*.

As I already noted, from the time of its publication in the *Complaints* volume in 1591, readers connected the Fox in *Mother Hubberds Tale* with William Cecil, Lord Burghley. By making his main villain a fox, Spenser alluded to Burghley, who was referred to as a fox before 1591. But not everyone knew that Burghley was connected to foxes; readers who were naïve with regard to the allusion to a nickname for Burghley would perhaps catch the allusions to earlier literary traditions of prosopopoietic foxes, and even readers not well read in those literary works would still know the folk culture's natural-historical ideas about foxes as dirty and wily, so that this symbolism would attach to a fox character as well.

Yet these allusions and symbolism alone might not have been enough to render the setting of *Mother Hubberds Tale* no longer a fictional beast-fable world, but a world suggesting clear parallels with the real world of sixteenth-century England. The situations in the fourth episode that are clearly analogous to situations in Spenser's England—an advisor to the monarch who shows favoritism toward his sons is greedy, holds plural offices, undertakes elaborate building projects, and controls access to the monarch—illustrated common complaints about Burghley with sufficient detail to help readers, primed by the genre of beast fable to look for connections, to make the identification. Despite the wealth of allusions, symbolism, and analogies, the satire is indirect, in the sense that Spenser does not use Burghley's name or official titles, but Burghley—presumably the "Superior awthoritie" referred to in 1591 by Sir Thomas Tresham who took the poem "in suche earnest" that he "called in" the entire collection in which the poem appeared—must have seen Spenser's poem as entirely too explicit a way of referring (Peterson, "Laurel crown," 7).

Bruce Danner's chapter on *Mother Hubberds Tale* illustrates the importance of small details; Danner contextualizes Spenser's references to the Fox's grand building projects as chief advisor to the Ape as false king (that is, the reference to "loftie towres" quoted above) by exploring the similarities to Burghley's excessive and expensive work at his estate Theobalds, and he notes that the Fox's building work does not connect to the rest of the narrative. The strangeness of the incongruous detail invites readers to consider real-world applications and satirical meanings. Writing of Aesopian discourse in England, Annabel Patterson comments that "The fable gives up its goods more generously when its details are recognized as *specifying*, not generalizing; and those details, in turn, constitute an unusual and untapped archive for the early history of political and social thought"

(Patterson, *Fables*, 43). Essentially, this is my method in excavating satirical meanings from the four-hundred-year-old poems I examine in this book: I look for strange details, words or images that don't quite fit or that introduce a remarkable degree of specificity into a passage—these are one form of what Annabel Patterson elsewhere calls "entry codes": textual material that serves to flag the presence of hidden satirical meaning (Patterson, *Censorship and Interpretation*). I then examine those small details to ascertain in what ways they may function as entry codes that create allegorical connections between the fictional world in the text and the real world of the writer and reader. I am especially interested in the ways that other authors used Spenser as source and inspiration for their own satirical poetry. Just as, for example, Spenser alludes to and adapts to his own purposes a number of different textual, generic, and cultural versions of the fox in creating his own Reynold the Fox, authors developing the indirect, Spenserian form of satire in the 1590s and beyond often use Spenserian allusions to function as entry codes, so that Spenser provides for such authors both satirical tools and a satirical tradition to link to through allusion.

A portrait of the artist as a satirist

Scholars have paid a great deal of attention to Spenser's satirical poetry, but in a fairly piecemeal and atomistic fashion, looking at individual texts or, in the case of *The Faerie Queene*, individual moments of satirical tone or meaning within the epic. The rest of this book will demonstrate this same sort of local-level attention to particular texts, with close attention to *Shepheardes Calender* and *Daphnaïda* in the next chapter, followed by close readings of the satirical inspiration provided to other authors by specific Spenserian texts. However, because the purpose of this whole book is to convey a sense of story—the story of Spenser as a satirist working within and responding to a print culture ever under the threat of possible censorship, and the story of how that story of Spenser as principled poet speaking truth to power inspired and influenced other poets in the 1590s and early seventeenth century—I want to create a narrative of "satirical Spenser," a storyline connecting key events in Spenser's career in which he adopted a more satirical stance in his poetry.

I do not wish to argue, or at least not to argue strenuously, against comments such as Richard Helgerson's that Spenser "studiously avoided" presenting himself as a satirist, keeping Colin Clout out of the satirical eclogues in *Shepheardes Calender* and dissociating himself as poet from

Mother Hubberds Tale (Helgerson, *Self-Crowned Laureates*, 85n37). Helgerson's and Patrick Cheney's (*Spenser's Famous Flight*) persuasive analyses of Spenser's self-fashioning as a poet, the ways that he presented individual works as part of a *career*, prioritize individual, self-consciously canonical works in ways that seem to me to fit with Spenser's own *stated* goals as a poet. Still ... by naming his poetic alter ego "Colin Clout"—even if he does then send Colin to an undisclosed location when it is time for a satirical eclogue—Spenser *already* alludes to satirical poetry by referencing John Skelton's most famous poetic narrator, as I will discuss in the next chapter. Although Spenser does not proclaim himself a satirist, or self-consciously link a series of satirical works into an *oeuvre* or career, he demonstrates a consistent, sustained interest in using his poetry to comment on and criticize the real world. This desire to make poetry matter, coupled with an equally strong desire to avoid punishment or censorship, leads to several discrete episodes in which we see Spenser trying to negotiate the boundaries governing licit poetic meddling in affairs, trying to find "the line" but not cross it, with greater or lesser success.

In *The Shepheardes Calender*, Spenser obviously succeeded, fabulously, in creating a work that would position him as the premier poet writing in English, a key work whose importance scholars analyzing Spenser's career universally recognize (e.g., Helgerson; Cheney; Rambuss, *Spenser's Secret*). And yet we don't know to what extent Spenser achieved his additional goal of criticizing specific abuses in England: he may have been satisfied that enough people, or the right people, sufficiently understood his indirect satirical critiques. Algrind's identity as Bishop Grindal, Morrell's as Bishop Aylmer, the bald-faced reference to Lettice Knollys, the wife of the Earl of Leicester, as "Lettice"—the ways that these and other allusions place Spenser as a firm Protestant and as connected with the Leicester circle have been well rehearsed, including book-length studies such as Paul McLane's sometimes too-ingenious allegorical readings in *Spenser's* Shepheardes Calender: *A Study in Elizabethan Allegory* and the more cautious readings advanced in Robert Lane's *Shepheards Devises*.

But did enough readers even at the time of publication understand, say, the story of Roffy and Lowder in the "September" eclogue, an allegorization of some event now utterly lost to us? We can recognize this episode as an instance of indirect satire by perceiving two allusive names, Roffy and Lowder. We know that Roffy refers to John Young, Bishop of Rochester and Spenser's employer at the time of composition, but we don't know to what person the name Lowder alludes, and although we presume that the plot was recognizable to knowing readers as an analogue of real-world events, we are unable to connect the analogue to any event we know of. Our ignorance, however, does not mean that "September" should be considered general satire—it doesn't make sense as general satire that can be understood by a general audience. The episode requires a knowledgeable audience; it is undeniably indirect satire, but we cannot understand it and probably never will.

Spenser makes so much of the secrets contained in his book through E.K.'s repeated references to secrets (e.g., the author's "labouring to conceale" "the generall dryft and purpose" of the work, the "few" things "whose speciall purpose and meaning I am not privie to," and numerous references within the notes [Spenser, *Shepheardes*, 19, 23; see Rambuss, *Spenser's Secret*, chapter 2]—did his contemporaries "get" enough of them? Or did Spenser wish for a fuller appreciation of his work as social criticism? William Webbe wrote a great deal about the *Calender* in his 1586 *A Discourse of English Poetry*, but he is willfully vague about the extent to which he himself succeeded in understanding the hidden secrets; instead, he focuses on some of the most general, banal messages a reader might take away from the collection, mentioning only briefly the potential for sharper critiques:

> The occasion of his worke is a warning to other young men, who being intangled in loue and youthful vanities, may learne to looke to themselues in time, and to auoyde inconueniences which may breede if they be not in time preuented. Many good Morrall lessons are therein contained, as the reuerence which young men owe to the aged in the second *Eglogue*: the caueate or warning to beware a subtill professor of freendshippe in the fift *Eglogue*: the commendation of good Pastors, and shame and disprayse of idle & ambitious Goteheardes in the seauenth, the loose and retchlesse lyuing of Popish Prelates in the ninth. The learned and sweete complaynt of the contempt of learning vnder the name of Poetry in the tenth. There is also much matter vttered somewhat couertly, especially ye abuses of some whom he would not be too playne withall: in which, though it be not apparant to euery one, what hys speciall meaning was, yet so skilfully is it handled, as any man may take much delight at hys learned conueyance, and picke out much good sence in the most obscurest of it. (E4v–F1r)

We know that the John Stubbs episode, which had nearly cost Spenser's publisher, John Singleton, his hand the month before publishing *Shepheardes Calender*, might have induced Spenser to exercise extreme caution. We know of no censorious objections or reactions to *Shepheardes Calender*. We do not know, however, whether Spenser was satisfied with the extent to which this volume of poetry allowed him to express his ideas about and criticisms of the world around him. His choice of the poetic alter ego Colin Clout, a name that in 1579 stood not for Spenser but for the satirical poem by John Skelton, and the decision to title his work after a book that, according to John Foxe in *Acts and Monuments*, had been "accused & detected" by Catholic persecutors of Protestants in the early sixteenth century (both of which I will discuss more fully in Chapter 2), suggest a greater commitment to poetic intervention into political and religious matters than he received credit for at the time. At any rate, with *Shepheardes Calender*, although we cannot know the extent to which Spenser achieved his rhetorical goals related to satirical allegory and critique, we do know that authorities did not judge that he had crossed the line into actionably offensive work.

Eleven years later, when *Complaints* was entered into the Stationers' Register, Spenser had a very different status than did the "new poet," "Immerito," at the time of *The Shepheardes Calender*. The success of that venture and the publication of the first installment of *The Faerie Queene* (1590) established Spenser as the premier English poet, and some have thus found surprising the publication of *Complaints*, with its multiple poems insulting to Burghley, in the following year. Scholars differ on whether or not Spenser participated in the publication of the work, with Jean Brink arguing that, because of the offensiveness of some of the poems, Spenser must have intended for them to remain in manuscript ("Who fashioned"). On the other side, Andrew Hadfield believes that the care taken with presentation and the handsomeness of the volume support the view that Spenser participated in and supported the publication process (*A Life*, 273–74, 283–84), and I have argued elsewhere that the multiple dedicatory materials included in the volume, especially to the Spencer sisters, constitute a self-conscious bid for patronage and support at the crucial moment in Spenser's career when he was waiting for approval of the pension he was ultimately to receive as reward for his labors on *The Faerie Queene* (Hile, "Auto/biographical fantasies").

Whether or not Spenser participated in the publication process for this volume, his writing of poems such as *The Ruines of Time* and *Prosopopoia; or, Mother Hubberds Tale* indicates that he felt a great deal of self-confidence (and perhaps also a great deal of self-righteous conviction that Burghley had responded unfairly to *The Faerie Queene*, as Bruce Danner argues). We can speculate what impact Spenser hoped to achieve with these poems, but we do not know whether he was surprised and dismayed by the censorious government response or whether he relished the knowledge that his barbs had bitten. At any rate, Spenser's book was punished, but not his body, and the scandal died down quickly. Thomas Tresham's letter, dated "the xixth of Marche 1590" (i.e., 1591 new style), describes the details of the contemporary scandal, with Spenser recently having returned to Ireland, authorities trying to collect all copies of the offending book, and booksellers profiting by selling the book at inflated prices (Peterson, "Laurel crown"). In the following year, Gabriel Harvey criticized Spenser for writing the work, because "Mother Hubbard, in heat of choller, forgetting the pure sanguine of her sweete F[ae]ry Queene, wilfully ouer-shott her malcontented selfe"; this work was entered in the Stationers' Register on December 4, 1592 (Harvey, *Fovre Letters*, 15). In Thomas Nashe's response to this criticism, he charges that "If any man were vndeseruedly toucht in it, thou hast reuiued his disgrace that was so toucht in it, by renaming it, when it was worn out of al mens mouths and minds" (Nashe, *Strange Newes*, 282). This work was entered in the Stationers' Register January 12, 1592 (i.e., 1593 new style), and thus we learn that the scandal, at least as it touched Spenser, was of relatively short duration. However, whereas the gossip was short-lived, the impact on *Mother Hubberds Tale* was not: Although the other *Complaints* poems were republished without *Mother Hubberds Tale* in 1611, that poem was not reprinted until 1612, following the death of Lord Burghley's son Robert Cecil, Earl of Salisbury (Lord Burghley having died in 1598).

This censorship episode certainly contributed to Spenser's credibility as a satirist to other poets in the 1590s, leading to other poets finding satirical inspiration in such poems as "March" and *Muiopotmos*, as I discuss in Chapter 4, in addition to beast fable and fox allusions more commonly recognized. This image of Spenser as a principled poet who was willing to take risks in order to express his ideas about the world around him affected not only how other poets in the 1590s thought of and responded to him, but also how Spenser thought of himself, and I believe this sense of himself, coupled with the self-confidence derived from his success as a poet, explains the presence of topical allegories, many with the bite of satire, in the 1596 installment of *The Faerie Queene*, which the 1590 books generally avoided. (The extended satirical critiques of the Roman Catholic Church in Book 1 hardly qualify as *dangerous* satire [see Waters, *Duessa*].)

Daphnaïda's satire, which I will discuss in detail in the next chapter, can be seen as intermediate, in that it was composed after the first installment of *The Faerie Queene* but before the censorship of *Complaints* (Weiss, "Watermark"). As a private satire of an acquaintance, this work presumably posed no real risk to Spenser, but his inventiveness in the poem—using genre and readers' generic expectations themselves to create indirect satirical meanings—indicates a further step in Spenser's development of the possibilities of indirect forms of satirical meaning-making. Similarly, Spenser avoids major risks with the satirical moments in *Colin Clouts Come Home Againe*, dedicated December 27, 1591, though not published until 1595. The criticisms of court life in *Colin Clouts Come Home Againe*, even though the court he targets clearly figures the English one, are much more cautious than the preceding *Complaints* poems or the 1596 *Faerie Queene* books.

Continuing this speculation on Spenser as satirist, we can imagine that, with the 1596 installment of *The Faerie Queene*, Spenser found a balance between the caution of *The Shepheardes Calender* and the rashness of *Complaints*, a balance that Aristotle might describe as true courage. He intervenes into court politics with his allegorical defense of Walter Raleigh against the displeasure of the Queen at his secret marriage. He offers multiple opinions on European political and religious struggles with his allegorizations of the situations in France and the Netherlands. Most famously, he supports the justice of executing Mary, Queen of Scots, by allegorizing her as Duessa and putting her on trial. This passage motivated King James VI of Scotland, who of course dearly hoped to become King James I of England, to attempt to influence Elizabeth to punish, not the book, but Spenser himself. A November 1596 letter from Robert Bowes to Burghley states:

> The K[ing] hath conceaved of great offence against Edward [sic] Spencer publishing in prynte in the second book p[ar]t of the Fairy Queene and ixth chapter some dishonorable effects (as the k. demeth therof) against himself and his mother deceassed ... he still desyreth that Edward Spencer for his faulte, may be dewly tryed & punished. (qtd. in Goldberg, *James I*, 1)[6]

Fortunately for Spenser, the queen declined to follow up on James's request. Spenser died just over two years later, so he was spared from finding out if James was able to hold a grudge for as long as Burghley could, and we missed out on the chance to learn how Spenser, fully mature as both a poet and a satirist, would have responded to King James I of England.

Yes, Spenser built his career in an arc leading to the highest poetic genre, so that he could claim the status of an epic poet. Over the centuries, as he became a specimen for anthologies and survey courses, he often became *only* an epic poet, or sometimes a pastoral poet as well. But

---

6 For additional discussion of this passage, see McCabe, "Masks," for an analysis of James's response, and Ashworth-King, *Ethics of Satire*, chapter 3, for a discussion of its meaning within the overall context of Spenser's satirical meanings in the Mercilla episode.

in his time, and for his contemporaries, his inventive muse led him to a larger array of genres, of experiments, of poetic stances, than he was to be remembered for. His satirical works were an important part of who he was, both for his contemporaries and for his own poetic self-image, and although too much time has passed, and not enough documentation exists, for us to understand fully everything that Spenser attempted to say, or that his contemporaries heard, in his satirical poetry, this book attempts to begin filling in some of the gaps in the story of Spenser as satirist.

2

Spenser's satire of indirection: affiliation, allusion, allegory

The previous chapter provided a preliminary analysis of how indirect satire works to create a sense of an allegorical connection to the real world and real situations and discussed how allusions, symbolism, and analogy prompted allegorical projections that inflected contemporaries' understanding of the message of *Mother Hubberds Tale*, Spenser's best-known satirical work. In this chapter, I will continue analyzing Spenserian indirection in satire, but with an additional concept in play by examining the way that Spenser presents affiliative ties with other poets as part of his own self-fashioning as a satirical poet. Just as, in the 1590s and the early seventeenth century, younger poets affiliated themselves with Spenser in their poetry in order to convey certain messages about their poetic and/or political values, Spenser, in 1579 and in the early 1590s, needed to define the type of poet he aimed to be with reference to other poets.

To the extent that satire depends upon allegorical processes of meaning-making, theories of allegory can be productively transferred to understanding satire. Maureen Quilligan's comments on the allegorical "pretext"—"the source that always stands outside the narrative ... the pretext is the text that the narrative comments on by reenacting" (*Language of Allegory*, 97–98)—can illuminate both Spenser's and younger poets' uses of earlier poets as satirical pretexts. I will discuss in this chapter a number of poetic affiliative ties Spenser emphasizes in *The Shepheardes Calender* to create a sense of his literary genealogy, and all of these contribute to his performance of a poetic identity, but his true allegorical and satirical pretext in the *Calender* is of course John Skelton's *Collyn Cloute*. This book takes the form that it does from my interest not just in the pretexts important to understanding Spenser's satirical writing but also in Spenser's satirical poems *as themselves pretexts* for younger poets. Young Spenser signaled something about the poet he wanted to be by claiming the name Colin Clout as his alter ego and thus linking himself to Skelton. For other poets, alluding to or modeling work on Spenser becomes a shorthand way of affiliating oneself with a well-defined poetic and even political stance, because of his well-known enmity to Lord Burghley. If Quilligan is correct that the existence of a pretext is a *sine qua non* of allegory, then so, too, of indirect satire, and thus this book becomes a series of backwards mappings: from Spenser to his satirical pretexts, and from younger poets to their Spenserian pretexts.

This chapter will analyze Spenser's satirical uses of pretexts in order to create and display a poetic persona. In *The Shepheardes Calender*, Spenser uses extensive allusions to define himself as the "new poet." Titling his work *The Shepheardes Calender* connects his work with *The Kalender of Shepardes*, the popular sixteenth-century almanac that John Foxe mentions as a work that was "accused & detected" as a Protestant book (Foxe, *Acts*, 808). By naming his poetic alter ego "Colin Clout," Spenser affiliates himself with John Skelton, the "new poet" and "British Catullus" of the early sixteenth century, as a way of signaling how his own poetic preoccupations differ from those of the "old poet" Chaucer, specifically to advertise himself as interested in focused and specific satire, not vague complaint. Twelve years later, in his *Daphnaïda*, Spenser once again pushes against the Chaucerian model by using a Chaucerian pretext, *The Book of the Duchess*, to create a targeted satire that criticizes Arthur Gorges for his excessive mourning for his dead wife.

From affiliative allusion to allegory: becoming Colin Clout

A retrospective view (and selective attention to only some of Spenser's corpus) allows us to see a purposeful, sure arc to Spenser's career, with clear authorial statements from the beginning showing, for example, his plan to model his career on the Virgilian rota or to describe his career in terms of a tradition of avian imagery, according to Richard Helgerson and Patrick Cheney, respectively (Helgerson, *Self-Crowned Laureates*; Cheney, *Spenser's Famous Flight*). But we can also see false starts and uncertainty—the early poems, now lost, that he discusses with Gabriel Harvey in their published letters, for example, or the confusing semiotic superfluity of the presentation of *The Shepheardes Calender* (Halpern, *Poetics*, chapter 5), including the use of three different names to represent or refer to the poet. Helgerson asserts that Spenser "abandon[ed] all social identity except that conferred by his elected vocation. He ceased to be Master Edmund Spenser ... and became Immerito, Colin Clout, the New Poet" (Helgerson, *Self-Crowned Laureates*, 63), but this narrative, to my mind, overstates the definitiveness of the transformation and reads Spenser's later poetic self-confidence backward to 1579.

Later, Spenser would "become" Colin Clout—an allegorical alter ego for the poet himself, freed somewhat from the constraints of his original fictional world—but in 1579 Colin Clout was a fictional character "under [whose] name this Poete secretly shadoweth himself," E.K. tells us (Spenser, *Shepheardes Calender*, 33). That is, in 1579 Colin has not yet become an allegory for Spenser, the poet; despite "shadowing" Spenser, Colin is primarily a character whose name serves as an allusion, an "entry code" that E.K. explicitly connects to John Skelton, whose poem *Collyn Cloute* uses an eponymous rustic figure to criticize and satirize abuses in the Church, with pointed attention to Cardinal Wolsey, and to Clément Marot, who used the name Colin in one of his eclogues.[1] Despite the avowed Marot connection, certainly for a sixteenth-century English audience, the addition of "Clout" to "Colin" would create a strong association with Skelton: *Collyn Cloute* was among Skelton's most popular works throughout the sixteenth century; in 1541, William Barnes named the narrator of his satirical pro-beard treatise "Collyn Clowte" (written in skeltonics), suggesting widespread recognition of this figure as a sort of everyman satirist (Griffiths, "'An ende,'" 717–18).

Thus, although by the end of his career, "Colin Clout" functioned for contemporaries as a poetic cognomen for Spenser himself, this is a phenomenon of the 1590s that can obscure our understanding of the Colin of 1579. Spenser himself begins the process of greater self-identification with Colin in 1591 in *The Ruines of Time*, where he apparently refers to himself as the "Colin Clout" who has not yet commemorated the death of Sidney. This Colin—"his Colin" to the great Astrophel/Sidney (Spenser, *Ruines*, line 225)—and the Colin of *Colin Clouts Come Home Againe* bear more biographical resemblance to Spenser than to the shepherd boy of *The Shepheardes Calender*, and the commendatory sonnet addressed to Colin that precedes the *Amoretti* in 1595 similarly points to the poet Spenser. The idea caught on quickly, so that many uses of "Colin" in literary works by other authors in the 1590s clearly refer to the poet, not the character. Evidence, though, that this conflation of Spenser and

---

1 For previous work connecting Spenser's Colin Clout with Skelton's, see McLane, "Skelton's *Colyn*," and Segall, "Skeltonic Anxiety." McLane believes that Spenser alludes to Skelton in order to highlight the significance of Skelton's animus against Cardinal Wolsey to an understanding of Spenser's indirect satire of Lord Burghley; Segall argues that Spenser chooses Colin Clout because Skelton's Collyn exemplifies an anxiety about the role of the poet that Spenser shares. For work connecting Spenser to Marot, see Prescott, *French Poets*, 10–13; and Patterson, "Re-opening."

Colin occurs primarily in the 1590s comes from George Peele's *Arraignment of Paris* (published 1584), in which the lovelorn Colin—surrounded by friends Hobinol, Thenot, and Digon—is simply a character: an allusion to Spenser, that is, not an allegorical stand-in for him.

But before he "became" Colin Clout, Spenser was the "New Poet" and, briefly, "Immerito." Although Lynn Staley Johnson correctly distinguishes the Colin of the 1570s from the Colin of the 1590s and wisely cautions against "view[ing] Colin Clout as simply a pseudonym for the poet" in the 1579 *Shepheardes Calender*, she errs, I think, in seeming at times to transfer that role to Immerito, repeatedly referring to the authorial voice in the work by the name of "Immerito" (Johnson, *Shepheardes*, 8). Following in Johnson's path, Jennifer Richards continues the conflation of Immerito with Spenser but with a more pointed analytical perspective, building an argument based on the contrast between the voice of "its supposed author 'Immerito' (Spenser's persona)" with those of the other characters, including "Colin (Immerito's persona)" (Richards, *Rhetoric*, 140). Thinking of Colin and Immerito in relation to one another adds nuance to our understanding of these two as fictional characters, but considering them both also in relation to the poet's other moniker as "the New Poet" can provide a sharper sense of how Spenser is using these three names to create a satirical auto-genealogy through allusion.

What does Spenser mean by having E.K. refer to the author of the work as "the new Poete," and how does this designation connect with Colin Clout and Immerito? We can easily answer the question "new in comparison to what?" E.K. clearly identifies the Old Poet as Chaucer: in the first paragraph of the Epistle he mentions "the olde famous Poete Chaucer" and refers to Pandar in the work of "that good old Poete" (*Shepheardes Calender*, 13). John King has argued that, in paying homage to Chaucer, Spenser aims to connect himself to the "Reformation tradition of the radicalized Chaucer," making of himself "the heir and peer of Chaucer. To do so means that he dons the disguise of the Reformation satirist" (King, "Spenser's *Shepheardes Calender*," 378, 379). Spenser's admiration of Chaucer is undeniable, but he creates himself as the "new" poet partly in *contrast* to Chaucer's "old," not simply in homage. The Protestant "tradition of the radicalized Chaucer" finds proto-Protestant ideas in his poetry, but certainly the manner in which Chaucer expresses his criticisms of the Church is milder than the manner in which John Skelton made similar critiques. In *Shepheardes Calender*, Spenser clearly connects his project to the work of Chaucer, but he also contrasts himself to Chaucer by aligning himself with an earlier "new poet": Skelton. I believe he means this contrast to emphasize his own more aggressive and satirical stance in using poetry to comment on abuses. Thus, answering the question "what is a New Poet?" provides a fine example of Spenser's allusive practice and gives a sense of the importance of satire, and especially Skelton, to the role he envisioned for himself in 1579.

Three times in the Epistle to *The Shepheardes Calender*, E.K. refers to the author of the work as the New Poet. More than a decade later, the 1591 *Complaints* volume featured the identification "Ed. Sp." on the title page, but William Ponsonby, in "The Printer to the Gentle Reader," invites the reader "graciouslie to entertaine the new Poet" (Spenser, *Complaints*, 224). In non-Spenserian texts, we find William Webbe in *A Discourse of English Poetry* (1586) referring to the author of *The Shepheardes Calender* four times as "the new Poet," perhaps because he did not know Spenser's real name. Regardless, the reference to him as the new poet rather than Immerito or Colin Clout reminds us that this epithet was equally important to the public's identification of the resolutely anonymous author of *The Shepheardes Calender*, who suppressed his name not only from the first edition of 1579, but also from subsequent editions of 1581, 1586, and 1591.

Before Spenser claimed the moniker "new poet" (through E.K., presumably because it would be unseemly to nominate himself, and thus he instead refers to himself as "Immerito"), England had another "new poet" in Skelton. In a commendatory poem included in the 1568 edition of Skelton, Thomas Churchyard tells his readers not to scorn "the works and sugred verses fine / Of our raer poetes newe" (Churchyard, "If slouth," A3v).[2] This appellation, offered after Skelton's death in a new edition of his works, would perhaps be insignificant except for the fact that it may allude to an even earlier "new poet," Catullus, with whom Skelton had compared himself—immodestly as usual—as the "British Catullus" in his *Garland of Laurel*:

> Skeltonis alloquitur librum suum
> Ite, Britannorum lux O radiosa, Britannum
> Carmina nostra pium vestrum celebrate Catullum!
> Dicite, Skeltonis vester Adonis erat;
> Dicite, Skeltonis vester Homerus erat.
> Barbara cum Latio pariter jam currite versu;
> Et licet est verbo pars maxima texta Britanno,
> Non magis incompta nostra Thalya patet,
> Est magis inculta nec mea Caliope.
> (Skelton, *Garlande*, lines 1520–28)

---

2 For details on Spenser's knowledge of and debts to Churchyard, see Scott Lucas, "Diggon Davie," 164n24.

Skelton speaks to his book. Go, shining light of the Britons, and celebrate, our songs, your worthy British Catullus! Say, Skelton was your Adonis; say, Skelton was your Homer. Though barbarous, you now compete in an equal race with Latin verse. And though for the most part it is made up of British words our Thalia appears not too rude, nor is my Calliope too uncultured. (Skelton, *Garlande*, 512n1519–32)

Whereas scholars such as James McPeek and Jacob Blevins have interpreted Skelton's self-identification with Catullus as "referring to the fame that Catullus enjoyed as an uninhibited lyric poet" (McPeek, *Catullus*, 95),[3] Juan Manuel Castro Carracedo argues that Skelton means to emphasize his own innovations, both formally and in the use of the vernacular, in line with Catullus's well-known status as a "neoteric" or "new poet."[4] According to Carracedo, "Skelton feels that his work is different from everything written before, even different from his contemporaries... . By calling himself the 'British Catullus' he demands the label of *New Poet*, he wants to be, for the English letters, what Catullus meant in his time" (Carracedo, "*Pium Vestrum*," 13–14). Certainly the *Garland of Laurel* passage quoted above focuses on innovation, specifically linguistic innovation in developing English as a poetic language, but there is evidence that Skelton also thought of Catullus as a satirical poet, not just an erotic one.

Carracedo argues that Skelton did not think of Catullus as a satirist, because Catullus does not appear in the list of "poettes saturicall" that Skelton provides in *Agenst Garnesche*, a list that includes "Persius and Juvynall, / Horace and noble Marciall" (Skelton, *Agenst Garnesche*, section v, lines 139–41; Carracedo, "*Pium Vestrum*," 6). Still, in Skelton's other reference to Catullus, we find evidence connecting him to the Latin satirists. In *A Replycacion*, after quoting Jerome's comparison of the psalms of David to the work of secular poets ("David, inquit, Simonides noster, Pindarus, et Alceus, Flaccus quoque, Catullus, atque Serenus, Christum lyra personat, et in decachordo psalterio ab inferis excitat resurgentem"), Skelton translates and expands upon Jerome's text, including "Flaccus nor Catullus with hym [i.e., David] may nat compare" (Skelton, *A Replycacion*, line 336). By quoting and expanding upon Jerome's linking of Catullus with "Flaccus"—that is, Quintus Flaccus Horatius, that is, Horace, who *is*

---

3   See also Blevins, *Catullan Consciousness*, 20–21.
4   These descriptions, the Greek "neoteric" in Cicero's *Letters to Atticus* and "poetae novi" in his *Orator*, are, as Julia Haig Gaisser notes, "used by Cicero in disgust and by modern critics in approbation," and this approval of Catullus as an innovator characterized his Renaissance reception as well (Gaisser, *Catullus*, 4).

included in Skelton's list of "poettes saturicall"—Skelton provides evidence for my argument that both Catullus's innovative practices *and* his harsh, even insulting poetic criticisms of his political and poetic enemies served as inspiration to Skelton, leading him to style himself the British Catullus.

Even more so than the monikers "Colin Clout" and the "New Poet," which connect Spenser to the past, but to a specific poetic lineage, titling his work *The Shepheardes Calender* connects him to the folk wisdom of the medieval past, but with a playful twist. The title *Shepheardes Calender* is self-consciously allusive, given that E.K. refers to it in the "Epistle" as "applying an olde name to a new worke" (Spenser, *Shepheardes Calender*, 19). *The Kalender of Shepherds*, translated from the French, was extremely popular in sixteenth-century England, going through nineteen editions between 1503 and 1631 (Driver, "When is a miscellany," 200), but Spenser scholars have found "little connection between that heterogeneous handbook of kitchen astrology and Spenser's sophisticated eclogues" (Heninger, "Shepheardes," 645). The form and content of the book differ substantially from Spenser's work, so Spenser clearly did not look to the *Kalender* for literary inspiration (however, see Shinn, "Extraordinary," 139–41, for discussion of some thematic connections). However, he might well have chosen to link his book to the *Kalender* not only because it, like the name Colin Clout, suggested a homely source of communal wisdom but also because of its reputation as a proto-Protestant book, as highlighted by John Foxe in his *Acts and Monuments*.

In a list of hundreds of names in a table in the *Acts* titled "Persecution in the Dioces of Lincolne," covering records for the year 1521, Foxe singles out "*The Shepheardes Kalender*" in the column "parties accused" for going "agaynst the bodely presence," "Because the same [John] Edmundes sayde that hee was persuaded by this booke, readynge these woordes: that the Sacrament was made in the remembrance of Christ" (Foxe, *Acts*, 808).[5] These persecuted Protestants, Foxe notes, were not "learned, being simple laborers and artificers, but as it pleased the Lord to worke in them knowledge and vnderstandyng, by readyng a few Englishe bookes, such as they could get in corners" (Foxe, *Acts*, 809), and they learned about the doctrine of consubstantiation "partly out of Wickliffes wicket, partly out of the Shepehardes Calender" (Foxe, *Acts*, 810).

Interestingly, however, although religion is clearly an extremely important part of the overall message of the work (Driver, "When is a miscel-

---

5 Immediately thereafter, spanning both the "Parties accused" and "Crime objected" columns, Foxe notes "The booke of William Thorpe likewise was muche complayned of both by thys Iohn Edmundes, and diuers other" (Foxe, *Acts*, 808).

lany," 211), there is not a great deal of evidence to support viewing *The Kalender of Shepherds* as espousing strongly Protestant views. The poem for October focuses on the month as the time for vintners to press wine, some of which will become sacred as "The blessed body of Christ in fleshe and blode / Which is our hope, refection and fode" (Copland, *Kalender*, B2v). Similarly, a passage on the Lord's Prayer explains the request for daily bread thus: "Here we aske of God to be susteyned with materiall breade for our bodyes, and spiritual bread for our soules, that is the bread of lyfe, the body of Iesu Christ, the whiche we receaue by faith, in mynde of hys passion" (Copland, *Kalender*, F4r). In brief, a person who finds the doctrine of consubstantiation in *The Kalender of Shepherds* is either a person already so thoroughly converted to Protestantism that she finds its theology in every book she reads or a person playfully trying to divert his Catholic persecutors on to a false scent.

We find this second interpretation in two texts from the second half of the sixteenth century, in which "finding it in the *Shepherds Kalender*" seems to be an idiomatic expression that means "making things up." The Anglican bishop John Jewel, in a contentious mid-century print debate with the Catholic priest and apologist Thomas Harding, mocks Harding's interpolation of a tale of shepherds who accidentally consecrated bread and wine and then were immolated—every one—by fire from an angry God in heaven. If all the shepherds were killed, Jewel wonders, what angel or other divine messenger told the tale; without any reference to the source of the story, Jewel believes that Harding's reader "wil suspecte, M. Hardinge founde it in the Shepeheardes Calendare" (Jewel, *A Replie*, 552). The phrase receives a similarly fantastic connotation in the work of John Harvey, brother of Gabriel Harvey, in his treatise against prophecies: "Neither shal I therfore néede to ransacke *Pierce Plowmans* satchell; nor to descant vpon fortunes, newly collected out of the old shepherds *Kalender*" (Harvey, *A Discoursiue Probleme*, 62).

Thus, we find in both the title and the monikers for the poet contained therein allusions that would push a reader in 1579 to look for indirect satire. If *The Kalender of Shepherds* had a double meaning—both a dangerous (to Catholics) book that was labeled a "part[y] accused" in Foxe and a fantastic source of whatever ideas someone wishes to read into a book—then naming Spenser's own book *The Shepheardes Calender* would both prod the reader to read searchingly *and* provide a playful cover of deniability. Likewise, E.K.'s reference to the "New Poet," coupled with the creation of a character named Colin Clout, doubly ties Spenser to Skelton and connects him to Catullus as well, creating a satirical auto-genealogy (see Falco, *Conceived Presences*, 51). Neither of these earlier poets shied from directly attacking their enemies in verse: in 16, Catullus offers to rape Furius and Aurelius, who say his verses are impure (Catullus, *Poems*, 22);[6] Skelton's flyting poems lack some of the shock value of Catullus, but, like Catullus, he names and directly insults his enemies.

Considering the "New Poet" and *The Shepheardes Calender* with reference to their namesakes would have prompted the contemporary reader of E.K.'s comment on the "Moral" eclogues, "which for the most part be mixed with some Satyrical bitternesse" and his explanation that there are a few of the eclogues "whose speciall purpose and meaning I am not privie to" to look for indirect satirical meanings. A reader thus primed would be alert to the numerous anagrams, nicknames, or actual names that appear in the *Calender*—Morrell, Algrind, Roffy, Lowder, Diggon Davy, Lettice, and so forth—and perhaps more likely to read them as intentional and allusive. Spenserian scholars' acceptance of such names as satirical entry codes is unambivalent, even when the specific interpretation is either unrecoverable or debatable centuries later. My project in this book is to extend attention to such indirect entry codes both to Spenser's works that have not been fully considered as having satirical meanings and to works by other authors that use Spenserian pretexts to create indirect satire. I begin with Spenser's *Daphnaïda*, a mostly unliked poem that I argue can be improved by reading it as a satire.

Spenserian indirection and readerly ingenuity: a reading of *Daphnaïda*

In Spenser's *Daphnaïda*, critics meet with the problem of accounting for what David Lee Miller calls "the poem's deliberate badness" (Miller, "Laughing," 245), the many features—from drearily repetitive poetry in Alcyon's too-long lament to the generic transgressions of a pastoral elegy in which the mourner refuses any possibility of consolation other than death—that have made the poem Spenser's least-loved work. Historical approaches to the poem seek interpretive help from information derived from the historical context; formal approaches look at issues of genre and intertextuality, but no one can agree on what Spenser was trying to accomplish with this poem. The dividedness of critical opinion on this poem indicates its slipperiness, serving to remind us of the importance of the *reader* in Spenser's satirical works. Readers who approach the work "straight," that is, as a serious attempt at pastoral elegy, provide us with one

---

6 The Loeb edition modestly translates only part of the poem.

set of interpretations;[7] readers open to ironic or playful readings, on the other hand, find diametrically opposed readings. Significantly, however, the poem allows either kind of reading, straight or satirical, and this is characteristic of indirect, Spenserian satire. Instead of viewing this work as a failed pastoral elegy, in this section, I argue for reading *Daphnaïda* as an intentional satire: through his caricature of the mourner Alcyon, Spenser creates not so much a reasoned critique of excessive grief as a vision of mourning or sorrow so extreme that it crosses from elegy into satire by means of allegory.

The most influential recent interpretations of the poem place varying degrees of emphasis on either text or context, with Donald Cheney's largely ahistorical reading of the poem as musing about the nature of poetry serving as an outlier to more typical attention to links between the poem and the historical situation of Arthur Gorges, the death of whose first wife, Douglas Howard, led Gorges into numerous legal battles with her relatives regarding inheritance (see Cheney, "Grief," for the former and Gibson, "Legal context," for the latter). Although Spenser does not here explicitly identify Gorges with Alcyon and Douglas Howard with Daphne, he invites speculation upon the connection by describing the work on the title page as "an Elegie vpon the death of the noble and virtuous Douglas Howard, *Daughter and* heire of *Henry* Lord *Howard, Viscount Byndon, and wife of* Arthure Gorges *Esquier*" (486). The dedication to the Marchioness of Northampton, Gorges's aunt, makes more compliments to Gorges and his deceased wife but again without explicitly connecting them to the characters portrayed in the poem itself. Although later, Spenser suggests in *Colin Clouts Come Home Againe* (dedicated 1591, published 1595) a one-to-one correspondence between Alcyon and Gorges and Daphne and Douglas Howard by referring to "Alcyon" and "Daphne" and identifying Alcyon as the author of Gorges's *Eglantine of Meriflure*, he avoids making such direct connections in *Daphnaïda* (*CCCHA*, lines 384, 386, 389).

Thanks to the litigiousness of Douglas Howard's relations, who tried to block both Gorges and their daughter Ambrosia from inheriting from Howard, the richness of the historical record vis-à-vis Gorges's marriage—Douglas Howard's death, Ambrosia's life and early death—has provided

7 Efforts to find in *Daphnaïda* a successful pastoral elegy have tended to seek consolation in numerological analyses of the poem's structure. See, for example, Røstvig, *Hidden Sense*, 82–87; and Kay, *Melodious Tears*, 49–52. Kay writes that "Spenser uses structure as a species of consolation, as a demonstration of the capacity of art to suggest meaning, order, and purpose" (52). The lack of consolation at the level of word and image seems to me a problem in approaching this work as a sincere pastoral elegy.

ample information on which to base interpretations of the poem with reference to the Gorges situation. William Oram finds in Spenser's fictional Alcyon a critique of excessive mourning directed at the real man Gorges by his friend and well-wisher Spenser (Oram, "Daphnaida"). Jonathan Gibson finds in Alcyon's bathetic sorrow the image of a man out of his mind with grief and hypothesizes that Spenser intended the poem to serve as something of a character witness in Gorges's ongoing legal squabbles with the Howard family—this grief-stricken widower bears no resemblance to the calculating gold-digger that Douglas Howard's uncle saw when he looked at Gorges (Gibson, "Legal context"; see Hadfield, *A Life*, 284–88, for details of the friendship between Spenser and Gorges). David Lee Miller sees in Alcyon a parody of the sort of histrionic emotional performance perfected by Sir Walter Raleigh, friend of both Spenser and Gorges, and speculates that Spenser, disgusted by such shows, involved himself poetically in Gorges's legal battle at Raleigh's instigation and protested by making Alcyon/Gorges look ridiculous (Miller, "Laughing").

In addition to these comparisons between poem and history, other scholars compare *Daphnaïda* to its source-text, Chaucer's *Book of the Duchess*, to Chaucer's source-text in Ovid's *Metamorphoses*, or to Spenser's own poetry (Cheney, "Grief"; Harris and Steffen, "Other side"; Steinberg, "Idolatrous idylls"). My own reading will focus on intertextuality, but with an emphasis not so much on what Spenser knew but on what he could expect his readers to know, because of the importance of providing just the right amount of information to enable one's reader to make a connection and read for satire. In addition to the interested parties who might have read this poem in 1591—such players as Gorges, Raleigh, the Marchioness of Northampton, or others involved with Gorges's legal battles—Spenser published *Daphnaïda* with a larger audience in mind. I will consider the poem with this imaginary 1591 reader in mind, paying attention to the expectations the text raises and the specific words and images that may have called other texts and other ideas to mind for this reader.

Spenser advertises the poem on the title page as an "Elegie"; in the dedicatory letter he refers to it as a "little Poëme" and a "Pamphlet" (pp. 486, 492, 493); later, in *Colin Clouts Come Home Againe*, Colin says that he "complaine[d]" (line 511) *Daphnaïda* to Mansilia, the shepherdess who represents Helena Snackenborg, the Marchioness of Northampton and Gorges's aunt. In the poem itself, Alcyon blames Daphne's death on "a cruell *Satyre* with his murdrous dart" (Spenser, *Daphnaïda*, 156). These words are not all mutually exclusive (and of course "complaine" is inadmissible as part of the experience of our hypothetical 1591 reader), but, taken together, they suggest an intentional generic instability, a sense that strengthens with the generically bizarre opening invocation. Spenser's more typical contributions to the English pastoral elegy—the "November" eclogue, *Astrophel*, and *The Doleful Lay of Clorinda*—indicate his familiarity with classical and continental models and certainly form part of the English tradition of this mode.[8] The beginning of *Daphnaïda*, however, jars against the reader's expectations of elegy. Instead of invoking a Muse such as Melpomene, as he does in "November," or avoiding invocation altogether, as befits a pose of rustic simplicity, as he does in *Astrophel*, Spenser banishes "the sacred Sisters," because "their heavie song would breede delight" (lines 11, 13). Instead, he invokes "those three fatall Sisters, whose sad hands / Doo weave the direfull threds of destinie" (lines 16–17).

David Lee Miller sees in this invocation a banishing not only of the Muses but also of Horatian *dulce et utile*, such that Spenser creates a "deliberately unpleasing" poem (Miller, "Laughing," 244). Glenn Steinberg tries to render this banishment less strange by arguing that Spenser's repudiation of the Muses here functions as Protestant iconoclasm, because he sees the Muses as "idolatrous symbols of art and beauty" ("Idolatrous idylls," 130). Spenser's devotion to the Muses elsewhere in his work makes this argument a hard sell, and it also ignores the invocation just a few lines later to the alternative muses of the Fates. The weirdness of this opening passage, however, becomes less weird when considered in light of the generic expectations regarding style and inspiration that readers brought to satires in the sixteenth century. John Skelton's "ragged" rhymes in *Collyn Cloute* (line 53); George Gascoigne's stated plan in *The Steele Glas* to win fame not through poetic merit but with "rymelesse verse, which thundreth mighty threates" ("The author to the reader," line 14); and Spenser's own "No Muses aide me needes heretoo to call; / Base is the style, and matter meane withall" in *Mother Hubberds Tale* (lines 43–44)— these denials of poetic merit develop by the late 1590s into aggressive satirical anti-invocations: John Marston's assertion that he "prostitute[s his] muse, / For all the swarms of idiots to abuse" (Marston, "In lectores," lines 61–62); Everard Guilpin's image of the "wits [who] haue got my Muse with Tympanie" and the "loose tayld penns" who will lance her swollen abdomen ("Satyre preludium," lines 96, 97); and Thomas Middle-

---

8 For a full recent discussion of Spenser's knowledge of and work within the tradition of pastoral elegy, see Kay, *Melodious Tears*. See also O'Connell, "*Astrophel*," for his argument that in *Astrophel* and *The Doleful Lay of Clorinda* Spenser exemplifies the two forms that consolation takes in elegy: poetic immortality and Christian apotheosis.

ton's promise to drink up the "devilish venom" of his detractors and then "belch" it up into their "throats all open wide" (*Micro-cynicon*, "The Author's Prologue," lines 28, 33). Spenser's banishing of both the Parnassian Muses and readers who find sense in pleasure or take delight in "this wretched life," and his promise of "no tunes, save sobs and grones" in "this dolefull teene," seems part of this same continuum of satirists advertising the ugliness of their verse (Spenser, *Daphnaïda*, lines 8, 9, 14, 21).

The strange invocation prompts the reader to question the genre of the poem, and Spenser also alludes to the source-text early in the poem, activating intertextual reading habits, by naming the main character in the first stanza. The reference to "sad *Alcyon*" might recall to the reader's mind either Chaucer's *Book of the Duchess* or Chaucer's source-text in Ovid's *Metamorphoses*; both recount the same story of Queen Alcyone, who dies from grief over the death of her husband, King Ceyx. Reader recognition of the Chaucerian source-text would obviously be more germane, and it is more likely as well, because the names Seis and Alcione were part of the title of the work we now call *The Book of the Duchess*. In the second half of the sixteenth century, publishers referred to the work as "The Dreame of Chaucer, otherwise called the boke of the Duches, or Seis and Alcione, with a balade to his master Buxton." A search of Early English Books Online indicates that most uses of the words "Alcyon" or "Alcyone" referred to the halcyon or kingfisher, or the associated "halcyon days" of winter—uses that emphasize the Ovidian metamorphosis of human into bird and thus a happy ending—but several refer to Alcyone in her human form as an exemplar of a mourning spouse. Lexicalization of eponymous terms (that is, the tendency for the source of a word in a story or name to be forgotten over time) means that, for some readers, the name "Alcyon" would call to mind a bird and nothing more, but, for most readers, the name would put in play ideas and expectations about mourning, specifically excessive grief.

After this introduction, which identifies the main character as Alcyon, banishes the Parnassian Muses, and engages the inspiration of the Fates as muses, the narrator begins his story. Oppressed in spirit by his own sorrow, he walks out into the fields one evening, but he doesn't get far before he encounters another person:

> I did espie
> Where towards me a sory wight did cost,
> Clad all in black, that mourning did bewray:
> And *Jaakob* staffe in hand devoutlie crost,
> Like to some Pilgrim come from farre away.

> His carelesse locks, uncombed and unshorne
> Hong long adowne, and beard all over growne,
> That well he seemd to be sum wight forlorne;
> Downe to the earth his heavie eyes were throwne
> As loathing light: and ever as he went,
> He sighed soft, and inly deepe did grone,
> As if his heart in peeces would have rent.
>
> (Spenser, *Daphnaïda*, lines 38–49)

Again, something is strange here, something that jars with generic conventions. The narrator has placed the scene in a pastoral landscape: "open fields, whose flowring pride opprest / With early frosts, had lost their beautie faire" (lines 27–28). Both the fields and the pathetic fallacy represent typical generic conventions of pastoral, as does indicating the time of day with reference to the sun: "the wearie Sun / After his dayes long labour drew to rest" (lines 22–23). Eventually, after the initial description just quoted, the narrator recognizes the figure as Alcyon, "the jollie Shepheard swaine, / That wont full merrilie to pipe and daunce / And fill with pleasance every wood and plaine" (lines 54–56), and this brings us back to typical imagery and language of pastoral. But the intervening lines quoted above do not fit the genre; instead, they echo the ways that Spenser introduces allegorical personifications in the first three books of *The Faerie Queene*, which, published less than a year earlier, Spenser could expect his readers to know.[9] Although allegorical *meaning* appears frequently in pastoral, as both Puttenham ("in rude speeches to insinuate and glance at greater matters"; *Art*, 128) and Sidney aver (poets "under the pretty tales of wolves and sheep" speak to larger concerns; *Apology*, 127), finding a *Faerie Queene*-like allegorical figure in a Spenserian pastoral poem is unusual. Although the narrator has named Alcyon early in the poem, in this description Spenser follows his typical practice in *The Faerie Queene* of delaying identification, using ekphrastic clues that focus on symbolic imagery before closing off identificatory speculation by providing a name. During the initial description, the reader does not know that this is Alcyon, the protagonist named in the first stanza; in

---

9 Adrian Weiss, by analyzing the paper and watermarks of various copies of *Daphnaïda* and the *Complaints* volume, has proved that *Daphnaïda*'s dedication date of January 1, 1591 is new style, not old style, and thus less than a year after the publication of the first installment of *The Faerie Queene* and in the same time period as the printing of *Complaints* (Weiss, "Watermark evidence"). Other critics have briefly noted the connections with allegory in the character of Alcyon: William Oram states that Alcyon "embodies with almost allegorical clarity the desire to grieve" ("*Daphnaida*," 143), and Glenn Steinberg writes that Alcyon "becomes almost an allegorical figure for 'lifes wretchednesse,' a projection of our own—and the narrator's—fear" ("Idolatrous idylls," 140).

light of this ambiguity, a reader might employ reading strategies developed through encountering the personifications in *The Faerie Queene*.

Such a reader would look for iconographic details that might help identify the figure and would also notice descriptive words that convey evaluative information. The figure wears black and carries a "*Jaakob staffe*" that makes him look "Like to some Pilgrim come from farre away" (lines 41–42). These details might link him to the Palmer in *The Faerie Queene*, whose name connects him with pilgrims; the Palmer goes "clad in black attyre" and uses a staff (*FQ* 2.1.7.2, 4). But another character in *The Faerie Queene* also wears black, looks like a pilgrim, and carries a staff: Archimago, whose staff is explicitly a "*Iacobs* staffe" (*FQ* 1.6.35.7; see 1.1.29.2 for the detail of his black clothes)—Archimago's and Alcyon's Jacob's-staffs are the only occurrences of the word in the works of Spenser. The reference to the Jacob's-staff is striking—it is an unusual word and a multivalenced one that deserves more scrutiny than Renwick's somewhat dismissive note "The *Jacob-staffe* was a navigating instrument, but Spenser here means simply a pilgrim-staff" (Renwick, *Commentary*, 176n41).[10] The *Oxford English Dictionary* lists three distinct meanings for the word current in the second half of the sixteenth century: the word can refer to a pilgrim's staff, an instrument for measuring celestial or terrestrial distances and heights, or a staff that conceals a dagger (s.v. "Jacob's staff, n."). A search of Early English Books Online for the keyword indicates that the majority of uses before 1600 refer to the Jacob's-staff's technical meaning for astronomy and surveying and that the unusual spelling "Jaakob staffe" occurs nowhere else. Indeed, the spelling "Jaakob" for the name "Jacob" appears *only* in biblical contexts during this time period. The word suggests rich possibilities for interpretation, to which I will return later.

The iconographic details of black clothing and the staff in the first stanza of description leave it unclear what emotional reaction Spenser expects his reader to have, but the unappealing description in the second stanza pushes the reader more strongly in the direction of a rejecting response to the figure. In *The Faerie Queene*, unkempt, unattractive figures represent or exemplify negative moral states, such that physical ugliness serves as shorthand for moral ugliness (Hile, "Disabling allegories"). The *Daphnaïda* figure's "carelesse locks, uncombed and unshorne, / [That] hong long adowne, and beard all over growne" connect him to unappealing *Faerie Queene* personifications such as Despair and

---

10 Oram et al. quote Renwick's interpretation of this word in the Yale edition (*Daphnaïda*, 495n41).

Occasion, both of whom have ugly hair hanging in front of their faces. Despair's "griesie lockes, long growen, and vnbound, / Disordred hong about his shoulders round, / And hid his face" (*FQ* 1.9.35.4–6), and Occasion's "lockes, that loathly were and hoarie gray, / Grew all afore, and loosly hong vnrold" (*FQ* 2.4.4.5–6). Andrew Escobedo's pithy summary of what "character" means in the Renaissance—"a category of narrative resource, not an individualized interior" (Escobedo, "Daemon lovers," 205)—aids in thinking about the incongruity of this figure in this poem. Spenser creates broad categories or types of character to populate the worlds that he creates, such as "negative allegorical personifications" and "simple shepherds." When Spenser creates a character who doesn't fit the world of the work he or she inhabits, as in the case of the figure described in these two stanzas in *Daphnaïda*, who is kin to *The Faerie Queene*'s allegorical personifications instead of Spenser's shepherd characters, he also creates irony. This irony of undermined expectations—the distance between what we expect and what Spenser provides—is a key method of creating satirical meaning.

Moving from this introduction into the plot, such as it is, of the poem, Spenser continues to undermine the reader's expectations of genre and character … and even of poetic merit. Some scholars have tried to redeem the poetry of Alcyon's lament; for example, Ellen Martin argues that critics who dislike the poem, or see it as inferior to *The Book of the Duchess*, create subjective assessments based on temperament, taste, and consistency (Martin, "Spenser"). But critical attempts at recuperating *Daphnaïda* as straightforward "good poetry" tend to focus on big-picture issues—numerological interpretations of structure, for example, as in Røstvig and Kay, or Martin's ideas of genre in relation to mourning and melancholia—and do not address directly the most obvious source of critics' distaste for the poem: the poetry of Alcyon's lament, which David Lee Miller bluntly calls "inexplicably bad" and which Duncan Harris and Nancy L. Steffen allude to politely by stating that the poem "depends … heavily for its effect on the reader's ability to recognize excess" (Harris and Steffen, "Other side," 27). Indeed, Alcyon's "intemperate complaint against everything in the universe" (Gibson, "Legal context," 24–25) includes a thirty-five-line summary of all the things Alcyon hates, such as the senses:

> I hate to speake, my voyce is spent with crying;
> I hate to heare, lowd plaints have duld mine eares;
> I hate to tast, for food withholds my dying;
> I hate to see, mine eyes are dimd with teares;

> I hate to smell, no sweet on earth is left;
> I hate to feele, my flesh is numbd with feares;
> So all my senses from me are bereft.
>
> (Spenser, *Daphnaïda*, lines 414–20)

The automaton meter, repetitive diction, and clichéd imagery are hallmarks of bad poetry—as Harris and Steffen note, Spenser expects the reader to recognize the excess of the poem, and this extends beyond Alcyon's emotions to the characteristics of his verse: excessively regular, excessively repetitive, and excessively trite. As I argue throughout this book, the satirist who writes in an indirect mode expects and demands more of the reader than the writer of more direct satire. Spenser creates in Alcyon a poet bad enough, he hopes, to enable a reader to have the confidence to judge that the acclaimed poet of *The Shepheardes Calender* and *The Faerie Queene* has put bad poetry into the mouth of this character, and to wonder why.

But the poetry is not just bad technically—we might call Alcyon's poetry, with its excessive, compulsive allegorizing, *ontologically bad*, because his poetry serves to distance him from reality. Leigh Deneef argues that Alcyon's most important characteristic is his status as poet, and that Spenser suggests the dangers of false poetry through Alcyon's stubborn misreadings of metaphor as literal truth: Daphne's *contemptus mundi* soliloquy, for example, or the pastoral cliché of nature's decline read as metaphor for human life (Deneef, *Spenser*, 48–49). However, the mirror image of this literalizing approach to metaphor is Alcyon's equally pronounced tendency to use metaphor and allegory to the near exclusion of literal statement; in this, he illustrates an extreme version of the stereotypical Renaissance love poet, who is also, not coincidentally, a figure of the bad poet. Shakespeare's speaker of Sonnet 130 mocks the clichéd metaphors of sonneteers by emphasizing the reality of his love's embodiedness, contrasting and privileging her fleshly imperfections against the idealism of the "false compare." The message is straightforward, with the wit arising from the cleverness of the contrast between reality and poetic idealizing; with Alcyon, the wit is in the creation of a parody, and the reader's pleasure comes from speculating on the rhetorical and satiric purposes of the parody.

Alcyon's metaphorizing and allegorizing impulses call to mind well-worn poetic tropes and imagery that Shakespeare mocks in Sonnet 130. Initially, she is a white lioness—a heraldic allusion to the Howard family—that Alcyon tamed "and brought away fast bound with silver chaine," after which she helped him to tend to his sheep (Spenser, *Daphnaïda*, line 119).

The narrator feels sympathy for Alcyon but confesses that he does not understand: "Yet doth not my dull wit well understand / The riddle of thy loved Lionesse" (lines 176–77). Deneef forgives the narrator for his frank confusion at the fable, noting, "This is not the naïve obtuseness of Chaucer's comic narrator: Spenser's narrator is totally cut off from Alcyon's meaning because he is given only a metaphoric vehicle; he does not, and cannot, know its tenor. He is led to assume, therefore, that the lioness is not metaphoric at all" (Deneef, *Spenser*, 45). Where Chaucer's narrator seems foolish for not recognizing that the Man in Black's reference to a game of chess with Fortune in which he lost his "fers" (i.e., the queen piece in medieval chess sets) is an extended metaphor, Spenser's Alcyon provides no such clues as the Man in Black's reference to "Fortune," which points Chaucer's reader to the presence of figurative language. But note the distinction between what Spenser's reader knows and what the narrator knows: whereas the reader can recognize the allegory because of the heraldic allusion, previous experience with beast fables' allegorical tendencies, and subtle echoes of Thomas Wyatt's "Whoso List to Hunt" (and his source in Petrarch's *Rime 190*)—because of extratextual and intertextual knowledge, that is—the reader does not expect the narrator, who after all lives in the pastoral world as an ignorant shepherd, to recognize this as allegory. Even more sustained than Alcyon's commitment to allegory, though, is his use of metaphors to describe Daphne, more of which I will discuss below. He describes Daphne with so many plant-themed metaphors as to be ludicrous. She is a "Primrose," "a flower," a "blossome," and "fruit blowne downe with winde" that still had green leaf, fresh rind, and a branch with blossoms (lines 233, 237, 252, 244).

In addition to suggesting Alcyon's weakness in poetic invention, his excessive metaphors for his lost love create a depersonalizing effect, especially when considered in contrast to Spenser's source-text, *The Book of the Duchess*, where the Man in Black provides a detailed portrait of his wife, White (i.e., John of Gaunt's deceased wife, Blanche), that conveys a sense of her human characteristics. Instead, Alcyon describes his Daphne in nonhuman terms—animal, plant, angel—and resists pursuing references to her as human; after the narrator's incomprehension forces him to explain his lioness allegory—"*Daphne* thou knewest … / She now is dead" (Spenser, *Daphnaïda*, lines 183–84)—he faints. After he revives and begins his formal complaint, he begins with a description of her as human—she excelled "In pureness and in all celestiall grace / That men admire in goodlie womankinde" (lines 211–12)—but then shifts immediately to comparing her to an angel ("seem'd of Angels race / … like Angell new divinde" [lines 213–14]) before moving into the series of plant metaphors quoted above.

Later, after repeating what Daphne said to him before her death, Alcyon moves to metaphorical descriptions of her words as weapons and allegorizations of her dead body. Not only are the words of her deathbed speech "piercing words / ... / ... like swords"; even the words she spoke at the beginning of their courtship "conquerd and possest" Alcyon's soul, extending the martial metaphor backwards and figuring Alcyon as Daphne's victim (lines 295–97, 300; military metaphors for love in sonnetry are of course commonplace: Alcyon's metaphors in general lack freshness). Contemplating the image of Daphne's face after death, Alcyon complains that "sad death his pourtraicture had writ" in her cheeks and "ghastly night did sit" on her eyes (lines 303, 305). Immediately after this, Alcyon spends a stanza describing her dancing among the other shepherdesses; this passage, along with the brief reference to "*Daphne* thou knewest" and Daphne as a paragon of womanhood (lines 183, 211–13), are the only references to her as a human. Later, when explaining why he shuns women, Alcyon veers away from describing Daphne in human terms, instead describing her as the "Starre" (line 424) of women. He recoils from remembering his wife as a woman, but, by doing so, he dehumanizes her through metaphor and allegory, and his inability to remember her in human terms serves as an index of his oft-noted lack of acceptance of his situation.

In contrast, the Man in Black's reminiscences of White in *The Book of the Duchess* show a change in his ability to deal with his loss. Although he, like Alcyon, distances himself from his loss by starting his conversation with the narrator with allegory and the extended chess metaphor in which Fortune has reft him of his fers, he eventually progresses to descriptions of a real person, creating a portrait of a flesh-and-blood woman with an actual personality. The 237-line passage in which the Man in Black describes White and recounts the story of their love includes details of her appearance, her mind, her virtues, and her personality. He occasionally uses metaphors to describe her (her throat, like the throats of so many other women celebrated in poetry, "Semed a round tour of yvoyre," line 946, but we can perhaps forgive Chaucer for writing this two hundred years before the sixteenth-century rage for sonnets wore it out), but these are rare, especially when considered as a proportion of the entire long narration. More typical is careful, detailed description that emphasizes the humanity and specificity of White, as in the following:

> Ryght faire shuldres and body long
> She had, and armes, every lyth
> Fattyssh, flesshy, not gret therwith;
> Ryght white handes, and nayles rede,
> Rounde brestes; and of good brede
> Hyr hippes were; a streight flat bak.
>
> (Chaucer, *Book*, lines 952–57)

If we think of the Man in Black's narrative mode as indexing the trajectory of his emotional response to his loss, the move from allegory (which I will discuss in a moment) to extended metaphor (the chess game with Fortune) to straight narrative and description suggests acceptance of loss and a willingness to allow memory to salve mourning. I believe that Spenser expects his reader to contrast Alcyon with the emotional trajectory of the Man in Black and to notice that Alcyon begins as an allegory and remains allegorical, permanently disconnected from reality by his stubborn commitment to grief.

At the beginning of the Man in Black's conversation with the narrator, he speaks allegorically through personifications, most interestingly personifying himself as sorrow: "For whoso seeth me first on morwe / May seyn he hath met with sorwe, / For y am sorwe, and sorwe ys y" (Chaucer, *Book*, lines 595–97). As already noted, he moves from this mode to the extended chess metaphor, and then to straightforward narrative. Alcyon, on the other hand, begins by appearing with the descriptive hallmarks of a Spenserian allegorical personification already discussed. In light of the Man in Black's self-allegorization in Spenser's source-text, Oram's observation that Alcyon "embodies with almost allegorical clarity the desire to grieve" can be pushed farther: both the narrator's description and Alcyon's own words support an identification of the abstract quality personified in Alcyon as "sorrow." But whereas we read the Man in Black's self-allegory metaphorically, if you will, Spenser "literalizes" it, in the sense that what is in Chaucer a verbal flourish becomes in *Daphnaïda* a shift of genre that underscores Spenser's serious ideas and critique about grieving, and allegorical interpretation thus becomes the key to reading this poem satirically. In this sense, then, to the extent that Spenser here mimics his own strategies for creating personifications in *The Faerie Queene*, requiring his readers to use interpretive strategies they learned by reading his allegorical epic the previous year, we can view *Faerie Queene* as one of the allegorical pretexts of this satirical poem.

Despite Chaucer's Man in Black's self-description as "sorwe," he finds consolation. Spenser's sorrowful Alcyon finds none, and in this we can see connections to another allegorization of Sorrow, Thomas Sackville's representation of Sorrow in his "Induction" to *The Mirror for Magistrates*. *Daphnaïda*'s opening scene presents a similar situation to that of Sackville's "Induction"—in both poems, a man walks out into the fields at day's end, brooding over troubling thoughts, and meets a figure in black. This is not remarkable, given the frequency with which medieval and early modern poems begin in a similar manner. Important, however, to a consideration of Spenser's oddly unconsolatory pastoral elegy is the fact that Sackville's Sorrow inhabits a thoroughly pagan fictional space: "Sorrowe I am, in endeles tormentes payned, / Among the furies in the infernall lake: / Where Pluto god of Hel ... / Doth holde his throne" ("Sackville's Induction," lines 108–11). She moans for the victims of Fortune and summarizes the trouble of life thus: "no earthly ioye may dure" (line 119). In the pagan hell to which she leads the narrator, no heavenly joy serves to compensate for the transience of earthly joy. Here we find another generic incongruity, in that the fall-of-princes trope does not require a Christian worldview, but Spenser's poem would seem to.

I suggest that we find in Alcyon and in *Daphnaïda* not so much allegorical satire as allegory *as* satire, a biting commentary on the dangers of *idées fixes* in the real world, with the pastoral world here standing as Spenser's literary representation of the real world, and the allegorical personification intruding, incongruously and indecorously. If allegory, then, is key to the satirical reading I advance in this chapter, what might have been Spenser's aims in making of Alcyon, that shepherd's swain, an allegorical personification who spouts allegories and metaphors compulsively?

Allegorical personifications are strange, but one becomes stranger still in the pastoral landscape: theoretical considerations of how such personifications work become intensified when considering one outside its natural habitat. The sense that the various actors in play in allegory represent the interaction of abstractions makes even the encounter between the narrator and Alcyon potentially meaningful. Linda Gregerson's distinction between "exemplary" and "catalytic" personifications—with an exemplary personification understood as one that "directly bodies forth the psychic or material condition for which it is named" and catalytic personifications functioning "as the precipitating cause or occasion of the condition for which it is named"—thus complicates our understanding of the meeting between the sorrowing narrator and a figure who in some ways personifies sorrow (Gregerson, *Reformation*, 55–56). This reading illuminates Oram's comment that "Alcyon surely embodies at one level an impulse within the narrator: the juxtaposition of his appearance with the narrator's brooding melancholy suggests an allegorical dimension to the character," just as "the Redcrosse Knight comes across Sans Joy when he is feeling neglected in the House of Pride" (Oram, "*Daphnaida*," 154).

Alcyon's dual function as both exemplary and catalytic complicates his identity, because it suggests the sort of shifting relevant to Spenserian personifications who share this doubleness, such as *The Faerie Queene*'s Malbecco and Despair, both of whom appeared in the first installment of the work and thus were part of Spenser's recent publishing past at the time he composed *Daphnaïda*. Gregerson argues that Malbecco functions both exemplarily and catalytically (Gregerson, *Reformation*, 56); Despair does as well, as suggested by James Nohrnberg's comment that "In hanging himself ... [Despair] moves in the opposite direction from Malbecco, that is, from human Despair to a despairing man" (Nohrnberg, *Analogy*, 99). Gregerson and Nohrnberg have slightly different foci, but both their comments highlight that sense of the capacity to shift, to change from human into ossified personification (or vice versa), which suggests here the narrowing of freedom illustrated through the figure of Alcyon. Escobedo notes that "Personification expresses the sense that the necessity imposed by the order of nonfictional ideas has gotten inside the character, shifting adjective to noun, imbuing her with an essence that compels behavior from within as well as without" ("Daemon lovers," 210). He is interested in choice and free will among Spenserian characters, but his comment, with its description of the shift along a continuum from "human" to "personification," can also inform our understanding of characters such as Malbecco and Despair who makes these shifts.

My overarching argument in this section is that the initial description of Alcyon imports the allegorical mode into this otherwise pastoral world, calling on the reader to exercise the same reading strategies he or she would bring to *The Faerie Queene*. Alcyon, as Sorrow, is a "character" in the Renaissance sense of a caricaturish personality type, and Spenser invites the reader to laugh at him just as audiences and readers were later to laugh at the satiric character portraits of the formal verse satirists and epigrammatists of the 1590s, Ben Jonson's humours comedies at the turn of the century, or Sir Thomas Overbury's *Characters* in the seventeenth century. Whereas the reader's pleasure with those later incarnations of the one-note character depended upon the wit and verbal brilliance (or outrageousness) of the author, Spenser's early version of the same preoccupation with the dividing line between human and caricature grows out of his own work in allegory. For the reader of *Daphnaïda*, the pleasure depends on the irony and incongruity of a personification within the sheep-fields and on bringing allegorical reading strategies to bear in an ostensibly pastoral poem.

However instructive it may be to think of Alcyon's resemblances to satirical "characters" or "humours"-driven figures, Spenser's preference for indirect satirical meaning-making leads to less obvious judgments than those more directly judgmental works. Reading Alcyon—like reading with attention to the possibility of satire in the Fox, Verlame, the Gnat, the oak and the briar, Diggon Davy, Duessa, and so on and so forth—involves sensitivity to unusual words, out-of-place images, and passages that call to mind other texts, that is, the same reading strategies prompted by allusion, symbol, and analogy's clues to read allegorically that I discussed at length in the first chapter. In this chapter so far, I have argued that Spenser includes things that don't fit the genre of pastoral elegy, such as invoking the Fates instead of the Muses and introducing a shepherd in the same way he introduces negative allegorical personifications such as Despair and Occasion; that Alcyon's poetry and thinking are both bad; and that Spenser's invention of this character may have begun with Chaucer's Man in Black's statement "y am sorwe, and sorwe ys y." In the remainder of the chapter, I will return to a consideration of Spenser's introductory description, connecting this figure to the Wandering Jew and the Old Man of Chaucer's *Pardoner's Tale*. I believe that reading the description of Alcyon emblematically and allegorically like this helps to tie together the whole poem, leading to an interpretation of Alcyon as not just one who sorrows, but one who sorrows without faith, one who sorrows culpably and thus brings on himself the same punishment of restless wandering and long life suffered by the Wandering Jew and Chaucer's Old Man.

I have already discussed the description of Alcyon with reference to other figures created by Spenser, and those connections, with their negative evaluative words, help the reader to know immediately not to admire the figure described thus. However, the fuller meaning of other details of the description do not become apparent until later in the poem, and thus the reader attempting to interpret the description of Alcyon iconographically, particularly his "*Jaakob* staffe," has to wait until more details emerge. I mentioned above the rareness of the spelling "Jaakob," which occurs, other than this use, only in Biblical contexts referring to the patriarch Jacob, or Israel. To spell the already unusual word "Jacob's-staff" as "*Jaakob* staffe" is strangely Hebraicizing, a choice that makes sense only later in the poem, when Alcyon describes his perpetual wandering:

> Yet whilest I in this wretched vale doo stay,
> My wearie feete shall ever wandring be,
> That still I may be readie on my way,
> When as her messenger doth come for me:
> Ne will I rest my feete for feeblenesse,
> Ne will I rest my limmes for frailtie,
> Ne will I rest mine eyes for heavinesse.
>
> But as the mother of the Gods, that sought
> For faire *Eurydice* her daughter deere
> Throghout the world, with wofull heavie thought;
> So will I travell whilest I tarrie heere,
> Ne will I lodge, ne will I ever lin,
> Ne when as drouping *Titan* draweth neere
> To loose his teeme, will I take up my Inne.
>   (Spenser, *Daphnaïda*, lines 456–69)

Although he does expect to die eventually, given that he instructs later pilgrims to mourn at his grave (lines 532–38), his constant references to his desired, delayed death convey a stronger impression of unwelcome immortality: "cruell death doth scorne to come at call, / Or graunt his boone that most desires to dye" (lines 356–57); "Why doo I longer live in lifes despight? / And doo not dye then in despight of death" (lines 442–43).

An unkempt man wandering endlessly with a staff matches the literary and iconographic details salient to the legend of the Wandering Jew, a medieval tale that gained new legs, if you will, in the early modern period when Matthew of Paris's *Chronica Majora* was published in London in 1571, leading to a new and more strongly anti-Semitic incarnation of the tale that began with a German version of 1603 (Anderson, *Legend*, 16–21, 60–66).[11] Spenser, however, presumably draws on the medieval version, told in Matthew of Paris's chronicle and adapted, perhaps, by Chaucer in his portrait of the deathless wandering man in *The Pardoner's Tale*. Despite changes in the interpretations accorded to the Wandering Jew story over time, serving to illustrate either a miracle of Christianity or the perfidiousness of the Jews, iconographically there is a great deal of similarity over time, with the unkempt beard and walking staff generally appearing in representations from the medieval and early modern period; Eszter Losonczi notes as well a frequent conflation of Wandering

---

11 For the version of the tale most likely to be familiar to Spenser, see Matthew Paris's *Matthaei Paris, monachi Albanensis, Angli, historia maior* (470–71 [from chronicle year 1228] and 1138 [from chronicle year 1252]).

Jew iconography with pilgrim iconography, relevant here to the pilgrim imagery used by Alcyon and the narrator (Losonczi, *Visual Patterns*, 46, 54, 58).

If Spenser considered the Old Man of the *Pardoner's Tale* as an iteration of the Wandering Jew legend,[12] this may help to make sense of Alcyon's puzzling conflation of the Orpheus/Eurydice and Ceres/Proserpina myths. Alcyon plans to do "as the mother of the Gods" when she searched the world for "faire *Eurydice* her daughter deere" (lines 463–65), an odd mixing and metamorphosing of relationships and sexes that emphasizes, as Donald Cheney notes, "the travel and the travail" of the search ("Grief," 130). It also oddly mirrors the mother–child imagery introduced by Chaucer's Old Man when he describes his efforts to be allowed to die:

> Ne Deeth, allas, ne wol nat han my lyf.
> Thus walke I, lyk a restelees kaityf,
> And on the ground, which is my moodres gate,
> I knokke with my staf, bothe erly and late,
> And seye "Leeve mooder, leet me in!
> Lo how I vanysshe, flessh, and blood, and skyn!
> Allas, whan shul my bones been at reste?"
>
> (Chaucer, *Pardoner's*, lines 727–33)

The image of the earth as a mother who denies the Old Man admittance reverses the mother–child relationship of Ceres and Proserpina, where the mother seeks the lost child who is in the earth, adding to the confusion of parent read as lover and wife confused with daughter; overall, reading Alcyon's conflated myth with reference to the Old Man's wandering and quest to be allowed to enter the earth, his mother, creates a jumbled and overdetermined set of relationships among artist and beloved, parent and child—the one clear thing that emerges from this reading, however, is an emotional effect of irremediable longing and suffering.

But how does Spenser expect the reader to respond to this suffering? Not with sympathy, I believe. In this chapter, I have read *Daphnaïda* with reference to several intertexts that Spenser's original audience would have known well: *The Faerie Queene*, *The Book of the Duchess*, the legend of the Wandering Jew, and *The Pardoner's Tale*. Many other scholars have examined the poem in relation to *The Book of the Duchess* and to

12 For an early statement of the argument connecting *The Pardoner's Tale* to the legend, see Bushnell, "Wandering Jew." George K. Anderson initially rejected the hypothesis ("Wandering Jew," 241n16) but later came to support this interpretation (*Legend of the Wandering Jew*, 31–32). Of course Chaucerians differ on how best to interpret the Old Man; for a summary of the multiplicity of interpretations of this figure, see Benson, "Explanatory notes," 905.

Spenser's more generically conforming examples of pastoral elegy, such as "November" of *The Shepheardes Calender* and *Astrophel*. There is general critical consensus that Alcyon is less appealing than Chaucer's Man in Black and that the deviations from the generic norms of pastoral elegy raise questions. I have argued here that Spenser connects Alcyon descriptively to negative allegorical personifications, which pushes the reader in the direction of a judgmental response to the character. Connecting him to the Wandering Jew, punished with eternal wandering for his lack of compassion to Jesus on the day of the Crucifixion, emphasizes Alcyon's lack of faith (which becomes over the course of the poem something like idolatry of Daphne, as Oram notes; "*Daphnaida*," 147).

Alcyon *is* sorrow, and sorrow is he, but he is supposed to be a man, or perhaps the pastoral equivalent, a "jollie Shepheard swaine." More so than the critical portraits of character types found in the formal verse satires of Joseph Hall, Thomas Middleton, John Marston, and others, Spenser's criticism of "the excessive mourner" seems to target a particular individual, Arthur Gorges. Yet the point he makes by reducing a putatively human character to a figure so "flat" that he resembles Spenser's allegorical personifications has applicability as general as the study of virtues found in *The Faerie Queene*. Read in this way, *Daphnaïda* becomes a more interesting work, an example of Spenser's allegorical and allusive satire that requires an active reader. Spenser provides some clues to the work's generic nonconformity, such as the invocation of the Fates rather than the Muses and the nonpastoral style of the initial description of Alcyon. Alcyon's bad poetry serves as another clue, given the narrator's comment that Alcyon, in former days, "wont full merrilie to pipe and daunce, / And fill with pleasance every wood and plaine" (lines 55–56). *Daphnaïda*, tedious as pastoral elegy, becomes a good game when read through the lens of satire.

3

Spenser and the English literary system in the 1590s

The previous two chapters have analyzed Spenser's methods of creating satirical meaning in his early poetry. It would now be sensible, and might even be expected, to devote a chapter to the satirical episodes in *The Faerie Queene*, especially the second installation of 1596, which includes a great deal more allegorical commentary on contemporary historical events than the first three books do. Instead, I veer in another direction entirely and in the remainder of the book will consider how other poets used Spenser as source material and used ideas about Spenserianism, shared with their audience, to help them signal their own satirical and topical meanings. Specifically, I will aim to discover what Spenser's contemporaries thought about him as a satirist by looking at how they adapted and alluded to poems from *The Shepheardes Calender* and from the *Complaints* volume. This focus on reception and influence precludes close attention to the satirical elements in *The Faerie Queene*, because Spenser's epic did not influence satirical poetry of the time period as clearly and significantly as did others of his works. To put it mildly, it would have appeared presumptuous in the extreme for a young satirist of the 1590s to use *The Faerie Queene* as a pretext. Although I argue in this chapter that Joseph Hall does precisely that in *Virgidemiarum Sixe Bookes*, it was a bold move, which he presents as such and mitigates through obsequiously emphasizing the value of Spenser among poets. In my study, I have found Spenser's earlier, shorter, more modest (in *rota* terms) poetry to be more productive of imitation and allusion among younger poets in the 1590s and early 1600s, and so I leave aside an in-depth analysis of satire in *The Faerie Queene* to focus, as my subtitle indicates, on a *tradition*.

My overall goal is to create a fuller and more nuanced view of Spenser's influence on satirical poetry in England in the 1590s and the impact of Spenser's role in the literary system on poets writing satire. Even though Spenser has never been thought of as primarily a satirist, his overwhelming importance to poetry in general by the last decade of his life means that he served as both an authorizer of and influence for poets who sought to fashion themselves as satirists. I believe that Spenser, as "Prince of Poets in His Time," by the 1590s exerted a disproportionate influence on literature, specifically satirical poetry, written during and after his life. His clearly defined authorial "brand" made "Spenser" a source of stable cultural meanings that poets could allude to or react against in order to clarify their own satirical messages while forestalling criticism, censorship, and punishment. In this chapter, after initial attention to the theoretical groundwork for thinking about the roles that Spenser played in his fellow writers' imaginings of the English literary system near the turn of the seventeenth century, I will focus on two friends' somewhat reductive treatments of Spenser in their own works. William Bedell's simplistic and repetitive Spenserianism clarifies what tropes and images predictably called the concept "Spenser" to the minds of writers and readers in the late sixteenth and early seventeenth centuries, while Joseph Hall's disgusting parodies of Spenserian images and language from *The Faerie Queene*, which serve to contrast his own aggressive indecorousness with Spenser's famous decorum, suggest the satirist's impatience with the epic poet.

Theories of literary interconnectedness

Itamar Even-Zohar's ideas on literary "interference" (i.e., influence), his conception of literature as a "polysystem" of numerous connected systems, and his ideas of center/periphery and canonical/noncanonical provide less historically and ideologically weighted perspectives on the complexity and connectedness of literary systems than those of Pierre Bourdieu. However, his ideas are not as well known within English studies as they are in the fields of comparative literature, especially translation studies, and so I will spend some time highlighting a few concepts that inform the chapters that follow.

Although Even-Zohar argues, somewhat tendentiously I think, against borrowing individual ideas piecemeal from his comprehensive theory ("Introduction," 4–5), one cannot avoid the reality that certain elements of his theory have more or less descriptive or explanatory power for particular situations, and thus I focus my attention on those points that provide the most help in conceptualizing the lines of influence connecting Edmund Spenser to other English satirists. Even-Zohar defines literary "interference" in a way that indicates its similarities to what is more typically called "influence": "a relation(ship) between literatures, whereby a certain literature A (a source literature) may become a source of direct or indirect loans for another literature B (a target literature)" ("Laws," 54). Not surprisingly, given the terminology of the definition, to date these ideas about literary interference have been explored primarily with reference to inter-cultural transfer and influence, such as conceptualizing, for example, the impact that a hegemonic culture can have on the cultural productions of a less powerful culture, as in comparatists' recent discussions of the disproportionate influence of the English-language literary system on the literary systems of other nations and peoples (e.g., Moretti, "Conjectures"; and Moretti, "More conjectures"). The word "interference" perhaps goes too far in providing a negative judgment of the phenomenon, and this stems, no doubt, from a desire to root for underdog literary systems in their battle for self-determination; Franco Moretti highlights this sense of the word when he glosses Even-Zohar's terms as "powerful literatures making life hard for the others—making *structure* hard" (Moretti, "Conjectures," 65). Despite this justifiable emphasis on inter-cultural exchange and transfer, I argue for the relevance of Even-Zohar's "laws of literary interference" at the intra-cultural level, because even within a single nation or group, the polysystemic nature hypothesized of the literary system means that there are more and less privileged and powerful genres, publishers, authors, critics, and so forth in relationships within a single polysystem. How, we might ask, does the hegemony of the novel at the present day interfere with poetry, or with short stories? What does the towering stature of Shakespeare within early modern English studies mean for graduate students considering dissertation topics? Interference, understood as the impact of one disproportionately powerful node in the literary polysystem on other nodes in relationship with it, happens frequently intra-culturally as well as inter-culturally, and so I see Even-Zohar's "laws" as important in thinking of the ways that Edmund Spenser, and especially his indirect form of satire, "interfered" with and influenced the work of other near-contemporary English poets writing satire. In the time period I focus on here, state censorship also comes into play, limiting the choices available to individual authors while also affecting authors' overall sense of what is permissible, safe, or effective in the literary subsystem of satire.

Spenser's importance to the literary system of satire in England in the 1590s derives, I believe, from two sources: Spenser's extremely high poetic status, earned by his work in high-prestige genres such as pastoral and epic, and his reputation as a courageous poet who has no fear of criticizing the powerful, earned primarily by his work's being censored in 1591. To start with Spenser's disproportionate status in his literary polysystem, consider the following "laws" in thinking about Spenser as a possible influence on other writers: "2.2. A source literature is selected by prestige. 2.3. A source literature is selected by dominance" (Even-Zohar, "Laws," 59). With the 1590 publication of the first three books of *The Faerie Queene*, followed in 1591 by his reward from Queen Elizabeth of a £50 annuity for life, Spenser's status as the premier English poet of his time was assured, but his poetic reputation was already quite strong before those events. We can gain a sense of his importance from the numerous references to him and his works in contemporary writings, as documented by R.M. Cummings (*Spenser*); Ray Heffner, Dorothy Mason, and Frederick Padelford (*Spenser Allusions*); and more recently by Jackson Boswell (*Spenser Allusions*). In 1586, for example, William Webbe assigned Spenser "the tytle of the rightest English Poet, that euer I read"; for Thomas Nashe in 1589 he was "diuine Master Spencer, the miracle of wit"; and so forth (Heffner et al., *Spenser Allusions*, 7, 13).[1] Spenser's dominance is also suggested by his importance—in his own time and through the eighteenth century— as a model for young men in particular, leading Richard Frushell to term him "the young poet's poet" (Frushell, *Edmund Spenser*, 12). To sum up, by the 1590s, Spenser had both "prestige" and "dominance" in the English literary system.

Additionally, with the publication of the epic *Faerie Queene*, Spenser did much to advance *English* literature as an independent national literary system and to fashion himself as a laureate poet, as Richard Helgerson has demonstrated (*Forms of Nationhood*; *Self-Crowned Laureates*). Significantly, though, part of his reputation in the 1590s derived from the fact that the *Complaints* had been censored, contributing to the sense of Spenser as a courageous writer who valued truth over flattery. For young poets writing in English, and especially for those working in the less prestigious genre of satire, Spenser had a lot to offer as a model and, in some sense, authorizer of the project of writing English poetry and/ or satire. In this regard, Even-Zohar's idea of literature as a polysystem is helpful, because it reminds us to consider the multiple types of nodes in the system (e.g., genres, publishers and publication formats, authors) and the hierarchies that exist within and among these nodes as systems in their own right, with their own sets of relations. Even-Zohar defines the literary system as "The network of relations that is hypothesized to obtain

---

1 See Radcliffe, *Edmund Spenser*, 9–11, for more discussion of Spenser's literary reputation with his contemporaries.

between a number of activities called 'literary,' and consequently these activities themselves observed via that network," thus emphasizing the dynamicity and relationality of the system ("Literary system," 28). We can think about the hierarchies that obtain within these relations—specifically vis-à-vis satire as a stepchild genre in Spenser's England—by means of Philippe Codde's clarification of Even-Zohar's hypothesized continua *central/peripheral* (textual models that influence the creation of new texts are central; those that do not are peripheral) and *canonized/noncanonized* (texts and textual models with cultural prestige are canonized; those without are noncanonized). Codde separates these two continua to create a more comprehensible set of (four) possibilities:

> (1) canonical + central: this would be the logical situation, where items or models that enjoy prestige in the system influence the production of other cultural items or models in the system ... ; (2) canonical + peripheral: here belongs the case of the Shakespearean sonnet [at the present day] and other models and items that are prestigious, though no longer influential; (3) noncanonical + central: this would be the case of models and artifacts that are popular and therefore occasion much imitation, even though they are far from prestigious (i.e., they enjoy no critical acclaim and are not taught in schools or colleges); (4) noncanonical + peripheral: this is the position of works and models that are generally considered inferior, both by other artists (who do not use them as models) and by critics and institutions (who do not grant them prestige). (Codde, "Polysystem theory," 104n18)

I can use this taxonomy to clarify a central claim of this book: Spenser by the 1590s was already canonized *as an author*, with *Shepheardes Calender* and *Faerie Queene* also to be viewed as canonized texts, and these works were also *central* in terms of inspiring other English poets to create pastoral and epic poetry modeled on Spenser's. But although satire as a genre lacked prestige in early modern England, "diuine Master Spencer" also published a number of satirical poems in the innocuous and medieval-sounding *Complaints* volume,[2] and these, not famous but

---

2 The classic analysis of complaint versus satire is John Peter's *Complaint and Satire in Early English Literature* (1956). Peter sees Spenser as important to the history of neither complaint *nor* satire: "Spenser again, whatever his interest in another context, is hardly a key-figure in the development of Satire. His allegorical method is distinctly medieval ... but its affinities are with political songs rather than complaints proper.... Beyond Drayton's *The Owle*, moreover, which will be mentioned later, [*Mother Hubberds Tale*] seems to have had very little contemporary influence" (132–33). Obviously, I disagree with this conclusion. The polarizing nature of satirical writing means that critics' own preferences can cloud their genre analyses; Peter, for example, likes complaint and dislikes formal verse satire, and this preference influences all of his judgments. On the other hand, to Kirk Combe, complaint sounds "frequently whiny and distressingly acquiescent," and,

notorious, served to connect the illustrious laureate poet Spenser with the genre of satire. These satirical works were never canonized texts, in part because the collection was called in by the authorities shortly after publication and in part because the poems in the collection worked within less prestigious genres than epic and pastoral.

But although these works were not canonical in late Elizabethan England, they were, still following Codde's taxonomy, *central*, not peripheral. That is, although other writers carefully avoided obvious imitation of Spenser's satirical poems (and Thomas Nashe's disgusted response to Gabriel Harvey's reference to the scandal just under two years later suggests a general preference not to mention the matter at all, to avoid "rekindl[ing] against him the sparkes of displeasure that were quenched" [Nashe, *Strange Newes*, 281]), other poets' use of his indirect satirical methods and their allusions—real but not obvious—to some of his satirical poetry clarify the ways in which his work in satire was central to poets working within the mode in the 1590s. So, when young satirists alluded to Spenser, modeled their works on his, or otherwise rode on his coattails, they did so as practitioners of an uncanonized and largely peripheral genre looking to the canonized author Spenser to add meaning to their works and some authority to their genre. Given that Spenser spent most of the 1590s living in Ireland, we must think of the influential force as textual and conceptual: that is, Spenser-as-author, the name "Spenser" serving as a means of classifying texts, discourses, and ideas, as Michel Foucault imagines "the author-function" (Foucault, "What is an author?"). Foucault reaches backward in time to borrow Jerome's criteria for what constitutes an "author"; I will embrace anachronism to connect Foucault's ideas about the author-function as depending in part on the quality and consistency of texts to the contemporary marketing concept of the "brand."

Linking ideas about branding to work in architecture and design, Peggy Deamer distinguishes between "fame," which is inaccessible and which requires a clear identification between author and product, and the "brand," which, on the other hand, depends on repeatability and accessibility (Deamer, "Branding," 42). To the extent that no one but Spenser could write works as enduring and valued as his own, Spenser had fame, but I speak of "branding" as a way of thinking about the numerous poets who *tried* to write like Spenser as well as the authors who connected their own works to their audience's idea of Spenser through allusion rather than imitation, including the handful I discuss in this book. Without a

so to his eyes, the seventeenth-century shift from complaint to satire was a good thing ("New voice," 75).

literary model that *seems* reproducible and accessible, no one would try to write a Spenserian poem. For this reason, the poetry of Spenser has spawned more imitators than, say, the plays of Shakespeare, presumably because poets see in Spenser's works, and in their ideas about "Spenser," elements that seem accessible for imitation or adoption as part of their own authorial personae. To return to Even-Zohar's laws of literary interference, he asserts that "Appropriation tends to be simplified, regularized, schematized" ("Laws," 59). As we will see, a coherent picture of "Spenser" develops from examining other writers' uses of him: politically, he is censored, unappreciated, and exiled (i.e., "oppositional"); culturally, he is high class; as a satirist, he is indirect, using allusion and allegory, especially pastoral and animal allegory, to create deniability for his attacks.

The way that other writers made use of this general understanding of the meaning of "Spenser" changed over time, however, as the political situation in England changed. After the censoring of the *Complaints* volume, poets did not closely imitate Spenser's satirical works during the remainder of Elizabeth's reign. Instead, poets signaled the importance of interpretive reading and aligned themselves with the values and political positions considered "Spenserian" through allusion, sometimes quite veiled allusions. Only later, in the early seventeenth century, following both the 1599 Bishops' Ban targeting formal verse satire (among other genres) and the 1603 death of Elizabeth, did satirists begin to connect themselves with Spenser by openly imitating those features of his writing that were most repeatable and accessible, the characteristic linguistic and generic moves recognizable to contemporaries as "Spenserian."[3] Only then do we find the directly imitative pastoral satires of the "Spenserian poets" or the allegorical beast fables examined by Hoyt Hudson ("John Hepwith's"). Although both of these ways of "using" Spenser in early modern English satires interest me, the bulk of this study will focus on the allusive practices of the 1590s.

Spenserianism simplified: two reductive responses to Spenser

In the chapters that follow, I will discuss some very artful and sophisticated uses of and responses to Spenser in satirical poems written by his near-contemporaries, but, first, I want to spend some time on two writers, friends and future illustrious bishops, whose uses of Spenser in their works provide a sense of the caricature version of what "Spenser"

---

3 Of course the very most Spenserian thing about Spenser is the "Spenserian stanza" of *The Faerie Queene*, which was imitated over and over again across the centuries. Because this stanzaic form is of only tangential interest for the topic of satire, I pass over it in the text.

Spenser and the English literary system 71

meant to his contemporaries in the late sixteenth and early seventeenth centuries. In the remainder of this chapter, I will explore how "Spenser" appears in poetry by William Bedell (pronounced like "beadle") and Joseph Hall. These remarkable men became friends while studying at Emmanuel College, Cambridge (Bedell admitted 1584, elected fellow 1593; Hall admitted 1589, elected fellow 1595), a college founded in 1584 by Sir Walter Mildmay to train staunchly Protestant young men for the ministry (for details of Mildmay's religious goals for the new college, see Bendall et al., *A History*, 17–25). Given the college's Puritan leanings, it is not surprising that Bedell and Hall were the only two bishops produced by Emmanuel before the Civil War, which suggests something of their religious moderation during those politically and religiously difficult times (Bendall et al., *A History*, 82, 84, 88). Between 1601 and 1607, both served in parishes in Suffolk—Bedell at Bury St. Edmonds and Hall at Hawstead—and continued their friendship (Bendall et al., *A History*, 84, 88). Hall wrote a commendatory verse for Bedell's poem on the Gunpowder Plot; both contributed verses to the 1606 obituary volume for Edward Lewkenor and his wife Susan (*Threnodia*, 27–28 for Bedell, 30 for Hall); and both took part in an epistolary exchange with James Wadsworth, a friend and former fellow minister whom they had known at Emmanuel and in Suffolk who had moved to Spain, converted to Catholicism, and become a pensioner of the Inquisition.

In the exchange with Wadsworth, which Bedell published after Wadsworth's death, we can see the contrasting personality traits of Bedell and Hall that appear as well in the poems I will discuss, with Bedell gentle and kind-hearted and Hall irascible and sarcastic.[4] Bedell seeks common ground with Wadsworth, with assertions such as "Incomparably more and of more importance are those things wherein wee agree; then those wherin we dissent. Let vs follow therefore the things of peace, and of mutuall edification"; he also offers reminders of their long friendship, as in "I hope you shall perceiue that setting aside our difference in opinion, I am the same to you that I was when we were either *Schollers* together in *Emmanuell Colledge*, or *Ministers in Suffolke*" (Wadsworth and Bedell, *Copies*, 160–61, 36). Wadsworth adopts a similarly conciliatory tone, leading Izaak Walton to comment that in the letter exchange, "there seems to be a controversy, not of Religion only, but who should answer each other with most love and meekness; which I mention the rather, because it too seldom falls out to be so in a book-war" (*Walton's*

---

4 For more on Wadsworth's life, see Marotti, *Religious Ideology*, 119–21, 123; and Questier, *Conversion*, 80–81.

Lives, 153). Hall, on the other hand, shows in his one letter included in the collection the tendency toward bitter taunts familiar to readers of his *Virgidemiarum*, written almost twenty years earlier. Although we do not have Hall's original letter to Wadsworth, Wadsworth characterizes it as "satyrical" and expresses particular hurt that Hall accused him of apostasy (Wadsworth and Bedell, *Copies*, 16, 2). The letter from Hall to Bedell included in the collection suggests the railing and harsh tone he may have taken in his lost letter to Wadsworth: "what a sorry crabb hath Master *Waddesworth* at last sent vs from *Siuill*? I pittie the *impotent malice* of the man; sure that hot Region, and *sulphurous Religion* are guiltie of this his choler. For ought I see hee is not onely turned Papist but *Spaniard* too" (Wadsworth and Bedell, *Copies*, 30–31). Though a moderate politically and religiously, his approach to controversy was anything but gentle, and his later published dispute with Smectymnuus (answered by John Milton) indicates that his truculence would last his whole life. Looking at Spenser from the perspectives of Bedell and Hall can give us a sense of what his contemporaries thought he "meant," in terms of both poetry and morality.

William Bedell's Shepherd's Tale of the Pouder-Plott:
reproducing the Spenser brand in a topical poem

William Bedell, future bishop of Kilmore in Ireland, was inspired by the successful foiling of the Gunpowder Plot to write a poem about it (published in 1713 as *A Protestant Memorial; or, The Shepherd's Tale of the Pouder-Plott*); he took such pride in the poem that, according to his son-in-law and biographer, Alexander Clogie, he read it aloud to his household each year on November 5 (Clogie, *Speculum*, 194).[5] Arnold

---

5 Karl Reuning argues against Bedell's authorship of the poem, but his evidence is weak and does not take account of Clogie's testimony. He offers a useful and very detailed discussion of the textual history of the poem, but his arguments against Bedell's authorship do not convince. Reuning tries to prove that the poem is an early eighteenth-century fake by analyzing handwriting and biographical details, but the argument ignores key evidence. Reuning uses the fact that Bedell's biographer Gilbert Burnet does not mention Bedell's poetry as evidence that the poem did not exist in 1685. Reuning cites the Shuckburgh edition that includes Alexander Clogie's biography but does not mention Clogie's reference to the poem (Reuning, "*Shepherd's Tale*"). Burnet himself acknowledges his overwhelming debt to Clogie, son-in-law and close associate of Bedell in the last years of his life (calling him "much more the Author of this book than I am"; Burnet, *Life*, 175), and thus we must view Clogie's reference to Bedell's annual reading of his poem as more authoritative than Burnet's failure to mention the poem one way or the other. Julius Hook summarizes Reuning's arguments uncritically (*Eighteenth-Century Imitations*, 75). Frushell follows Reuning, adding his opinion that the poem was composed as a satire in response to the political situation in 1713. Surely, the 1712 "Bandbox-Plot," an attempt on the life of Robert Harley, Earl of Oxford, that was foiled

Davenport creates a convincing timeline for the composition of this poem—to account for the dedicatory poem by Bedell's friend Joseph Hall, Davenport hypothesizes that Bedell wrote the poem and shared it with his friend at some point between the discovery of the plot in 1605 and Bedell's departure for Venice with Sir Henry Wotton in 1607, because, during that time, Bedell and Hall lived only four miles from each other (Davenport, "Commentary," 269–70n15).

The 1713 published version of the poem opens with Joseph Hall's poem to his friend, in which he sets the Spenserian stage by opining that "Collin dying, his Immortal Muse / Into thy Learned Breast did late infuse" (C1r; a footnote identifies Collin as "Spenser" for the eighteenth-century audience). In Bedell's poem, we find a précis of what contemporaries considered the hallmarks of Spenser's poetry. To call Bedell a "poet" would overstate his talents, but his status as "imitator" can tell us much of interest, because his unskillful imitation highlights what seemed, following Peggy Deamer's formulation of the brand, reproducible and accessible in the work of the master. These details—shepherds, sheep, and foxes—can provide us with insight into what "Spenser" meant to his contemporaries.

Bedell's poem begins with a typical pastoral dialogue between Willy and Thenot (later, a character named Perkin will appear with no introduction): Willy wants to "Pipe and Play" to celebrate the lucky escape from "the darkest Day / That ever lowerd on the *British* Shore," but Thenot has not heard the happy news of the foiling of the thinly allegorized story of the Gunpowder Plot (Bedell, *Shepherd's Tale*, 1–2). After a few speeches back and forth, the dialogue turns into Willy's 443-line interpolated tale of the Catholic plot to blow up "the Senate of Shepherds" (13). The low quality of the poetry will become apparent from the quotations I include, and this need not trouble us here. In general, as an imitator, Bedell focuses on key Spenserian characteristics such as archaic language and alliteration, and easily copied pastoral poetic forms such as the roundelay form seen in, for example, "August" of *The Shepheardes Calender*. In terms of Spenser's satirical methods, Bedell apes Spenser's well-known use of pastoral and animal allegories, but, because Bedell's poem is politically safe, he does not need to make his allegories actually difficult to decipher: one part panegyric of the victorious king plus one part satire

---

by the quick wits of none other than Jonathan Swift, resembles in important ways the story of the Gunpowder Plot (Harley received a package containing pistols that were to be triggered by the box's opening), but these similarities can explain the 1713 *publication* of Bedell's poem without requiring us to deny his authorship of the poem.

of the perpetrators (who have already been drawn and quartered) and the Catholic Church (which requires no particular courage to criticize in seventeenth-century England) equals an utterly transparent allegory.

Bedell shows his awareness of the fictional space and time of pastoral that appear regularly in pastoral, but this awareness flags as he warms to the topic of the Plot. Spenser, following his own models in earlier pastorals, pays attention to verisimilitude in creating the pastoral world in which his shepherds exist, so that, for example, the sun sets, leading shepherds to finish their talk and lead the sheep to the fold, thus closing an eclogue. In the eclogue most concerned with the city, "September," Spenser maintains the pastoral setting through frequent changes of speaker—Diggon Davy's lament never becomes a monologue—and extremely frequent references to sheep. During the lengthy narration about the Plot, Bedell seems to recognize that he has lost track of the pastoral setting and frame story and attempts to correct the oversight by having Willy interject one comment that reminds readers of the setting and the supposed audience for Willy's monologue—"But let me see; whereof said I this? / Ah! well bethought" (Bedell, *Shepherd's Tale*, 19)—before wrapping up his narration. Too little, too late, though: during Willy's monologue, readers lose track of the pastoral frame setting, and the scene and story both feel firmly bound to the city, despite Willy's references to the King, Queen, and members of Parliament as "shepherds."

Still, Bedell creates a reasonably effective allegory in the extended metaphor of the "sickness" of Catholic "sheep" reminiscent of the allegorically ailing sheep belonging to such Spenserian shepherds as Colin Clout and Diggon Davy. Perkin describes the view he used to hold of the Catholic sheep:

> I had yweend; and so had many more,
> They had been simple, souple, meek, and poor;
> And eek as other Sheep, methought, they bleat,
> Albe for sick they did forsake their Meat.
> At most I would have thought they scabbed were,
> Or fly-stung so they gadded here and there.
> Their ragged Pelts I pityed all to rent,
> Whilst in the bushy Thickets they miswent.
>
> (Bedell, *Shepherd's Tale*, 25)

Perkin has realized the error of this view and now understands that these sheep have "monsters" within their breasts and cannot be cured. Willy concurs, advising that shepherds should chase or kill the monstrous sheep and work to preserve the health of the good flocks:

> To make strong Fence, and sure, that may hold
> These Leapers, and keep them in Pasture and Fold.
> For souverain'st Medicine is sweet and clean Feed
> On virtuous Hearb, without rank and fowle Weed.
> Such can preserve the Flocks in good Plight,
> And heal their Diseases, and well acquite
> The tender Lambs from ill Eys, as I guesse,
> And all the Charms of the false Sorceresse.
>
> (26)

The false sorceress, naturally, is the Roman Catholic Church, about whom more later.

The pastoral frame story thus contains certain familiar conventions, such as the insistent sheep metaphors and imagery at the beginning and after the end of Willy's monologue, as well as the movement from country to city and back again with news, as occurs in "September" of *The Shepheardes Calender* and in *Colin Clouts Come Home Againe*. Willy can tell Thenot about the events of the Plot and its foiling because he was in the city five days earlier and saw for himself "the Bonfires, the Mirth, and the Jollity; / The Ringing and Singing, and all the Glee" (20). Additionally, the poem that Willy recites at the end, a roundelay with one voice speaking the lines of Psalm 124 and the undersong connecting the psalm to the Gunpowder Plot, clearly derives from Spenser's "August" not just in the form but in the language used to describe it: "his Fellow Swain, / The under-Song him answerd again" (27). Spenser coined the term "undersong" in "August" of *The Shepheardes Calender* (line 128), and the *Oxford English Dictionary* records no other use of the word before Spenserian poets Michael Drayton in 1606 and William Browne in 1616 (although the editors ignored Spenser's own repetitions of the word in *Daphnaïda* [line 245] and *Prothalamion* [line 110]), so the word itself suggested Spenser when Bedell wrote the poem between 1605 and 1607 (s.v. "undersong"; see also Hollander, *Melodious Guile*, chapter 8, titled "Spenser's Undersong").

We find another word likely to remind readers of Spenser in Willy's reference to "Lobbin," the source of his details about the Plot: "Of many good Shepherds I heard the same, / And from the sage *Lobbins* own Mouth it came; / The wise *Lobbin,* that Fame doth resound, / As true a Shepherd as lives on the Ground" (Bedell, *Shepherd's Tale,* 21). Bedell here provides readers with an allusion considerably harder to decipher than, say, the reference to the Monteagle letter ("So said this Letter. I heard his Name neven, / *Mount* it began with to whom it was given"

[17]).[6] The presumed counterpart of Spenser's Lobbin in "November," Robert Dudley, Earl of Leicester, was of course long dead by the time Bedell wrote. His son and heir, Robert Dudley (1574–1649), left England forever in July 1605, and thus he cannot be Lobbin (Adams, "Dudley"). Edmond Malone cites Bedell's use of the name Lobbin to support his contention that the identity of the Earl of Leicester was generally known, arguing that Bedell uses the name Lobbin to connect his Lobbin (whom Malone believes to be Robert Cecil) with Spenser's Lobbin by means of their shared given name (Malone, "Life," 202n5). Cecil seems an adequate identification, though it jars somewhat to think of a Spenserian shepherd praising a Cecil.

The Shepherd's Tale of the Pouder-Plott clearly owes more to *The Shepheardes Calender* than to Spenser's *Mother Hubberds Tale* as a model, yet Bedell's heavy-handed use of animal imagery and allegory at times suggests conscious allusion to Spenser's beast allegory. Of course we find animals in pastoral as well, and, predictably, the animal imagery in the pastoral frame story feels less like "beast fable" and more like shepherding concerns, but with some foreshadowing of the obsessive use of animal allegory in the interpolated tale of the Plot. For example, Thenot's question about Willy's reason for celebrating serves to introduce the phrase "false Fox," which Willy will later use twice to refer to Guy Fawkes: "What might the Danger be, that was so dern? / … . / Or hath some wicked Woolf, or Beast more stern, / (As Beare, or Boare) been spied in Halk or Hern? / But if false Foxes be, that would us shend, / We have true Currs that shall them well defend" (2).

Willy twice refers to the allegorical version of Guy Fawkes as the "false Fox" (14, 19): "False was his Name, I remember well, / As well it fitt him, they say that can tell. / A false *Fox* it was in Mans-shape ydrest, / Enclosing a false Fiend in his Breast" (14). Richard Hardin notes that poetry of the Gunpowder Plot often punned on the names of the perpetrators, but the puns Hardin cites for Fawkes connect him with *fallax* or falseness, not with foxes ("Early poetry," 65). Bedell thus connects his poem to other Gunpowder Plot poetry with the standard pun "false," but he connects himself as well to Spenser through the phrase "false fox," which occurs four times in *Mother Hubberds Tale* and twice in the "Maye" eclogue of *The Shepheardes Calender*. Although, as Thenot's reference to the danger from "false foxes" acknowledges, foxes are part of the pastoral world, with Willy's description of this human fox we can perceive a shift

---

6 For more details on the letter, see Nicholls, *Investigating*, 6–8, 174–75.

in how Bedell uses animals to convey his ideas: Thenot fears real foxes, but Willy speaks of beastly humans, and thus we enter the realm of the beast fable in the interpolated tale of the plot. Within the allegory of the interpolated tale, the sorceress who represents the Catholic Church turns men to beasts with her enchanted cup:

> What Mouth of that Cup once kisse the Brimm,
> Albe he seemeth a Man, as before;
> Inly a Beast he is and no more:
> A fierce Lion, a Woolf ravenous,
> Or cruel Tiger, or Fox cautelous,
> Or grizly Beare, or Dragon hideous,
> Or other like Monster outrageous.
>
> (Bedell, *Shepherd's Tale*, 6)

This sorceress is far more "cunning" than Circe, who could "transform Men to Doggs, / Woolves, Foxes, Beares, Lions, Tigers, Hoggs / .... / Soon as they drunk of her charmed Wine, / Right anone were they changed into Swine" (5). But Circe could change only the body, not the mind, whereas this (Catholic) sorceress leaves men's bodies unchanged on the outside, but transforms them within to beasts. However irenic Bedell may have been in his correspondence with James Wadsworth, his real antagonism to the Roman Catholic Church (if not to individual believers) appears in this allegory and fits with his other published writings.[7]

This tale of origin renders it unnecessary to explain the motives of the plotters: the Catholics—"these misformd Monsters," "that beastly shaped Crue" (12)—are no longer human and thus act on behalf of the sorceress. Later, after the conclusion of the interpolated tale, when the pastoral dialogue resumes, the discussion of what to do about the sick sheep, quoted above, hearkens back to this tale of origin about what makes Catholics different and why efforts to "cure" (that is, convert) them are a waste of time: "Within their Breasts such Monsters doe they keep," and so the best course of action is "to chasen these Monsters away, / Or doe them dead without more Delay" (25, 26).

Bedell knows how to imitate the most recognizable features of Spenserian satire: allegories of shepherds and animals create a clear comment on a recent important event, the Gunpowder Plot. Surely, though, Bedell

---

7   See Milton, *Catholic and Reformed*, 40–42, 112, 161–62. Despite his anti-Catholicism, Bedell showed pastoral concern for the Irish Catholics when he was Bishop of Kilmore. Although laws promoted the English language and English customs, Bedell preferred to appoint Irish-speaking over monolingual ministers, because, he said, "those people had souls which ought not to be neglected till they would learn English" (qtd. in Jones, *A True Relation*, 44).

misses the spirit of Spenserian satire, which uses indirection and ambiguity to manage the risk of criticizing or even mocking people with real political power. Bedell takes no risks with this poem, because the satire targets a reviled out-group, English Catholics and the subset of English Catholic Gunpowder Plotters, and works to create a strong sense of group solidarity and self-congratulation among English Protestants, in line with Fredric Bogel's argument that satire functions socially to demarcate and police the boundary between social insiders and outsiders (Bogel, *Difference Satire Makes*). The first two stanzas of the closing roundelay, alternating lines from Psalm 124 and summary of the Gunpowder Plot, exemplify the effort to connect the English Protestants with the people of Israel and to strengthen the sense of group cohesion:[8]

> S. *When Men against us did arise,*
> F. *Cruel Beasts in Shapes of Men,*
> S. *And to destroy us did devise.*
> F. *We had bin devoured cleane,*
>
> S. *Had not the Lord bin on our side;*
> F. *Now may Britain justly say,*
> S. *Had not the Lord bin on our side,*
> F. *In that dark and dismal Day.*
>
> (28)

Whereas the circuitousness of Spenser's satires provides intellectual pleasure in the form of puzzles to solve, Bedell aims to provide the emotional pleasure of vindication and victory for his side and complete dehumanization of the enemy camp. Still, this somewhat tin-eared imitation provides a summary of what, in its simplest form, "Spenserian satire" meant to one of Spenser's near-contemporaries who admired his work enough to want to imitate it.

Joseph Hall and the anxiety of Spenser's satiric influence

Bedell's friend Joseph Hall, on the other hand, although he repeatedly mentions his admiration for Spenser, approaches Spenser much more critically in his own work than does Bedell, presumably because of his generally more choleric temperament. In 1597, Joseph Hall published the first installment of *Virgidemiarum Sixe Bookes. First Three Bookes, Of Tooth-lesse Satyrs 1. Poeticall. 2. Morall. 3. Academicall*; the second half, the *Byting Satyres*, followed in 1598. With this work Hall initiated

---

8 See Guibbory, *Christian Identity*, for discussion of the development of this imagined connection across the century.

the fashion of modeling English satires on the satires of the Roman author Juvenal. The fad was short-lived, however, because in 1599 the Bishops' Ban, after listing a number of satires to be called in and burned, including Hall's at the top of the list, would decree "That noe Satyres or Epigramms be printed hereafter" (qtd. in McCabe, "Elizabethan satire," 188).[9] Whereas scholars have considered how the Bishops' Ban led poets to alter their approaches to satirical writing, the impact of Spenser's 1591 censorship episode on satirical poetry in England has been less carefully studied. Even though Spenser's personal danger had blown over within a year or two, the censorship cast a sufficient pall on literature that no beast fables were written in England for the rest of the decade, and I know of no literary allusions to *Mother Hubberds Tale* made during the 1590s, despite the popularity of the poem in manuscript during the two decades that the poem was out of print (Beal, *Index*, Vol. 1, part 2, 527–28). For an author writing satire in the middle of the decade, it might have seemed safer to avoid acknowledging even the existence of previous satires in English, and Hall takes that course. In the Prologue, he boasts:

> I First aduenture, with fool-hardie might
> To tread the steps of perilous despight:
> I first aduenture: follow me who list,
> And be the second English Satyrist.
> (Hall, *Virgidemiae*, I.Prologue.1–4)

This puffed-up tone must betray some anxiety, and Hall's insistent allusions to Spenser in "His Defiance to Envie," which opens the collection, and in several of the satires of the first three books, suggest that Spenser may stand as the most important source of this authorial anxiety. Significantly, however, Hall alludes in his satires to *The Faerie Queene*, not to any of the poems in the *Complaints* volume, despite the fact that he surely knew of the book, not only because the author of Book 1 of *Virgidemiae*, focusing on abuses in poetry, had a strong grip on the English literary scene in the 1590s, but also because he specifically references *The Ruines of Time* in 1605, in a sidenote of his satirical utopian work *Mundus Alter et Idem* (translated in 1613 by John Healey as *The Discovery of a New World*; see Heffner et al., *Spenser Allusions*, 99; Boswell, *Spenser Allusions*, 374).

So although Hall presumably knew of the critical and politically charged poems of the *Complaints* volume, instead of engaging with that side of Spenser in his works as the supposed first English satirist, he

---

9 Note that *Virgidemiae*, along with Thomas Cutwode's [Tailboys Dymoke's] *Caltha Poetarum*, was "staid" and not burned along with the others (McCabe, "Elizabethan Satire," 190).

instead tilts at a purposefully simplified Spenser, the Spenser of decorum and *politesse*. Hall probably differentiates his work both stylistically and generically from the satirical poetry of Spenser at least in part to avoid the same fate for his work—ultimately unsuccessful, of course—but I believe also that Hall's self-consciously anti-Spenserian passages offer a muted critique of Spenser's own authorial persona as insufficiently harsh, too conciliatory, a criticism that could easily be transferred to Spenser's characteristic indirection in satire as well.

The question of Hall's attitude toward Spenser vexed a number of twentieth-century critics, and with good reason. All of Hall's direct references to Spenser praise him—for example, "At *Colins* feete I throw my yeelding reed" (Hall, *Virgidemiae*, "Defiance," line 107) and "But let no rebel *Satyre* dare traduce / Th'eternall *Legends* of thy *Faery Muse*, / Renowmed *Spencer*" (I.iv.21–23). However, some passages that appear to allude to Spenserian themes or images acquire a negative valence in the context of Hall's satire and thus convey a sense of ambivalence regarding Spenser. Critical responses to the issue often betray an unwillingness to engage with this doubleness, leading to such unambiguous assertions as "Spenser was Hall's literary idol"; Hall "declares Spenser off limits for the satirist"; and "all … the indubitable references that Hall makes to Spenser are laudatory."[10] Ronald J. Corthell addresses the ambivalence more directly than others; he finds "a weariness with Spenserian motifs" in Hall's declaration that he will not "scoure the rusted swords of Eluish knights, / Bathed in Pagan blood: or sheath them new / In misty morall Types: or tell their fights, / Who mighty Giants, or who Monsters slew" ("Defiance," lines 49–52) (Corthell, "Beginning," 51). Additionally, Corthell interprets Hall's comments on pastoral in "His Defiance to Enuie" as indicating that Hall chooses to begin his career with satire rather than pastoral because of a concern that "pastoral perspectives, while sharing some concerns

---

10 The quotations are, respectively, from Salyer, "Hall's Satires," 150; Jensen, "Hall and Marston," 81; and Davenport, "Introduction," xlii. Part of scholars' confusion regarding Hall's attitude toward Spenser stems from a probable misattribution of *Certain Worthye Manuscript Poems of Great Antiquitie* … (1597) to Joseph Hall. Dedicated "To the worthiest poet Maister Ed. Spenser," the book is the only printed work dedicated to Spenser. Andrew Hadfield ("Spenser and John Stow") argues that the editor of the collection was in fact John Stow, but he understates the evidence for a connection to Hall: the poetry collection was registered along with the first three books of *Virgidemiarum* in the Stationers' Register on March 31, 1597, and some volumes extant have the poetry collection bound together with *Virgidemiarum*; see Davenport (lxi), who explains the Stationers' Register error as a mistake caused by the clerk's misunderstanding of the "sixe bookes" part of the title, when only the first three books were in fact ready for press in 1597.

with satire, must be skewed in order to contribute to a true image of the times" (Corthell, "Beginning," 51).

Corthell's comment on pastoral, satire, and the historical moment leads to the glaring omission in all accounts of Hall's ideas about Spenser: no one has previously considered Hall's response to Spenser as himself a satirist. I believe that Spenser's place within the satirical landscape of the 1590s explains both Hall's ambivalence and his anxiety to distance his work from that of Spenser. On the one hand, it is prudent for Hall to distinguish his work formally from the most famous recent case of censorship at the time; on the other hand, Hall implies that Spenser, with his decorum and allegory, did not go far enough to arouse the kinds of reader reactions that would lead to real reformation of vice. This explains as well the higher proportion of Spenserian allusions in the first installment than in the second of *Virgidemiarum*: these satires may be "toothlesse," he seems to say, but not as toothless as those of Spenser.

There is no critical consensus regarding either the reasons for the inclusion of Hall's satires in the list of books to be called in and burned or the reasons why Hall's book (along with Thomas Cutwode's [Tailboys Dymoke's] *Caltha Poetarum*), though still prohibited, was not burned. Scholars with specific theses regarding the motivation of the Bishops' Ban are not able to make Hall's work fit. For example, Clegg explains the ban as an attempt to protect the Earl of Essex from criticism, but she does not connect Hall's work to this thesis (Clegg, *Press Censorship Elizabethan*, 198–217). John Peter, with his emphasis on obscenity as the bishops' motivation, hypothesizes that *Virgidemiae* was reprieved from burning when the bishops realized that it wasn't as obscene as the other works on the list (Peter, *Complaint and Satire*, 149, 150). Hall's work can fit more easily with broader claims by authors such as Andrew McRae and Richard McCabe that view the bishops as responding to satire's ability to create political instability, with McCabe pointing specifically to Hall's anti-enclosure comments in satire iii of Book V (McRae, *Literature, Satire*, 5–6; McCabe, "Elizabethan Satire," 191).

Although *Virgidemiae* is not obscene, Hall delights in using disgusting imagery and harsh language to make his points. In this, he differs from the decorousness of Spenser, though the two men shared a moderate reformist Protestant political and religious perspective (see King, *Spenser's Poetry*; and McCabe, *Joseph Hall*). Hall emphasizes his intention to create a tone strikingly different from Spenser's by using offensive language and imagery in passages of the satires that clearly allude to Spenser. I will discuss three examples of this before turning to an analysis of what may have motivated Hall to add the element of disgust to these allusions.

Spenser frequently referred to the Muses in making criticisms of contemporary poetry, and Arnold Davenport argues that Hall's satire on the Muses alludes to both Spenser's translation of Jan van der Noot's *A Theatre for Worldlings* (1569) and Spenser's *Teares of the Muses*, which was part of the *Complaints* volume (Davenport, "Commentary," 164–65). The idea of connecting a decline in poetry to mishaps that have befallen the Muses is certainly not original to Spenser—in his third satire, Juvenal speaks of the woods going begging because the Muses have been evicted ("eiectis mendicat silva Camenis," 3.16)—but Hall's readers would be more immediately familiar with Van der Noot's allegory of the Muses being swallowed up by the earth and Spenser's complaint by Euterpe that "a ragged rout / Of *Faunes* and *Satyres*, hath our dwellings raced / And our chast bowers, in which all vertue rained, / With brutishnesse and beastlie filth hath stained" (Spenser, *Theatre*, epigram 4; Spenser, *Teares*, lines 267–70; see Corthell, "Beginning," 55, for discussion of close verbal parallels between Spenser's *Teares of the Muses* and Hall's description of the Muses). However, whereas the home of Spenser's Muses is invaded against their will, in Hall's satire, the problems in poetry arise from the fact that the Muses have turned from "Vestall maides" (Hall, *Virgidemiae*, I.ii.1) into whores:

> Some of the sisters in securer shades
> Defloured were:
> And euer since disdaining *sacred shame*,
> Done ought that might their heauenly stock defame.
> Now is *Pernassus* turned to the stewes.
>
> (I.ii.13–17)

The poem closes:

> But since, I saw it painted on *Fames* wings,
> The Muses to be woxen Wantonnings.
> Each bush, each banke, and each base Apple-squire,
> Can serue to sate their beastly lewd desire.
> Ye bastard Poets see your Pedegree,
> From common Trulls, and loathsome Brothelry.
>
> (I.ii.33–38)

In both "His Defiance to Enuie" and the first satire of Book I, immediately preceding this poem, Hall had already declared that he was not competing with Spenser: "At *Colins* feete I throw my yeelding reed," he writes, and

Spenser and the English literary system 83

he will provide only "refuse rimes," not a "song" (Defiance.107, 113, 112). Furthermore, because the Muses have all left the Granta River (near Cambridge) to "haunt the tyded *Thames* and salt *Medway* / Ere since the fame of their late Bridall day" (alluding to the Thames–Medway marriage episode in Book 4 of *The Faerie Queene*), the best he can hope for near the Granta is a "baser Muse" (I.i.29–30, 27). Following these warnings, then, not to expect anything of the quality one might find in Spenser, Hall displays something else one would not find in Spenser: an image of whorish Muses selling their favors to sate their lusts.

The next poem, satire iii of Book I, continues the project of distinguishing Hall's work from Spenser by alluding to the story of Chrysogone from Book 3 of *The Faerie Queene*. Chrysogone, mother of the twins Amoret and Belphoebe, conceived them "Through influence of th'heuens fruitfull ray" when, as she slept, "The sunbeames bright vpon her body playd / ... / And pierst into her wombe" (*FQ* 3.6.6.2, 3.6.7.5, 7). The narrator explains that "reason teacheth that the fruitfull seades / Of all things liuing, through impression / Of the sunbeames in moyst complexion, / Doe life conceiue and quickned are by kynd" (*FQ* 3.6.8.3–6). Spenser here reiterates extremely common ideas about the origin of life that date to the classical period (see Lemmi, "Monster-spawning"; and Cumming, "Ovid"). Certainly the pervasiveness of references to the idea that, in the words of Himmet Umunc, "the origin of physical life was principally due to the generative effects of heat and moisture upon matter," suggests the importance of caution in identifying Spenserian allusions in references to the generation of life through sunbeams ("Chrysogone," 153). Nevertheless, Spenser's example of the sun's power of generation was surely the most fully developed and memorable example of this idea in the minds of Hall and his readers. In Hall's reworking of this idea of the sun's power in a satire on Christopher Marlowe, drunkenness, and literature, we see again the pattern of taking an image or idea that was beautified in Spenser and making it disgusting:

> As frozen Dung-hils in a winters morne,
> That voyd of vapours seemed all beforne,
> Soone as the Sun, sends out his piercing beames,
> Exhale out filthy smoke and stinking steames:
> So doth the base, and the fore-barren braine,
> Soone as the raging wine begins to raigne.
> (Hall, *Virgidemiae*, I.iii.3–8)

We see direct verbal parallels here with the references to "piercing" and "sun ... beams" and a general similarity in the idea of the importance of interaction between sun and moisture in creating change.

I will discuss one more example of Hall's pattern of alluding to Spenser, but with a disgusting twist, a passage that begins with a verbal Spenser allusion in the characteristic "who knows not ...?" rhetorical question in another satire on drunkenness:

> When *Gullion* di'd (who knowes not *Gullion*?)
> And his dry soule ariu'd at *Acheron*,
> He faire besought the Feryman of hell,
> That he might drinke to dead *Pantagruel*.
>
> (III.vi.1–4)

A search of Early English Books Online for the phrase "who knows not" confirms that "who knowes not Gullion?" imitates a phrasing characteristic of Spenser. This sort of parenthetical rhetorical question appears only twice before Hall's use of it, and both are from Spenser. In "August" of Spenser's *Shepheardes Calender* (1579), Cuddie asks Willye and Perigot if they would like to hear "a doolefull verse / Of Rosalend (who knowes not Rosalend?) / That Colin made" (lines 140–42). Spenser follows the same pattern in Book 6 of *The Faerie Queene* (1596): "That iolly shepheard, which there piped, was / Poore *Colin Clout* (who knowes not *Colin Clout*?)" (6.10.16.3–4). The only other appearance of this structure before 1600 occurs in another one of the satires banned in 1599, Thomas Middleton's *Micro-Cynicon: Sixe Snarling Satyres* (1599), where "Who knowes not *Zodon*" presumably imitates this Spenserian verbal structure, just as Hall does.

Following his request to drink to Pantagruel, the gluttonously thirsty Gullion proceeds to drink the river Acheron, all of it, such that Charon can no longer transport the ghosts.

> Yet stand they still, as tho they lay at rode,
> Till *Gullion* his bladder would vnlode.
> They stand, and wait, and pray for that good houre:
> Which when it came, they sailed to the shore.
>
> (Hall, *Virgidemiae*, III.vi.19–22)

Here again we see the pattern of a clear reference to Spenser followed by a disgusting and indecorous image. Hall's image of a river created by a drunkard's piss certainly aims at a different reaction from the reader than Spenser's considerably more polite allegory of bodily waste in his creation of Port Esquiline in the House of Alma. He uses allusion to conjoin Rabelais and Spenser, linguistically calling to mind the pastoral world of Colin Clout while creating the Rabelaisian image of Gullion's excess. The two examples I discussed earlier occur at the beginning of the collection of *Toothless Satyres*, the second and third satires of the first book. The satire on Gullion appears as the penultimate satire of the third book, and thus near the end of the installment that was published in 1597.

So ... why? And so what? Why does Hall allude to "renowmed Spenser" at his most disgusting moments? I believe that he does so because inviting the reader to contrast Hall's disgusting images with Spenser's famous decorum creates the implicit argument that Hall's apparent indecorousness stems not from ignorance but from moral outrage. Wayne Rebhorn, in his analysis of how three Renaissance rhetoricians treated the concept of decorum, notes that such English writers as Thomas Wilson and George Puttenham identify indecorousness as a marker of low birth and social status and thus advise their rhetor against, in Wilson's words, "scurrilitie, or ale-house jesting" and "Ruffine maners" (qtd. in Rebhorn, "Outlandish fears").[11] Spenser endorses this view in *Teares of the Muses*, when Thalia complains of the "scoffing Scurrilitie" and "rymes of shameles ribaudrie" that go against "due Decorum" in comic poetry (lines 211, 213, 214).

If Hall does not put forth a rationale for using scurrilous language, he risks being interpreted as merely one of the barbarous, ignorant rhymers that the Muse Thalia weeps about. Part of his argument that he is not indecorous, but instead adheres to the decorum of satire, appears in critical comments throughout the satires, as R.B. Gill notes ("Purchase of glory").[12] Equally important, though, are the ways that he distinguishes himself from the ignorant by demonstrating his knowledge of and ability to adapt creatively the works of both classical and English authors.[13] Certainly Hall's creative allusions to Spenserian motifs and quotations function in this manner. Through these allusions, Hall shows that he

---

11 Rebhorn unpacks the significance of the word "scurrilitie" with reference to the Latin word *scurra*: "By speaking of 'scurrilitie,' Wilson both invokes the lower class clown of Rome, thus connecting his treatise to the classical past it imitates, and brings the *scurra* up to date by identifying him with the lower class habitues of the Renaissance tavern, that is, with thieves, coney-catchers, impoverished second sons, and declasse knights, with characters such as Shakespeare's Bardolph, Pistol, Poins, and Falstaff" (paragraph 13).
12 Alvin Kernan, considering Spenser's *Mother Hubberds Tale* as an example of what Elizabethan readers would recognize as a decorous "base style" for satire, compares John Marston's language to the standard of *Mother Hubberds Tale* and concludes that "Marston's diction lies for the most part entirely outside the area recognized as suitable for poetry of any kind." One could argue the extent to which Marston's language is more disgusting than Hall's, but Hall's language is certainly closer to Marston's than to Spenser's (Kernan, *Cankered Muse*, 100n8).
13 Regarding Hall's demonstrations of learnedness, see Davenport, "Interfused sources"; and Arnold Stein, "Joseph Hall's imitation."

knows and understands Spenser's practice of decorum and consciously chooses to follow a different idea of decorum, one appropriate to a satiric response to a corrupt world. The first three books of *Virgidemiarum* focus primarily on cultural critique and the final three books rather more on political critique, but the tone of moral outrage remains fairly consistent throughout the collection.[14] Hall's engagement with Spenser seems to imply that for one who couches his religious and political commentary in allegories of "Eluish knights" and "striuing shepheards," the "stately Stanzaes" of Spenser are appropriate and decorous ("Defiance," lines 49, 85, 55). For hmself, though, who wishes to score more direct satirical hits, only "refuse rimes" will do ("Defiance," line 113).

Although the meaning of "Spenser" as a bundle of ideas about the man Spenser was relatively stable, his meaning to and influence on individual authors varied by person, based on numerous factors including political and religious commitments, anxieties about censorship, ideas about genre, and so forth. The ideological diversity of the authors considered in this book suggests something of the importance of Spenser's position in the literary system of late Elizabethan England: even authors who presumably found little to appreciate in Spenser's ideas about religion or politics—such as the Catholic Tailboys Dymoke or Thomas Nashe, whose *Choise of Valentines* suggests a critical stance toward the political faction with which Spenser was associated—found it worthwhile for their projects to engage with Spenserian works to create satirical meanings.

Poets more closely aligned with Spenser in terms of their loyalties respond to Spenser not only as a figure with disproportionate visibility and status within the literary system, but also as an ally. Under the capricious and sometimes harsh censorship of the Elizabethan government, the ability to circuitously signal one's own alignment with the religious and political beliefs associated with Spenser by alluding to him, as I argue that Thomas Middleton does, becomes an additional way to create and convey meaning in a deniable way. Later, as authors try to find the new lines not to cross under the Jacobean government, Spenser retains his value as a toweringly significant author understood to stand for a particular set of meanings and values. Throughout the period, his status as a canonized and central author helps us to understand the use made of him by other authors writing in the noncanonized and peripheral area of satire.

---

14 See McCabe (*Joseph Hall*, 56–66), for fuller discussion of Hall's political and religious sympathies that appear in the *Virgidemiarum*, including opposition to enclosure and sympathy for the poor.

4

Spenserian "entry codes" to indirect satire

In his own satirical poetry, Edmund Spenser criticized indirectly, requiring readers to interpret clues carefully to access satirical meanings. For some readers, such as Joseph Hall and William Bedell, Spenser's reputation as a decorous, conservative poet seemed to obscure awareness of him as also demonstrating an interest in or affinity for satirical writing, as discussed in Chapter 3. This chapter offers a corrective in the form of "case studies" of three poets who were quite sensitively attuned to the potential for satirical readings or uses of Spenserian intertexts. Analyzing Thomas Nashe's *Choise of Valentines* with reference to Spenser's "March" eclogue from *The Shepheardes Calender* and Tailboys Dymoke's *Caltha Poetarum* alongside Spenser's *Muiopotmos* gives a sense of the code of indirect satire as a flexible vocabulary of subterfuge and innuendo. In Nashe's, Dymoke's, and (in the chapter's "coda") Shakespeare's responses to and reworkings of Spenserian images and narratives, we see the overwhelming significance of Spenser in the literary field of the 1590s.

Hunting love and catching Cupid in Spenser's "March" and Nashe's *Choise of Valentines*

In *A Choise of Valentines*, Thomas Nashe playfully uses Spenser's "March" eclogue from *The Shepheardes Calender* as an intertext for his own poem. Nashe imitates the methods of Spenserian satire to create a bawdy poem that mocks the ideas about love put forth by Spenser and Spenser's own source-texts while nevertheless endorsing the dichotomies of city and country that are staples of pastoral satire. The poem is outrageous and funny, especially if we consider the possibility that Nashe satirizes both Frances Walsingham and Queen Elizabeth with his bawdry, but, in the contrast between country and city, Nashe implicitly accepts pastoral's valorization of the moral superiority of the country. Reminiscent of Colin

Clout in the "neighbor towne" ("Januarye," line 50), Nashe's Tomalin learns to hate the distortion that the urban space enforces on pastoral love.

Until recently, critics have not been kind to Thomas Nashe's bawdy poem *A Choise of Valentines* (written ~1592; published 1899).[1] The poem has disappointed those hoping to glean some juicy biographical tidbits, with G.R. Hibbard complaining that "Nashe's attitude to sexual matters is too normal and healthy to be anything but dull"; Charles Nicholl determining only that "the man who wrote it was certainly no virgin"; and Stephen Hilliard discovering the unshocking fact that "the poem, like much pornography, mechanizes sex and demeans women" (Hibbard, *Nashe*, 57; Nicholl, *Cup of News*, 92; Hilliard, *Singularity*, 199, respectively). More fruitfully, scholars have identified numerous classical, Continental, and English sources and intertexts for the poem. Although Hibbard dismisses the poem as "largely derivative" (57), the learnedness and creativity required to combine and rework such a variety of inspirations as Ovid, Maximianus, Chaucer, Aretino, and Marlowe suggest the need for a revaluation of the poem's literary merit.[2] I will add here to the list of Nashe's influences by arguing that Spenser's "March" eclogue from *The Shepheardes Calender* serves as an important intertext for the poem. Reading Nashe's poem as a satire, in conversation with "March" and its sources, allows us to understand *The Choise of Valentines* as *both* a serious use of satire to explore ideas about love *and* a mean-spirited satire probably targeted at Frances Walsingham, widow of Sir Philip Sidney and, at the time of the poem's composition, wife to Robert Devereux, Second Earl of Essex.

In the 316-line poem, the narrator goes to his "ladies shrine" on Valentine's Day but finds that "Iustice Dudgein-haft" has frightened her from her usual place, and she has taken refuge in a brothel, where he goes to seek her (Nashe, *Choise*, lines 17, 21). The madam shows him some "prettie Trulls" (line 50), but he asks instead for his sweetheart by name: "Fetch gentle mistris Francis forth to me" (line 56). She appears, the madam leaves them, and foreplay ensues, but the narrator's penis fails

---

1 See Nicholl (*Cup of News*, 90) for evidence for 1592 as the likely year of composition.
2 M.L. Stapleton has extensively analyzed the classical sources for the poem, with special attention to Ovid in "Nashe and the poetics of obscenity" and to Maximianus in "A new source." For discussions of Chaucer as a source for the poem, see, for example, Hibbard, *Nashe*, 58; Evans, "Nashe's 'Choise'"; Clark, "Writing sexual fantasy." David O. Frantz argues for Aretino as inspiration more than source ("'Leud Priapians'"). Nicholl argues for Marlowe's translation of Ovid as "not so much the model as the precedent for Nashe's *Dildo*" (*Cup of News*, 94).

to become erect. The sweetheart gently suggests, "Com, lett me rubb and chafe it with my hand. / Perhaps the sillie worme is labour'd sore" (lines 132–33). She does so, and a bout of intercourse follows; although it lasts for fifty-six lines before the narrator reaches a poetic (and physical) climax in which he likens his emission to Jove's "golden shoure" (line 194), the time is insufficient for his sweetheart, and she begs for more: "Staie but an houre; an houre is not so much, / But half an houre; if that thy haste be such: / Naie but a quarter; I will aske no more" (lines 215–17). The narrator's penis obdurately refuses to comply with the sweetheart's wishes, at which point she swears off men, gets out her dildo, and delivers a paean to it as she finishes the job left undone by the narrator. The poem ends with the narrator delivering a wrathful diatribe against dildos before paying the madam and slinking away from the brothel. The poem is indeed, as Gabriel Harvey sniffed, a "pack of bawdry" (Harvey, *Pierces Supererogation*, 45), but all this is not without meaning.

The dedicatory sonnet "To the right Honorable the lord S" (generally though not universally believed to refer to Ferdinando Stanley, Lord Strange)[3] provides the first hint of Spenser's importance to an understanding of the poem. Hibbard points out parallels between this poem and Spenser's "To the right Honourable the Earle of Oxenforde," one of the dedicatory sonnets to *The Faerie Queene*, while Stapleton notes a generalized Spenserianism in the diction, including "the Spenserian trademark 'Ne,' a line of mellifluous monosyllables, filler adjectives ... that do very little to modify the nouns they precede, and the distorted word-order to fit the rhyme: all can be found in practically any passage of Spenser" (Hibbard, *Nashe*, 56; Stapleton, "Nashe," 38). The satirical import of a dedicatory sonnet to Lord Strange that alludes to Spenser becomes clearer read alongside Nashe's nearly contemporary sonnet to Spenser in reference to Lord Strange (that is, "Amyntas") in *Pierce Penilesse His Svpplication to the Diuell* (1592). Andrew Zurcher provides a careful analysis of Nashe's satire of Spenser in *Pierce Penilesse*: mockery of the disorderly publication of the dedicatory sonnets—in the back, with variable numbers of dedicatees, presumably because Spenser made the mistake of forgetting Lord Burghley in the first round of dedications—serves as the general backdrop for specific criticism of Spenser for failing to honor Lord Strange (Zurcher, "Getting it back to front"). Either explicitly or implicitly, both sonnets pit Lord Strange against Spenser, and Nashe sides with Lord Strange.

---

3 See McKerrow, "Commentary," IV.150–51 and V.141n1, for his analysis of the evidence in favor of Lord Strange as the dedicatee of *Choise*.

When the poem itself begins, we sense the influence of both Chaucer and Spenser:

> It was the merie moneth of Februarie
> When yong-men in their iollie roguerie
> Rose earelie in the morne fore breake of daie
> To seeke them valentines so trimme and gaie.
>
> (Nashe, *Choise*, lines 1–4)

The situation of choosing a sweetheart on St. Valentine's Day parallels Chaucer's *Parliament of Fowls*, but the Spenserianism of the dedicatory sonnet primes the reader to read the Chaucerianism of the opening lines as "Chaucer's manner as refracted through the medium of Spenser" (Hibbard, *Nashe*, 58). Further, these lines echo the opening of the interpolated tale that Thomalin tells his friend Willye in the "March" eclogue of *The Shepheardes Calender*:

> It was upon a holiday,
> When shepheardes groomes han leave to playe,
>   I cast to goe a shooting.
> Long wandring up and downe the land,
> With bowe and bolts in either hand,
>   For birds in bushes tooting.
>
> (lines 61–66)

The identification of "March" as an intertext becomes stronger when we learn that the narrator of Nashe's poem is named Tomalin. Katherine Duncan-Jones connects the name of Nashe's speaker to Tam Lin, the elfin hero of early modern ballads, but I believe a Spenserian derivation is more plausible (Duncan-Jones, "City limits").[4] A Thomalin appears as a speaker in "March" and "Julye" of *Shepheardes Calender*, and we see the name and its variant Tomalin signaling pastoralism (and Spenserianism) in several poems published afterward: for example, a Thomalin appears in William Browne's *The Shepheards Pipe* (1614), and Phineas Fletcher includes Thomalins in *The Purple Isle* (1633) and the *Piscatory Eclogues* (composed 1606–15; published 1633). The spelling Tomalin also appears in pastoral: Andrew Marvell creates a conversation among Hobbinol, Phillis, and Tomalin in his "Second Song" on the marriage of Lord Fauconberg and the Lady Mary Cromwell (written ~1657; published 1681), and the anonymous poet of *A pastoral occasion'd by the arrival of His Royal*

---

4 Note that Richard Lynn argues that Spenser himself uses the name Thomalin to allude to Tam Lin in order to intensify a topical satirical take on the marriage of the Earl of Leicester and Lettice Knollys ("Ewe/who?").

Highness Prince George of Denmark (1683) names his speakers Tomalin, Willie, and Hobbinol. The name Tomalin thus indicates a pastoral setting, and Nashe here signals pastoralism in order to satirize or critique it, as Jonathan Crewe suggests when he argues that the poem allegorizes the loss of "an ideal pastoral order" in which a shift from country to city emerges as "a moment of profound dislocation and loss. The city emerges not as positive material or social entity to be written 'about,' but always paradoxically as a place of deficiency and negation" (Crewe, *Unredeemed Rhetoric*, 48, 53).

Nashe uses the name Tomalin and the opening of the poem to call the reader's attention to "March" as an intertext for *A Choise of Valentines*; having done this, he then repeatedly alludes to "March" and to Spenser's source-texts in one of Bion's idylls ("Fragment XIII") and Ronsard's adaptation "L'amour oyseau."[5] The plots in Bion/Ronsard, Spenser, and Nashe all include the following elements: a boy or young man goes hunting, finds love (or Love), and learns of its dangers. Bion's hunting boy finds Cupid in the form of a beautiful bird in a box-tree; he fails to trap the bird and tells the story to an old man, who tells him he is lucky not to have caught the dangerous bird of prey (Ronsard changes the old man to an old woman). Spenser's Thomalin finds Cupid "within an Yvie todde" ("a thicke bushe," E.K. informs us); he is a "naked swayne / With spotted winges like Peacocks trayne" (lines 67, 79–80). Thomalin shoots arrows and throws stones but fails to catch the winged boy. Cupid gets his revenge by shooting Thomalin with one of his arrows; now the wound "ranckleth more and more, / And inwardly it festreth sore," and Thomalin doesn't know "how to cease it" (lines 100–2). Nashe's Tomalin, along with the other young men, goes hunting "To seeke ... valentines" (line 4). "Good Iustice Dudgein-haft" has scared his sweetheart Frances away from her usual spot, and she has sought refuge in a brothel. Tomalin apparently finds love (small *l*) in the first half of his sexual encounter and Love

---

5 Although Spenser is generally understood to owe more to Ronsard than Bion as source for Thomalin's story in "March," he knew both versions of the story. Leo Spitzer notes a plot detail present in Bion but not Ronsard that suggests that Spenser drew upon the Greek poem ("Spenser," 504n5). Spenser certainly knew the Ronsard version, as indicated by his use of peacock imagery for Cupid, which Ronsard used in editions of this poem before 1560: "Son plumage luisoit plus beau / Que n'est du Paon la queüe étrange" (quoted in Harrison, "Spenser," 141). See Prescott (*French Poets*, 109, 263n50–52) for a summary of scholarship on Spenser's uses of sources for Thomalin's story in "March." Spenser himself obviously wanted to highlight his ancient Greek source in Bion more so than Ronsard, given that E.K. notes, incorrectly referring to Theocritus instead of Bion, "THIS Æglogue seemeth somewhat to resemble that same of Theocritus, wherein the boy likewise telling the old man, that he had shot at a winged boy in a tree, was by hym warned, to beware of mischiefe to come" (62).

(capital *l*) in his neo-Platonic effusions during intercourse, but his failure to satisfy Frances, and the consequent shame at being supplanted by the dildo, teach him of love's dangers. He ends the poem "quitte discourag'd ... / Since all my store seemes to hir, penurie" (lines 299–300). When Nashe refers to the earlier sources, he uses the allusion to provide a contrast or implied critique of the idealism and innocence of the earlier texts.

Where love/Love is found differs importantly but not randomly in these poems. Spenser alters his sources' box tree into an "Yvie todde." Leo Spitzer hypothesizes that Spenser's innovation stems from a "desire not only to acclimate our episode in England, but also to enforce the 'dormant' aspect of Love ... the statue of Cupid covered with ivy represents then the minimum of Love's effectual force" (Spitzer, "Spenser," 500). I would argue instead that Spenser makes the change in order to complicate the bird imagery of his Cupid. Spenser compares his Cupid explicitly to a peacock, with references to his "winges like Peacocks trayne" and "winges of purple and blewe" (lines 80, 33). And yet, in English bird symbolism, the ivy tod belongs to the owl. The *Oxford English Dictionary* provides three sixteenth- and seventeenth-century examples connecting owls with ivy tods,[6] but Robert William Dent found many more in a study examining only dramatic writing (Dent, *Proverbial Language*, II.567). Certainly, for Spenser's readers, "like an owl in an ivy-bush" (or "ivy-tod") was common enough to be proverbial. Both of Spenser's sources place Cupid in a box tree (Bion: "pyxoio," from pyxos, "Fragment XIII," line 3; Ronsard: "Buys," "L'amour oyseau," line 22), so the shift to ivy demands attention. The strong connection between owls and ivy tods suggests Spenser's aim to connect Cupid with the owl. Spenser's bird imagery thus becomes much more specific, and complex, than Bion's simple "mega ... orneon" ("big bird") or even Ronsard's reference in early editions to a "paon," or peacock. The peacock, which Spenser connects to both Juno and Cupid in *Muiopotmos* through comparison with Clarion's wings, symbolizes the appealing aspect of love, but Spenser innovates on his sources by also providing a specific bird image for the dangerous side of love. In Bion, the old man says of the bird, "kakon esti to thērion" ("The creature is evil"), and in Ronsard, the old woman describes it as "L'oiseau de mauvaise rencontre" ("the bird of bad meeting"). By locating Cupid in an ivy tod, Spenser alludes to the owl, thus importing into the poem

---

6 The *Oxford English Dictionary Online* (s.v., "ivy-tod, n.") provides the following examples: "as owles out of an yuye todde" from T. Becon's *Relikes of Rome* (1553); "Your Ladiship, Dame Owle, Did call me to your Todd" from W. Warner's *Albions England* (1592); and "Men of Britain, Like boading Owls, creep into tods of Ivie" from J. Fletcher's *Bonduca* (1625).

the ominous symbolism associated with this bird. In both occurrences of the word "owl" in *Shepheardes Calender* ("June," line 24; "December," line 72), Spenser uses the adjective "ghastly" to modify the noun, suggesting the ill-omened nature of the owl. Spenser makes another change to his sources in changing the lime twigs and snares of Bion and Ronsard to arrows and rocks, which Thomalin uses, and especially the "fowling net" in which Willye's father caught Cupid. The image of the net connects the entrapment of Cupid with the cliché of the sonneteer caught in the golden net of his lady's hair, as for example in sonnet 12 of Sidney's *Astrophil and Stella*, where Astrophil calls Stella's "locks" Cupid's "day-nets" (line 2) and in *Amoretti* 37, where Spenser himself describes the beloved's hair as a "net of gold," a "golden snare," and a "guilefull net" (Spenser, "Sonnet XXXVII," lines 2, 6, 10).

I have taken time to detail these patterns of imagery and symbolism in Spenser and in his sources, Bion and Ronsard, both to highlight the playful inventiveness of Nashe's allusions to these sources and to support my argument that Nashe's alterations create a consistent satirical message mocking naïvete in love. Bion's box tree as perch for Cupid becomes Nashe's "Good Iustice Dudgein-haft"; Spenser's bird imagery for Cupid becomes in Nashe's poem avian metaphors for the dildo; and Nashe transforms the "fowling net" used to catch Cupid in Spenser into the "duskie nett of wyres" of Frances's pubic hair.

"Good Iustice Dudgein-haft," who frightens Frances so that she seeks refuge in a brothel, has a remarkable name, one that indicates the stern rigor of the magistracy:

> For she was shifted to an upper-ground.
> Good Iustice Dudgein-haft, and crab-tree face
>   With bills and staues had scar'd hir from the place;
> And now she was compell'd for Sanctuarie
>   To flye unto an house of venerie.
>
> (lines 20–24)

Critics have generally read Frances's move as a shift from the country to the city, based on J.B. Steane's reading of "upper-ground" as referring to Upper Ground Street, "a street of low repute in Southwark," in contrast to the "toune-greene," "fields," "village," and "Contrie" mentioned as part of the setting before the shift to the brothel (lines 6, 8, 9, 13) (Steane, "Introduction and notes," 459n11). In this case, Iustice Dudgein-haft lives in the country, but he seems to represent the type of judicial official who would enforce the suppression of brothels in London that occurred after 1570 (Moulton, *Before Pornography*, 171 and 242n35). Whether in the country or the city, Iustice Dudgein-haft represents an allegorized character inimical to love, and this provides the key to understanding how his name fits within the complex system of plant and bird imagery developed in Spenser and his sources' treatment of the basic story, because "dudgeon" refers to the root of boxwood, the same box tree in which the boy finds Cupid in Bion and Ronsard (s.v. "dudgeon, n.¹").[7] Through this odd name, Nashe alludes to the location of Cupid in Spenser's sources in a way that underscores the implications for love of the shift from the pastoral to the urban setting. What was once natural is transformed through human artisanship into something violent and oppressive, and the social and judicial pressure from Iustice Dudgein-haft transforms Frances from a valentine into a whore.

Similarly to this playful alteration of the tree imagery, Nashe also builds on Spenser's innovation of the fowling net to convey his critique of naïvely idealizing ideas about love. Whereas Spenser's fowling net to catch Cupid calls to mind the sonnet topos likening a woman's hair to a net to catch men, Nashe creates a more bawdy and unappealing twist to this image by shifting attention from the hair on a woman's head to her pubic hair. Following an idealizing description of Frances's belly, Tomalin descends:

> At whose decline a fountaine dwelleth still,
> That hath his mouth beset with uglie bryers
> Resembling much a duskie nett of wyres.
> (lines 112–14)

In sonnetry, the "nets" or "wires" of women's hair must be golden to be appealing, leading to Shakespeare's satire on sonnet clichés: "If hairs be wires, black wires grow on her head" (Shakespeare, "Sonnet 130," line 4). Ian Moulton compares Frances's "duskie nett" to Acrasia's veil in *The Faerie Queene*, to the Palmer's "subtile net" that captures her, and to Vulcan's net that captured Venus and Mars (Moulton, *Before Pornography*, 174). Although Moulton focuses strictly on net imagery with negative connotations, the poem's Spenserian intertextuality means we need to consider the ways that this ugly image also references, in order to satirize, the more appealing images of a fowling net to catch Cupid and women's golden hair as a net to trap men.

Finally, Nashe uses two of Spenser's three bird images in "March" to connect the dildo to Cupid, which, given the low esteem in which the

---

7 In addition to the examples provided in the *OED*, see also Wilkins, who defines "Dudgeon" as "Root of Box" and "dudgeon-dagger" as "Short Sword whose handle is of the root of Box" (*Alphabetical Dictionary*, Eee4v).

narrator holds the dildo, serves as a clear critique of Cupid and the ideologies of love associated with him. As already noted, Spenser makes the bird imagery connected with Cupid in "March" much more specific than that found in Bion or Ronsard, with explicit reference to the peacock and the crow and the suggestion of the owl by placing Cupid in the ivy tod. Nashe alludes to this bird imagery and also develops his own, still with reference to "March." First, the bird imagery used to refer to Frances herself bifurcates the sense of hunting for love found in "March." Whereas Spenser's Thomalin "cast[s] to goe a shooting / ... / For birds in bushes tooting" (lines 63, 66) and finds only Cupid, not an actual woman, Nashe's Tomalin seeks an avianified woman. Tomalin, along with the other men, rises early in the morning "To seeke ... valentines" (line 4), but Tomalin of course cannot find Frances, because she "was compell'd ... / To flye unto an house of venerie" (lines 23–24; here, the pun on "venery," which can also refer to hunting, contributes as well to the imagery of hunting real birds).[8] At the brothel, he speaks to the madam, who "us'd to take yong wenches for to tame" (line 30). He attempts to hire Frances, and the madam tells him it will cost him, for "he that will eate quaile's must lauish crounes" (line 63; see Williams, "Quail," for contemporary uses of "quail" as slang for a prostitute, including this one). The quest for love, allegorized in Spenser and his sources as a hunt for Cupid, becomes closer to an actual hunt here, given that the "quail" is a human character, not an anthropomorphized and deified abstraction. The quail has been flushed, and she alights after her flight in a place that, in "taming" her, obliges her to be caught by anyone who will pay. She thus becomes, briefly, a perfect fantasy: a pure sweetheart, but one required to have sex with Tomalin because she took sanctuary in a brothel.

Any sense of Frances as a victim of the hunt for love dissipates, however, when she begins not only to assert herself sexually but to berate Tomalin for his unimpressive performance. We can assume that Nashe assumes a male reader, and that this male sixteenth-century reader would feel for Tomalin when Frances apostrophizes his penis thus:

> Adiew faint-hearted instrument of lust,
>   That falselie hast betrayde our equale trust.
> Hence-forth no more will I implore thine ayde,
>   Or thee, or men of cowardize upbrayde.
> My little dilldo shall suplye their kinde.
>
> (lines 235–39)

---

8 I am indebted to Yulia Ryzhik for this observation.

By this point she has metamorphosed from hunted quail to brazen strumpet, and here Nashe initiates the use of bird imagery for the dildo itself, thus linking it with Cupid in Spenser's "March" while giving it pride of place: Frances tells Tomalin that the dildo "playes at peacock twixt my leggs right blythe" (line 243). In response to Frances's paean to the dildo, Tomalin execrates it at some length, calling it among many other things "blinde mischapen owle" (line 288). Frances in her enthusiasm for the dildo uses the image that Spenser used for the beautiful aspect of Cupid, and Tomalin in his anger and shame at being supplanted by it uses one of the bird images that Spenser used to convey a sense of the danger of the bird that the innocent boy finds. The bird imagery links the dildo to Cupid, but, according to Tomalin, the dildo is more powerful than both Priapus and Cupid. Priapus's "triumph now must falle" unless he "thrust this weakeling to the walle" (lines 247–48). As for Cupid, the dildo "wayte's on Courtlie Nimphs, that be so coye, / And bids them skorne the blynd-alluring boye" (lines 255–56). The inanimate object thus becomes not only personified but almost deified by comparison with these other gods of sex and love.

Comparing Ronsard's—and, later, Spenser's—version of the story with that of Bion, Don Cameron Allen concludes, "It must be confessed, I think, that when we reach the end of Ronsard's poem our veins are less warmed and our sensibilities less charmed than they were when we had only Bion in our emotional history. Love has become more distasteful. It is associated with birds of ill omen, with witchcraft, with wounds, with bitterness" (Allen, "Three poems," 184). It must also be confessed that when we reach the end of Nashe's poem love has become even *more* distasteful, associated with prostitution, impotence, premature ejaculation, insatiable female desire, and especially the dildo.

Both love and Love take a beating in Nashe's satirical treatment of Spenserian idealizations of love and women, but "March"—with its sly allusion to Lettice Knollys, whose secret marriage to the Earl of Leicester led to their banishment from court upon its discovery in 1579—also provides us with a clue to another of Nashe's satiric intentions. If the name Tomalin in *The Choise of Valentines* calls attention to Spenser's "March" as an intertext, then the name Lettice in "March" ("And learne with Lettice to wexe light," line 20) cues us to consider the possibility that the name Frances in *A Choise of Valentines* refers to an actual person. Based on internal evidence of Frances's wealth and high status in the poem and external evidence of what personal satirical targets might be most amusing to Lord Strange, the dedicatee of the poem and Nashe's patron at this time,⁹ I speculate that the name refers to Frances Walsingham, who was in 1592 the wife of Robert Devereux, Second Earl of Essex, having been widowed in 1586 by the death of her first husband, Sir Philip Sidney.

In the poem, Frances dresses neither like a country lass nor like a prostitute, but like a great lady. The madam, in telling Tomalin of Frances's high price, notes:

> And mistris Francis in hir veluet goune's,
> And ruffs, and periwigs as fresh as Maye
> Can not be kept with half a croune a daye.
>
> (lines 64–66)

When Frances enters the room, Tomalin watches her:

> Sweeping she coms, as she would brush the ground,
> Hir ratling silke's my sences doe confound.
>
> (lines 77–78)

The Countess of Essex would surely be the most famous Frances at the time to wear "ratling silke's," and the connections between Frances, Countess of Essex, and Lettice Knollys, alluded to in Spenser's "March," strengthen the sense that Nashe had Spenser's bold reference in mind in naming his valentine-whore Frances.

Whether one agrees with Charles Mounts that Spenser's potentially inflammatory reference to "Lettice" was an accidental holdover from an earlier manuscript or with Richard Rambuss that alluding to the Earl of Leicester's marriage serves as a means of advertising his discretion by showing he "knows—and 'keeps'—the secret" (Mounts, "Spenser," 199–200; Rambuss, *Spenser's Secret*, 24), we can expect that savvy sixteenth-century readers would doubt E.K.'s obfuscatory note glossing "Lettice" as "the name of some country lasse" (63n20). Richard Lynn, in a very detailed reading of the poem, argues that "March" is a much more specific—and mean-spirited—satire than has previously been thought, criticizing Lettice Knollys for marrying the Earl of Leicester, thus damaging his standing with the Queen. Identification of the "Lettice" of "March" with the Countess of Leicester would be even more likely because of the near contemporaneity of the scandal: *The Shepheardes Calender* was entered in the Stationers' Register in December 1579, just two months after the Queen learned, in early October, of the Earl of Leicester's secret

---

9 See Nicholl (*Cup of News*, 87–90) for details about the patronage relationship between Nashe and Lord Strange.

marriage to Lettice Knollys (MacCaffrey, *Queen Elizabeth*, 261–62).

Several details connect Lettice Knollys and Frances Walsingham, both of whom secretly married favorites of the Queen, leading to public scandal. Before her marriage to the Earl of Leicester, Knollys was the widow of Walter Devereux, First Earl of Essex, to whom she bore Robert, Second Earl of Essex; she was thus mother-in-law to Frances Walsingham. Additionally, Knollys's daughter, Penelope Devereux, was Sidney's Stella before his marriage to Walsingham, which may have been, but probably was not, known to Thomas Nashe in 1592. Walter Friedrich notes that the identification of Stella as Penelope Devereux Rich was not widespread until 1598, when the folio edition of Sidney's works brought the sequence's Sonnet 37 into print for the first time, and notes that before—and even after—that date, writers, including of course Spenser in *Astrophel*, frequently misidentify Frances Walsingham as Stella (Friedrich, "Stella"). In his introductory note to Thomas Newman's unauthorized 1591 edition of Sidney's *Astrophil and Stella*, Nashe says nothing about the identity of Stella (Nashe, "Somewhat to read," A3r–A4v). Given the Countess of Pembroke's anger over the piracy of her dead brother's works, leading to the impounding of the edition and the removal of Nashe from involvement in the subsequent edition (Nicholl, *Cup of News*, 83), we can assume that Nashe did not receive private communications from the family about the true identity of Stella before penning *The Choise of Valentines* the following year.

Assuming that Nashe mistakenly believes Frances Walsingham to be Stella helps to explain the imagery of suns, stars, and planets in *Choise*'s sex scene. But whereas Sidney's Stella was a star-woman, and whereas Nashe describes Sidney himself as "Englands Sunne" ("Somewhat to read," A3v), in *Choise* Frances is the sun, and Tomalin the star:

> On him hir eyes continualy were fixt,
>   With hir eye-beames his melting looke's were mixt,
> Which lyke the Sunne, that twixt tuo glasses plaies
>   From one to th'other cast's rebounding rayes.
> He lyke a starre, that to reguild his beames
>   Sucks-in the influence of Phebus streames,
> Imbathe's the lynes of his descending light
>   In the bright fountaines of hir clearest sight.
>
> (lines 155–62)

Making Frances the sun (or a planet, as line 163 figures her) to Tomalin's star puts her into the masculinized role of a desiring sexual subject. Although the Petrarchan cliché of the mistress's eyes like sunbeams does suggest feminine possibilities for solar imagery, such is not the case with Frances's fieriness, which is altogether too *hot* to be anything but masculine: she has "fierce and feruent ... radiance," she darts "fyrie stake's ... at euerie glance," and Cupid likes to play with "euerie atomie / That in hir Sunne-beames swarme aboundantlie" (lines 169, 170, 175–76).[10] Considering Nashe's lusty Frances as a parodic version of Sidney's chaste Stella would have been hilarious to a reader like the poem's dedicatee, Lord Strange, whose Catholic leanings and political aspirations made the Leicester and Sidney faction inimical to him.[11]

In 1592, when Nashe penned his poem, the scandal of the Earl of Essex's secret marriage to Frances Walsingham Sidney, which the Queen learned of in 1590, was farther in the past than the Leicester discovery was when Spenser published *The Shepheardes Calender*. However, Nashe may have aimed, not at referring to old news, but at providing a satirical back-story for the newest news: the Queen's punishment of Sir Walter Raleigh and Elizabeth Throckmorton for marrying without her permission. If Nashe wrote the poem after March, when the birth of Damerei Raleigh ended the secret part of the Raleigh secret marriage, then he would seem to be using the allusions to two other famous scandals of royal favorites marrying ladies-in-waiting to the Queen without her permission to make a larger point about the Queen. Lettice Knollys, lady-in-waiting to the Queen, drew the Queen's ire by marrying her favorite, the Earl of Leicester. Frances Walsingham Sidney, lady-in-waiting to the Queen, infuriated the Queen by marrying her favorite, the Earl of Essex. Elizabeth Throckmorton, lady-in-waiting to the Queen, won a trip to the Tower for marrying the Queen's favorite, Sir Walter Raleigh. Nashe brings all three of these scandals into play in his poem—writing in 1592, when the Raleigh scandal was fresh; alluding to "March," which names Lettice and thus makes reference to the Leicester scandal; and naming Frances to call to mind the Essex marriage scandal. When we read with all three stories in mind, Elizabeth becomes the brothel-keeper, the "foggie three-chinnd dame, / That us'd to take yong wenches for to tame" (lines 29–30), and the brothel in the city where the valentine Frances takes refuge becomes the court. This view of Elizabeth aligns her firmly with Venus, not Diana, as Tomalin indicates by invoking the aid of Venus ("venus be

---

10 Moulton (*Before Pornography*, 181–82) provides a more detailed discussion of the connection between humours theory and Frances's heat to argue for Frances as masculinized to an early modern audience.
11 See Nicholl (*Cup of News*, 189–96) for details regarding Lord Strange's connections with Catholicism and Catholic plots to bring him to the throne.

my speede," line 43) while being led by the madam to the place "Where venus bounzing vestalls skirmish oft" (line 48).

If I am correct, it is no wonder that Nashe made no efforts to publish the poem, but its transmission to the present through six distinct manuscripts, in addition to the fact that his enemy Gabriel Harvey knew enough of the poem to have an opinion about it, suggests something of the pleasure that many of his contemporaries took in the poem, pleasure heightened, I argue, by Nashe's transformation of the innocent hunting boys of Bion, Ronsard, and Spenser into the disappointed Tomalin, whose hopeful ideas about love are shattered by Frances's insatiable desire, and the dildo she uses to quench it.

Satirizing the quean: Venus as Elizabeth in Spenser's *Muiopotmos* and Dymoke's *Caltha Poetarum*

In the previous section, I suggested the possibility that Thomas Nashe's madam, associated with Venus, may have glanced at Queen Elizabeth and her famous jealousy of courtier-favorites who fell for (and married) ladies-in-waiting. In this section and the "coda" that follows, I continue to explore the satirical potential for mocking the Virgin Queen, Elizabeth, by associating her—more or less circuitously—with Venus. I will look at two poems, Spenser's *Muiopotmos; or, The Fate of the Butterflie*, which, though part of the recalled *Complaints* volume, has never been perceived as the target of the censorship, and Tailboys Dymoke's *Caltha Poetarum*, a nearly forgotten poem whose chief claim to fame is having been named in the Bishops' Ban of 1599.

If the easy and obvious way to compliment Elizabeth is to celebrate her chastity and compare her to Diana, then Venus becomes the easy and obvious route to satire, and we find this occurring in both *Muiopotmos* and *Caltha Poetarum* in their plot points of a jealous Venus seeking revenge on beautiful maidens.[12] I do not aim to argue strenuously that Spenser intended to satirize the Queen with his brief interpolated tale of Venus and Astery, because the matter must rest in the realm of speculation, though a few critics have noted in passing the possibility of a correspondence between the Venus of *Muiopotmos* and Queen Elizabeth (see, e.g., Lemmi, "Allegorical meaning," 740–41; Harris, "Butterfly," 305; Herron, "Plucking," 100). Rather, I wish to read these two poems side by side not only to prove that at least one contemporary reader, Tailboys Dymoke,

---

12 For discussion of contemporary critiques of Elizabeth that hinged on supposed inchastity, see Levin, *Heart and Stomach*, 66–90.

did believe that Spenser intended his Venus to refer to the Queen, but also to consider Spenser's role as satirical inspiration for Dymoke's poem, which alludes insistently to *Muiopotmos* while pushing the indirect allegorical satire of the Queen much, much farther than Spenser's does.

The cold trail on *Caltha Poetarum* went cold again after Leslie Hotson's 1938 article identifying Tailboys Dymoke as the author of the poem, which in 1599 was published under the name "Thomas Cutwode," banned by the bishops, and then reprieved from being burned. Although being named in the Bishops' Ban rescued the poem from complete oblivion in the succeeding centuries, the poem has nevertheless languished in critical obscurity for two reasons: (1) Tailboys Dymoke died at some point before February 1603 and thus did not follow up this poem with a more substantial body of work (Larkum, "Dymoke"); (2) the poem is obviously allegorical, and it is more difficult to create allegorical interpretations of a work written by an unknown author. Still, even after 1938, when *Caltha*'s author ceased to be an unknown author, he remained lacking in fame, and critics are simply less interested in deciphering the allegories of un-famous authors. For example, Arthur Henry Bullen, in an early *Dictionary of National Biography* (*DNB*) entry on "Thomas Cutwode," published before Hotson discovered Cutwode's identity, for example, dismisses the poem as follows: "The poem shows some skill of versification and archness of fancy; but as the veiled personal allusions are now unintelligible, it is tedious to read through the 187 stanzas" ("Thomas Cutwode," 370). Hotson attempts to make the poem less "tedious" by identifying some of the allegorical figures and places, but, because he fails to notice the pervasive Catholic imagery, he misses the mark repeatedly, for example in reading Diana as representing Queen Elizabeth and Ephesus as London (Hotson, "Marigold," 61). Thus, Hotson's conclusions as a whole are weakened by some of his overconfident assertions regarding what are in fact highly speculative identifications.

Hotson's early twentieth-century preference for assertiveness in identifying topical allusions appears in his contemporaries' innumerable attempts to unravel the allegory of Spenser's *Muiopotmos*, giving the lie to Bullen's suggestion in the *DNB* that incomprehensible allegories are therefore inherently tedious. Summing up more than a century of *Muiopotmos* criticism in 1970, Franklin Court writes: "For at least the past one hundred thirty-four years, it has been subjected to so many various interpretations that even a cursory study of the scholarship written about it gets tedious and discomforting" (Court, "Theme and structure," 1). A small selection of examples from the period of the "Old Historicism" will suffice to convey a sense of the variety of interpretations of this apparently incomprehensible allegory: early twentieth-century critics argued for interpreting the butterfly Clarion and the spider Aragnoll as Spenser and Lady Carey, Raleigh and Essex, Sidney and Burghley, Sidney and the Duc d'Alençon, and Essex and Burghley (respectively, Long, "Spenser's"; Lyons, "Spenser's"; Hulbert, "New interpretation"; Lemmi, "Allegorical meaning"; Harris, "Butterfly"). *Muiopotmos* criticism eventually moved on to other concerns, but this scattershot approach to allegorical interpretation proves that incomprehensible does not necessarily mean uninteresting, if the author is famous enough.

It is not my aim here to provide identifications for every little flower and bee in *Caltha Poetarum*; however, while granting that the allegory is extremely obscure, I think there is much more to say about this poem than has yet been said, and I believe that considering its intertextuality with *Muiopotmos* can help us to make sense of this poem as a satire, rather than just labeling it "obscene" and moving on, as the poem's few critics have tended to do. John Peter cites three page numbers (without quoting or describing the events, which include descriptions of the Bee sucking honey from Caltha, the nondescription of the metamorphosed Caltha's genitalia, and Musaeus's sexual encounter with Venus) that render this a "wanton work" (Peter, *Complaint*, 149), though he sees it as sufficiently mild that he speculates that the bishops, upon examining the work, may have reprieved it because they found it not obscene enough to merit the flames. The focus on obscenity fits with his overall thesis about the Bishops' Ban: "That it was very largely with obscenity that they were concerned there can surely be no doubt whatever" (Peter, *Complaint*, 150).

Richard McCabe, with an opposing thesis, that the target of the ban "was neither eroticism nor lewdness but satire itself," quickly dispenses with the one work in which he finds no satire by referring to the "one undoubtedly obscene work, Thomas Cutwode's *Caltha Poetarum*" before moving on to more comprehensible satires included in the ban (McCabe, "Elizabethan satire," 189). Cyndia Susan Clegg does find satire in the "primarily erotic" poem, but not satirical intention (*Press Censorship Elizabethan*, 213). Her overall argument posits offensiveness to the Earl of Essex as the connection among all of the works named in the ban. Although she cannot find any pointed satire on Essex in *Caltha*, she notes that a contemporary manuscript poem connected Essex with bee imagery—she mentions "The bussin Bee's Complaint" but could have included another possibly Essex-authored poem, "It was a time when silly Bees could speak." To the extent, then, that Essex was associated with bee imagery in the popular imagination, *Caltha Poetarum* may have been read as satirizing the Earl, leading to its scrutiny by the bishops (Clegg, *Press Censorship Elizabethan*, 214).

Overall—and this comes as no surprise, given that practically no one reads this poem—the critical enterprise regarding *Caltha* has been characterized by insufficient care since the time of Hotson. Clegg does not cite Hotson and thus does not engage with his argument when she creates her own allegorical interpretation. Hannah Betts does cite Hotson in passing, but her brief treatment of the poem focuses only on the erotic blazon of Caltha and its debts to Spenser's less explicitly erotic blazon of Belphoebe in *Faerie Queene*, Book 2, canto 3. She notes Hotson's identifications of the bee with Dymoke himself and Caltha as a lady-in-waiting, closing with one of Hotson's incorrect identifications: "Diana, unsurprisingly, represents the queen" (Betts, "The image," 173). William R. Jones, in a confusing passage that cites Betts apparently erroneously, repeats Clegg's identification of the bee with Essex without citing Clegg before arriving at an identification of Venus with the Queen that he does not own but that does not come from either Clegg or the source cited immediately thereafter, that is, Betts p. 173 (Jones, "Bishops' Ban," 337).

In short, no one has engaged in a serious and sustained way with the allegory of *Caltha Poetarum* since Hotson, and Hotson's eagerness to make positive identifications too often impeded his critical acumen. I will argue a number of interrelated theses here: (1) Dymoke reads the Venus–Astery episode in Spenser's *Muiopotmos* as satirizing Queen Elizabeth's notorious jealousy. (2) He helps his readers to understand his own satire by calling their attention to his poem's intertextuality with *Muiopotmos* through multiple plot and thematic parallels, suggesting that other contemporary readers also read Spenser's Venus as a satire on the Queen. (3) He departs—radically—from his Spenserian prototype to create a Catholic-themed satire that is quite shocking in its allegorical animus against the Queen.

Given the obscurity of the poem, a plot summary is in order. The poem opens in a garden in the North; Hotson's success in identifying the poem's *personal* satire, which was animated by the contentious relationship that Tailboys Dymoke and his brother Sir Edward Dymoke, the Queen's Champion, had with their uncle, Henry, Second Earl of Lincoln, aids in recognizing the setting as Lincoln. And yet this garden in Lincoln bears striking resemblance in some respects to Queen Elizabeth's court in London: Venus rules over this garden in which the plants and flowers play at love, but she gets very angry when the inhabitants of the garden do not play at love as she wishes them to. She becomes angry with the Marigold, Caltha, for two reasons: Caltha is "the Viccar of a vaine vsurping Queene" (Dymoke, *Caltha*, 32.4)[13]—that is, Diana—and she does not return the love of the woodbine. Venus persuades Cupid to shoot Caltha, but at the last moment, the Bee accidentally gets in the way and is shot. Overwhelmed by love, he starts a new, idolatrous religion, Calthanism (a parody of Petrarchanism using Catholic imagery), and persuades his hive to become coreligionists with him. Venus, like Elizabeth angered by love that she has not sanctioned and outraged as well by this heretical religious sect, goes to war against the bees using spiders as her foot-soldiers. The Bee becomes trapped in a spiderweb, which makes it possible for Venus and Cupid to take him prisoner. The Bee stings Cupid and then escapes.

Meanwhile, Diana comes to Caltha to rescue her from the wrath of Venus. She metamorphoses Caltha into a human and takes her away from the garden. Venus has succeeded in destroying the Bee's hive, and so the Bee dresses as a pilgrim and sets off alone, still practicing Calthanism and "Blessing his Marygold with Aue-maries" (116.5). He ends up in Ephesus (i.e., Rome), and, once there, his worship immediately shifts from Calthanism to Roman Catholic worship practices. He makes his way to the garden where Diana and Caltha are; because of the Bee's excitement at seeing her, Caltha is able to recognize him as the Bee who saved her from Cupid's arrow. To reward him, Diana transforms him into a man and—wonder of wonders!—gives him a penis, because, having lost his sting to Cupid, he metamorphoses without genitals. She also grants him a wish; apparently cured entirely of Calthanism, he asks not for love but for the gift of music. Diana grants the wish and renames him Musaeus. In human form, Musaeus heads back to the garden in the North to take revenge on Venus. Venus asks Musaeus to watch over her while she sleeps, to protect her from her enemy the Bee. He agrees and plays the fiddle until she falls asleep:

> And downe he lies, and leanes vpon her hips,
> And licorously he kist the Ladies lips.
>
> Now whether that this Lady slept or no,
>   or winked wild, as little wantons vse:
> There will I leaue you, for I do not know,
>   iudge of it as you list, for you may chuse:
> And me I pray you heartily excuse.

---

13 Quotations from the poem will be cited parenthetically in the text by stanza and line number.

> But there the fidler found an instrument,
> That makes him mirth & much mad meriment.
>
> (175.6–176.7)

There is certainly sufficient erotic material in the poem to explain *Caltha*'s inclusion in the works named in the Bishops' Ban—although we are talking of bees and flowers, the poem is definitely sexier than the also-banned *Pigmalions Image*, by John Marston. However, representing Queen Elizabeth as Venus and then having her raped—or faux-somnolently seduced—by a vagrant musician within the context of a barely concealed pro-Catholic agenda creates offense of an entirely different order.

Dymoke offers readers two signposts for interpreting the poem's allegory: the cue to search for Catholic meanings suggests the author's general stance on political and religious issues, and indications to read with Spenser's *Muiopotmos* in mind lead the reader to understand Venus as allegorically representing Elizabeth, which is, I believe, the key to understanding the poem as a whole. Dymoke alerts the reader to be attentive to Catholic readings in the second stanza, in which he invokes the goddess Flora to be his Muse and to bring him flowers "For to attend my Virgin Mary-gold" (2.6). This is the first of many examples of Catholic concepts and imagery. Early in the poem, Dymoke creates a smokescreen for his pro-Catholic stance by using Catholic imagery to convey a negative judgment in the idolatrous Calthanist worship practices, similar to Spenser's use of Roman Catholic props to indicate to readers of *The Faerie Queene* that Archimago does not merit trust. Later, however, in Ephesus/Rome, Dymoke presents Catholic liturgical and worship practices as unambiguously positive. Although we have nothing other than the poem on which to base an assessment of Dymoke's personal religious affiliation, his parents were Catholic recusants, lending support to internal evidence that the author of *Caltha Poetarum* endorsed Catholicism. The *Catholic Encyclopedia* names Sir Robert Dymoke (*d*. 1580) a "confessor of the faith"; notes his associations with the Catholic priests Richard Kirkman, William Lacy, and Edmund Campion (including retaining Kirkman in 1579 as a tutor for his sons, perhaps including Tailboys, who was eighteen years old at the time); and details his death in prison for recusancy ("Dymoke"; Camm, "Robert Dymoke"; Wainwright, "Bl. William Lacy"; Rabenstein, "Kirkman").

Reading the poem with the author's probable Catholicism in mind leads one to make different allegorical interpretations than one might otherwise make. That a Catholic would use a poem by the staunch Protestant Spenser to sharpen and focus his satire may seem surprising, but it suggests how influential Spenser was as an allegorical satirist in the 1590s.[14] Dymoke creates numerous parallels between his poem and Spenser's *Muiopotmos* to highlight the importance of the earlier poem as an intertext. Both are Ovidian poems of metamorphosis, in which "two mightie ones" (Spenser, *Muiopotmos*, line 3) interact or interfere with the lives of mortals, including in each poem two metamorphoses. In *Muiopotmos*, although there has been a great deal of debate regarding the identity of the two mighty ones, Don Cameron Allen's influential interpretation of the allegory as referring to the progress of the soul has led to general acceptance of his identification of them as Venus and Minerva (Allen, "On Spenser's"). In *Caltha*, on the other hand, the two mighty ones are Venus and Diana. The metamorphoses in *Muiopotmos* occur because of envy—either Venus's envy of Astery leading to her transformation of the girl to a butterfly or Arachne's envy of Minerva as cause of her own metamorphosis into a spider (Bond, "*Invidia*")—and lead to a diminution or debasement of a human. In contrast to this trajectory in *Muiopotmos*, Dymoke creates his stories of metamorphosis to highlight the Catholic concept of grace as exemplified in Diana, representing the Virgin Mary, and the transformations she effects move in the opposite direction from *Muiopotmos*: from flower and bee to human. In *Caltha*, unlike *Muiopotmos*, Venus has no supernatural powers: she needs help from the woodbine to heal her son Cupid from the Bee's sting, for example, and so metamorphosing those who offend her is out of the question. Diana, on the other hand, grants metamorphosis as a boon: she changes Caltha into a human to protect her from Venus, and she makes the Bee human to reward him for saving Caltha from Venus.

We also find numerous plot parallels connecting the two insect protagonists, *Muiopotmos*'s butterfly Clarion and *Caltha Poetarum*'s unnamed Bee. Where Clarion has a mock-epic arming before setting out into the garden (lines 56–91), the Bee's hivemates help him with his epic disarming when he returns from the garden after being shot by Cupid and falling in love with Caltha (stanzas 63–64); here, as with the knights of *The Faerie Queene*, "the disarming of the hero is ... a metaphor for a yielding of the self to lust" (Moulton, *Before Pornography*, 177). The Bee

---

14 Numerous scholars have explored the significance of Protestant thought to *Muiopotmos*; for example, see Weiner ("Spenser's *Muiopotmos*") for an analysis of the poem as illustrating Protestant skepticism of allegory; Brown ("The allegory") for an argument that Spenser explores eschatological questions through the poem; and Anderson ("Spenser's *Muiopotmos*," 119–23) for a discussion of the impact of Calvinist and Reformation thought on *Muiopotmos*.

disarms immediately after indulging in the lustful pleasure of tasting the flower Caltha (stanzas 60–61), a scene that pushes to clear eroticism the incipient lustfulness that many scholars have noted in Clarion's greedy tasting of flowers. In *Muiopotmos*, Clarion

> casts his glutton sense to satisfie,
> Now sucking of the sap of herbe most meete,
> Or of the deaw, which yet on them does lie,
> Now in the same bathing his tender feete.
>
> (lines 179–82)

Similarly but more explicitly, in *Caltha Poetarum* the Bee approaches Caltha:

> Vpon her flew the flie and suckt her sweet,
>   and plaid full peartly with that pretie one,
> And there full featly labourd with his feet,
>   and kist her, least he shuld be deemd a drone:
> Now blest be loue, for there was loue alone,
> The Bee begins to find and stir his sting,
> Beleeue me (loue) thou art a wanton thing.
>
> (stanza 60)

In the next stanza, with his sting apparently fully stirred, "in her circle vp and downe he hops" (61.3). The final plot parallel—the entrapment of the hero in a spiderweb (*Muiopotmos* lines 417–40, *Caltha Poetarum* stanzas 75–79)—is of course the final event in Clarion's life. However, through the grace of Diana, the Bee goes on to have a much more rewarding, and quite literally more human, life after escaping from Venus's henchmen, the spiders, and leaving the garden.

In addition to the mythological framework and the plot parallels between the two insect heroes, Dymoke also models his poem generically on Spenser's, with several genre markers to encourage his reader to interpret this as a mock-epic. Although twentieth-century critics engaged in considerable debate over generic classification for *Muiopotmos*, Dymoke appears to be one early modern reader for whom the mock-epic elements had priority. Thomas Nadal in 1910 argued that *Muiopotmos* was mockheroic as a way of arguing against it being allegorical; he compared it with Chaucer's *Sir Thopas* and the *Nun's Priest's Tale*, a source-text that Judith Anderson has also explored (Nadal, "Spenser's"; Anderson, "Spenser's *Muiopotmos*"). Isabel Rathborne continued this dichotomization of allegory versus mock-epic by calling the poem an unfinished mock-epic and comparing it to the pseudo-Homer's *Batrachomyomachia* and Heywood's

The Spider and the Flie (Rathborne, "Another interpretation"). From the 1970s, there has been scholarly consensus that *Muiopotmos* is a mock-epic, but without the assumption that this genre is incompatible with allegorical meanings (e.g., Dundas, "*Muiopotmos*," 33; Brinkley, "Spenser's *Muiopotmos*," 668; Rustici, "*Muiopotmos*," 165; Wilson-Okamura, *Virgil*, 196). Dymoke creates generic parallels with *Muiopotmos*, parallels that reinforce an interpretation of both poems as mock-epics, by including an invocation (Dymoke invokes Flora, appropriate for a tale with a happy ending set in a garden), by treating an insect as an epic hero, and by treating something quite natural (i.e., a spider catches a butterfly or bee) with language appropriate for an epic battle.

Without the parallels with *Muiopotmos*, there is surely enough to get this poem censored—the erotic language alone might have been enough. The poem may also have offended by using language of crookedness and crippling, which by 1599 was strongly associated with satires on Robert Cecil, whose hunchback offered satirists a ready target for mockery (Croft, "Reputation"). After his escape from the spiderweb, the Bee's "legs & knees as camocks wer all crooked / That vp & down did carie him with care" (55.2–3).[15] Later, when Musaeus, the former Bee, prepares to return to the garden, he ties to his back a "bumfiddle," which "sags vpon his shoulders til they crack: / That made the little fidling fellow hutch, / As he had gone his crookback with a crutch" (155.5–7). Because this crook-backed Musaeus will later rape Venus/Elizabeth, interpreting him as Cecil would add extra insult. Whatever the potential for offense created by the poem's frank treatments of sex or the possible mockery of Robert Cecil's disability, we should consider as well the value of reading *Muiopotmos* as intertextually important to Dymoke's satire, given the care Dymoke took to connect his poem with Spenser's. Doing so, in addition to providing the key to Dymoke's satire on Elizabeth, also helps us to understand how Spenser's contemporaries read *Muiopotmos*.

One sixteenth-century reader, Sir Thomas Tresham, saw *Prosopopoia; or, Mother Hubberds Tale* as the cause of the offense that led to the calling-in of Spenser's *Complaints* volume in 1591 (Peterson, "Laurel crown"); the fact that the other poems in the *Complaints* volume were reprinted in 1611, but that *Mother Hubberds Tale* was not reprinted until 1612, after Robert Cecil's death, has been taken as corroboration that it was indeed the principal offender in the volume. Certainly, *Mother Hubberds*

---

15 *Oxford English Dictionary*, s.v. "cammock, n.²": "**1.** A crooked staff, a crook; *esp.* a stick or club with a crooked head, used in games to drive a ball, or the like; a hockey-stick; hence, the game played with such a stick."

Tale presents a clear and detailed satire on William Cecil (and to a lesser extent his son Robert), but the invented myth of Venus and Astery in *Muiopotmos* can be read as a milder and vaguer criticism of Queen Elizabeth herself. That Dymoke creates so many parallels with *Muiopotmos* in a poem that creates a harsh and quite damning satire on the Queen suggests that he believed that other sixteenth-century readers also saw in Spenser's Venus a veiled reference to the Queen.

Many recent critics have read *Muiopotmos* as allegorically representing the Elizabethan court. For example, Robert Brinkley asserts that "the fate of the butterfly offers an appropriate image for one of the fates at Gloriana's court" (Brinkley, "Spenser's *Muiopotmos*," 668), and Ayesha Ramachandran argues that "By associating the Elizabethan court with the romance garden rather than the epic battlefield, Spenser reveals and redefines the power relations that are at stake: romance is the world of Circe's bed, of Acrasia's garden and Aragnoll's web, a world where the artfulness of *women*, the duplicity and dissimulation associated with female power, prevails over single-minded epic might" (Ramachandran, "Clarion," 81). With one exception, even the Old Historicists, however, generally hesitated to identify Venus allegorically, despite their often breathless enthusiasm for hypotheses regarding the true identity of Clarion. C.W. Lemmi, as part of his argument that Clarion represents Philip Sidney, created the following chain of associations: "If Asterie stands for Penelope Devereux, how are we to interpret the episode? *Colin Clouts Come Home Again* would be sufficient to tell us that Stella was of Elizabeth's train of maidens. Venus must therefore stand for the Queen; and the occurrences allegorized in the episode must be connected with the Court" (Lemmi, "Allegorical meaning," 740). Lemmi moves from this identification to an unacceptably inventive string of hypotheses that depend upon it, but his interest lies in the allegory of Sidney, rather than possible satire of the Queen. Other critics took Lemmi to task for his speculations (e.g., Denkinger, "Spenser's *Muiopotmos*"; and Strathmann, "Allegorical meaning"), with Emma Denkinger directly addressing the Venus/Elizabeth identification (and taking it as axiomatic that Spenser would never satirize Elizabeth): "If Elizabeth is Venus, and Lettice Knolles is Psyche, Leicester automatically becomes Cupid and Elizabeth's son, which seeing they were of even age, is not only impossible but ungallant to boot!" (Denkinger, "Spenser's *Muiopotmos*," 272). More recently, Elizabeth Mazzola has built upon Lemmi's work to create a more measured and less speculative assessment of the possibility that Spenser used Clarion to refer to Sidney, but she does not deal with Lemmi's Venus/Elizabeth hypothesis.¹⁶ Denkinger's refusal to entertain the hypothesis that Spenser might create an "ungallant" allegory depends, of course, upon the now-doubted assumption that Spenser harbored no ambivalence toward the Queen (see, e.g., the essays in Walker, *Dissing Elizabeth*).

Judith Anderson notes the significance of the placement of the Venus–Astery episode immediately after the narration of the Court Ladies' envy of Clarion's wings: "The Court Ladies' cupidity, their mean possessiveness, takes form in the myth of Astery, precipitating the very myth that it introduces" (Anderson, "Spenser's *Muiopotmos*," 117). Anderson suggests that Spenser connects the ladies of the court with the envious nymphs, and this provides a clue to the possible fruitfulness of reading the Astery episode with the Elizabethan court in mind. The tale itself—invented by Spenser¹⁷—provides a myth of origin for the beauty of butterflies' wings: Venus's beautiful nymph Astery, by virtue of being "nimbler joynted" and "more industrious" than the other nymphs, gathers more flowers (Spenser, *Muiopotmos*, lines 121, 122). When Venus praises Astery, the other nymphs, envious, tell her that Cupid offered "secret aide" (line 127). Venus remembers Cupid's secret love for Psyche, becomes enraged, and transforms Astery into a butterfly. I find here no specific details to support an identification with Queen Elizabeth; rather, the situation, in broadest outline, simply feels *familiar*: a goddess with more power than discretion becomes—not once but twice—infuriated when her male favorite secretly associates with a beautiful woman. For two decades, Elizabeth's male courtiers worked around her famous jealousy by secretly marrying; when the secrets were revealed, husband and wife dealt with the ensuing rage, with the brunt often falling on the wife.

Bolder than Spenser in *Muiopotmos*, Dymoke provides *Caltha Poetarum* with multiple "entry codes," in Annabel Patterson's sense of clues that alert a reader to consider the possibility of hidden meanings (*Censorship and Interpretation*, 57). These include a frank admission in G.S.'s commendatory poem that, though concealed, "Persons of good worth are ment" (A8r); the heavy use of Catholic-associated language and imagery; and the numerous parallels with *Muiopotmos*, especially the plot element of a jealous Venus who revenges herself on beautiful young women. Dymoke builds upon Spenser's generalized satire of Eliza-

---

16 Mazzola briefly discusses the episode, arguing that Clarion owes his existence to a "mother's worries about her own reproductive powers" (Mazzola, "Sidney, Spenser," 77).
17 Andrew Weiner summarizes the appearances of characters named Astery elsewhere in myth to confirm the originality of Spenser's story, which is notable "for Venus' jealous over-reaction to the envious lies told about her innocent and devoted votary, whose punishment is totally undeserved" (Weiner, "Spenser's *Muiopotmos*," 215).

beth's jealousy to create a focused, harsh attack on Elizabeth that uses satirical allegory to make two points, both related to false religion: (1) as the symbolic enforcer of conformity to the Church of England, Elizabeth engages in injustice to support a damnable heresy; (2) as the idol of Elizabethan Petrarchanism, Elizabeth conflates love, worship, and politics in ways that degrade the right practice of all three. Dymoke makes these points through the allegorical presentation of two distinct false religions: the religion endorsed by Venus for the whole garden (a sort of state religion), and the idolatrous religion of Calthanism, created by the Bee under the influence of Cupid's arrow, which corresponds to Petrarchanism.

In the time before the action of the poem, Venus used marigolds extensively in the practice of her state religion, as Cupid reminds her when urging her to quell her desire for revenge. Cupid's lengthy description of garlands of marigolds for Venus herself, for the birds who drew her chariot, and for the crowds going to her church (stanzas 46–48), includes explicitly religious language:

> How often haue the buds bene laid abroad
>   vpon the traces whereas you should tread:
> How oft haue they thy stately altars strawd,
>   and we exalting there thy holy head,
> Whilst *Hymnes* wer sung, & sacred Psalms were sed:
> Me thinks I see how all the rabble runs,
> Vnto thy Church, with chaines of golden suns.
>
>   (Dymoke, *Caltha*, stanza 48)

This history of including marigolds in the state-sanctioned worship practice helps to explain Venus's fury that the marigold Caltha is now "the Viccar of a vaine vsurping Queene" (i.e., Diana) who "disdain[s] both the heuenly powers" (32.4, 6). Venus's efforts to take revenge on Caltha for her religious defection involve pressuring Cupid to shoot her with one of his arrows, and this limited recourse to violence in response to one religious nonconformist becomes all-out war when she learns of the Bee's creation of the rival religion of Calthanism:

> The fame of these [i.e., the "Caltheans"], and of this new religion,
>   was spred abroad with passing great report,
> And rumor of it, rattles through each Region,
>   till that it came to Lady *Venus* cort,
> God speed my pen for heere begins the sport:
> For now doth *Venus* bite and beate her fists,
> To be reuenged on these Calthanists.
>
>   (stanza 73)

She sends spiders to defeat the Calthanist bees (stanzas 75–79); when this does not succeed, she smokes the bees out of their hives (stanzas 112–13).

Venus's insistence on religious conformity would easily remind a Catholic reading audience of Elizabeth's dealings with Catholic recusants, and Dymoke strengthens the sense of Venus as the figurehead of a false religion by contrasting Venus's complete lack of supernatural power with Diana's miraculous powers. Dymoke's Venus lacks not only supernatural power but also even basic knowledge that any early modern mother would have: When the Bee stings Cupid in the face, Venus has no skill to heal him. She goes "vp and downe the Garden … / to gather all the coolest hearbs that grow: / To phisick and to leach her wounded lad" (84.1–3, 6), and yet we quickly learn that she does not know what plants can heal: after "trying many precious plants," she arrives at the woodbine tree and asks him "what phisick ther might bee / To take away the stinging of the flee" (85.4–5). Diana, in contrast, over and over again practices benign and wholly efficacious magic: metamorphosing Caltha into a human (stanzas 92–99), the Bee into the human Musaeus (stanza 139), and the void of Musaeus's genital region into "his priuie knacks" (142.5). At first glance it may seem odd that Dymoke has chosen to describe Diana's magic with language reminiscent of witchcraft. During her metamorphosis of Caltha, Diana

> mumbels in her mouth with whisper talk,
> And there in circle wise about did walk.
> As Tragetors for spirits set their spels,
> To coniure vp the Fairies or the Elues.
>
> (92.4–7)[18]

She uses "blessed bookes of diuination" (139.2) to transform the Bee, and in her creation of his penis she seems even more witchlike: "From forth the Hawthorne hedge she plucks a thorne, / and works and makes his picture all of wax," then "she pricks the hawthorn wher his secrets laks," and his genitals appear (142.1–2, 4). Odd as this witchlike language may appear in relation to Diana, who here represents Catholicism or the Virgin Mary, this embodied magic—as opposed to the acts of pure will we associate with gods and goddesses in myth—makes her more similar to the Catholic priest, whose sacramental "magic" involves not mere will but the "mumbling" of words and the use of objects (water, oil, bread, wine) to metamorphose things and people from one spiritual state to another.

---

18 *Oxford English Dictionary*, s.v. "tregetour, n.": "One who works magic or plays tricks by sleight of hand; a conjurer; a juggler; hence, a trickster, a deceiver."

As the instigator of the cupidinous arrow that leads the Bee to become an idolatrous Calthanist, Venus bears responsibility for another false religion. In his treatment of Calthanism, Dymoke satirizes the clichés of Petrarchanism by literalizing them. The Bee literally worships the marigold. His idolatry begins after he has metaphorically made love to her ('in her circle vp and downe he hops," etc., as quoted earlier, stanzas 60–61), at which point he begins to elevate her status: "For now no more he cals her Marygold, / but newes from Lady *Caltha* is he bringing" (62.3–4). This Petrarchan devotion to the lady begins to take on a religious cast, but the reference to "his Goddesse Lady *Caltha*" (65.7) still falls short of the development of an actual religion, which occurs when he builds a chapel. The passage is worth quoting at length:

> In meane while this same mightie bumble Bee,
>   is framing of a Chappell for his Queene,
> With strange and costly Archetectury,
>   the rarest sight that euer yet was seene,
> Of waxen worke, was neuer like I weene:
> Pillers of hony combes with Piramis,
> And strong pilasters of great statelinesse.
>
> And at one end there stands a proper steeple,
>   dawbing his height with hony for his lime:
> And bels to ring in these same pretie people,
>   when as they take it to be seruice time,
> To say their praiers, their Mattens & their prime
> And when this Chapell ended was and wald,
> *La santa Caltha,* this same bee it cald.
>
> With Virgin wax he makes a hony alter,
>   and on it stands, the torches and the tapers,
> Where he must sing his Rosarye and Psalter,
>   and pray deuoutly on his holy papers,
> With book, with candlelight, with bels & clappers,
> And in the praise of Goddesse *Caltha* sing,
> That all the holy quier & Church may ring.
>   (stanzas 68–70)

These stanzas create a strong sense of Catholic worship practices, and shortly afterward, the Bee creates a Catholic-like hierarchy when he "maketh Priests and Presbiters, and some / of Fryers & Monks he makes a rabble rout, / Of Clarks & Limitors to kneele and lowt" (72.3–5). Even after Venus destroys his Calthanist community by smoking the beehives, and even after Caltha disappears from the garden (rescued and then metamorphosed by Diana, unbeknownst to the Bee), the Bee remains true to his pseudo-faith, dressing himself as a pilgrim and leaving the garden himself. He "meanes to wander vncoth waies" and "seek strange countries far, that be vnknown" (115.4, 7; surely an echo of Chaucer's "to seken straunge strondes / To ferne halwes, kowthe in sondry londes"; *General Prologue*, lines 13–15).

Dymoke connects Calthanism to Petrarchanism through some typical clichés, such as the blazon of the metamorphosed Caltha (stanzas 95–99). Hannah Betts makes an excellent analysis of connections between this passage and Spenser's blazon of Belphoebe in *Faerie Queene* (2.3.22–30), but I disagree with her conclusion that, by emphasizing the sexual allure of Caltha, Dymoke "consigns the blazon to the category of writing about prostitutes" (Betts, "'The image," 174). Rather, the blazon, by describing Caltha's sexual desirability in terms of both her physicality and religious devotion, connects her body metaphorically to the chapel that the Bee already built for her:

> Her thighes like pillars of faire Allablaster,
>   that do support the body of this Saint:
> Where men must kneel them down & Idolaster
>   vnto the Image of this Queene so quaynt,
> That *Caltha* she may pittie their complaint,
> And heare their happie Orysons and prayer,
> When as her priest and people do come there.
>
> (stanza 99)

The standard Petrarchan blazon thus circles back to Dymoke's literalization of the well-worn metaphor of love as religious devotion. Similarly, Dymoke literalizes the hair-as-net metaphor by having the Bee become actually caught in the metamorphosed Caltha's beautiful hair: "So is this Bee entangled in her locks, / and fetterd in these golden yealow strings" (130.3–4). Through these playful references to Petrarchan clichés, Dymoke clarifies that, although he uses Catholic terminology and imagery to describe Calthanism, his satire targets not Catholicism but the Petrarchan love games of Venus/Elizabeth's court.

Further proof that Catholicism is the solution, not the problem, comes when the Bee is cured of his idolatrous Calthanism immediately upon arriving in Ephesus. Whereas Hotson believes that Ephesus represents London, Dymoke identifies it as Rome by associating it with Diana and by using the plane tree as the symbol of the city. The Bee arrives in Ephesus, "where chaste *Diana* and her vestals bee," and rests in "*Platanus*,

/ an aged and an auncient hollow tree" (121.2, 3–4).¹⁹ Upon waking the next morning, the Bee performs his "Mattins" and "lauds and Letanies" before moving on to the Psalms, "With *Pater Noster,* and with *Auie Marie*" (122.2, 4, 7). There is no suggestion of Calthanism in this stanza; though the Bee still loves Caltha, as we recognize when he finds her in Diana's garden immediately after this, he no longer loves her idolatrously. Proof of his complete conversion from Calthanism comes when Diana, after metamorphosing him into a man, tells him to make a wish, asking, "What pleasure couldst thou wish to passe thy daies?" (147.5). Surprisingly, his wish has nothing to do with Caltha; instead, he asks Diana to make him into a good musician and thus is transformed into the human Musaeus.

Despite being called in by the authorities, the poems of Spenser's *Complaints* volume had sufficient presence (either through copies that were not turned in or through manuscript copies; Peterson, "Laurel crown"; Beal, *Index,* Vol. 1, part 2, 527–28) to influence other satires written in the nearly two decades before the collection was printed again. At least some contemporary readers must have read Spenser's Venus in *Muiopotmos* as satirizing Queen Elizabeth, because Dymoke makes this identification key to understanding his satire. He takes some pains to obfuscate his targets—using Catholic language to criticize Calthanism, for example, obscures his strongly pro-Catholic message, and the common use of Diana to allegorize Elizabeth makes it less likely that some readers would instead connect Venus to Elizabeth. With these efforts at self-protection from censorship, the intertextual connections with *Muiopotmos* become essential in comprehending Dymoke's satirical message.

Coda

I close this chapter not by connecting more dots, but by drawing out threads, spinning an imaginative web that might suggest a connection between Shakespeare's *Venus and Adonis* (1593) and the poems discussed in this chapter.²⁰ We find in Shakespeare's Adonis an iteration of those boys, beginning with Bion's, who would rather hunt than love, and in

---

19 According to Rembert Dodoens, "The Plane is a strange tree, the whiche in time past hath bene of great estimation in Italie and Rome" (*A Nievve Herball,* 755). Further, the Catholic writer Richard Verstegan, in a series of odes based on "Epithets of Our Blessed Lady," includes an ode to the Virgin Mary as the plane tree, "Quasi Platanus" (*Odes,* 48).
20 Patrick Cheney provides a good list of references up through 2004 for scholars who have looked at Shakespeare's debts to Spenser in *Venus and Adonis* (Cheney, *Shakespeare,* 88n23); see also Harwood ("*Venus*").

his Venus further development of *Muiopotmos*'s jealous and powerful goddess as possible satire on the Queen. Addressing his poem to the Catholic Earl of Southampton, Shakespeare may satirize the Queen with the same doubts about her chastity that the Catholic author Tailboys Dymoke would express six years later in explicitly creating his Elizabethan Venus as the antitype to the Marian Diana. The argument can only be speculative, based on what Anne Lake Prescott calls "vibes" in her own study of Spenserian influence on Shakespeare, but the vibes suggest interesting and worthwhile interpretations of Shakespeare's fascinating poem (Prescott, "Equinoctial," 169).

In his immaturity and his lack of interest in Venus, Adonis differs significantly from Shakespeare's sources (Dubrow, *Captive Victors*, 43). We can speculate from their dedications to Henry Wriothesley, Third Earl of Southampton, that Shakespeare and Nashe were acquainted during this period, suggesting the possibility that Shakespeare was aware of Nashe's parodic adaptation of Spenser's young hunter Thomalin.[21] In the ephebe Adonis we can imagine, almost grown up, the hunting boy that I traced from Bion through Ronsard and Spenser to Nashe. Shakespeare's Adonis expresses as his own the antipathetic views on love taught to the boy by the more experienced adults to whom he turns for help:

> "I know not love," quoth he, "nor will not know it,
> Unless it be a boar, and then I chase it.
> 'Tis much to borrow, and I will not owe it,
> My love to love is love but to disgrace it;
>   For I have heard it is a life in death,
>   That laughs and weeps, and all but with a breath."
>   (*Venus and Adonis*, lines 409–14)

If Shakespeare sought to satirize the absurd courtship games between the aging Queen and her reluctant but obliged political "suitors," the character type of the boy who would rather hunt than love provides an admirable allegorization of the male participant in the games. Patrick Cheney notes the opposition of values between Venus and Adonis, with Adonis espousing goals and perspectives that make of him a "Virgilian figure of pastoral and epic ... voicing an aesthetics that resembles Spenser's" (Cheney, *Shakespeare*, 91). But whereas Cheney sees in Venus's character the exemplification of "Marlowe's Ovidian aesthetics" (Cheney, *Shakespeare*, 91)—and Cheney creates a persuasive case for reading Venus's

---

21 Shakespeare dedicated *Venus and Adonis* to the Earl in 1593 and *The Rape of Lucrece* in 1594; Nashe dedicated *The Unfortunate Traveler* to him in 1594. See Nicholl, *Cup of News*, 160–62, for discussion of the possible acquaintanceship.

rhetoric as Marlovian—I speculate that the idea to use Venus to satirize the Queen came from Shakespeare's reading of *Muiopotmos*.

At least one sixteenth-century reader did interpret Shakespeare's Venus as allegorizing Queen Elizabeth. Leslie Hotson, who discovered the identity of Tailboys Dymoke and learned most of what we know about his life and writings, also found in his archival work a letter by William Reynolds describing Shakespeare's poem as "a nother booke made of *Venus* and *Adonis* wherin a queene represents the person of *Venus*." He continues at some length to describe the plot of the poem, including his observation that there is "much ado wth red & whyte" and highlighting the references to Venus as a "phery nimpfe" (qtd. in Hotson, *Shakespeare's*, 143). Unfortunately, we cannot take Reynolds as a typical Elizabethan reader: Hotson describes him as suffering from "persecution mania," and Katherine Duncan-Jones expands upon the biographical information supplied by Hotson, emphasizing Reynolds's outrage at his treatment as a former soldier, his religious enthusiasm, and his tenacity in sharing his opinions with the Queen and her counselors (which led to numerous stays in prison) to come to a tentative post hoc diagnosis of paranoid schizophrenia (Hotson, *Shakespeare's* 142; Duncan-Jones, "Much ado," 480–86).

Modern critics have been more circumspect than Reynolds in considering the possibility that Elizabethan sexual politics inform Shakespeare's characterization of Venus. Heather Dubrow, for instance, suggests that "Venus' assertions of power may well reflect resentment of Elizabeth herself.... Hence in this epyllion ... ambivalence about an unsuccessfully manipulative heroine encodes ambivalence about a brilliantly manipulative queen" (Dubrow, *Captive Victors*, 34); and Judith Anderson refers somewhat coyly to "those critics who suspect that Shakespeare's poem might have a satirical relation to courtship, especially under a Queen who affected a Petrarchan role" (Anderson, "*Venus and Adonis*," 211). In other words, actual *readings* of *Venus and Adonis* as satire are difficult, perhaps impossible, to make, but many readers have the *impression* that satiric "vibes" exist in the work. I am equally unable to make an actual argument that Shakespeare read *Muiopotmos*, although A. Kent Hieatt has argued that Shakespeare did read the *Complaints* volume of 1591, demonstrating Shakespearean allusions to Spenser's *Ruines of Rome: by Bellay* and suggesting possible familiarity with *Mother Hubberds Tale* (Hieatt, "The genesis"). Still, for me, Shakespeare's lusty, large, and somewhat ridiculous Venus calls unavoidably to mind Spenser's jealous and petulant Venus in *Muiopotmos*, as well as Dymoke's more obviously Elizabeth-targeting Venus, who combines the worst qualities of both.

Critics have found Spenserian echoes in Shakespeare's image of Venus leaning over Adonis, clasping him in her arms while "glutton-like she feeds, yet never filleth" (line 548), with Judith Anderson paying the most careful attention to the repetition of this image in Books 2 and 3 of Spenser's *Faerie Queene*; she analyzes the posture's significance when it appears in Acrasia, Cymoent, Belphoebe, Venus, Argante, and Britomart in order to comment on its significance to *Venus and Adonis* (Anderson, "*Venus and Adonis*," 209–11). Elsewhere, Anderson provides a fascinating argument for Argante as the lustful antitype to the chaste Belphoebe; that is, in addition to the "most royall Queene or Empresse" figured by Gloriana and the "most vertuous and beautifull Lady" allegorized in Belphoebe (*Faerie Queene*, 716), the many other mirrors of Elizabeth include Argante as a parodic double. Anderson's evidence for the connection comes from Layamon's use of the name Argante for the elf queen on whose island Arthur recovers from an injury. Anderson concedes that a reader would be unlikely to make the connection between Argante and the Faerie Queene without recourse to Layamon's *Brut* (Anderson, "Arthur," 130). We might find, though, in the similarity that Prescott notes between "a sweating goddess in pursuit of a reluctant *ephebe*" and "Spenser's lustful giantess Argante chasing down young squires" (Prescott, "Equinoctial," 170) a suggestion that *Shakespeare* made the connection.

This tangled web connecting Adonis to Spenser's and Nashe's Tomalins and their predecessors and *Muiopotmos*'s Venus to Elizabeth, *Faerie Queene*'s Argante to Elizabeth, and both to Shakespeare's Venus may seem too speculative—one of the unavoidable hazards of considering indirect satire of Elizabethan England. My purpose, though, is not to create an argument about one-to-one correspondences and identifications, à la the Old Historicist accounts of *Muiopotmos* and *Caltha Poetarum* cited in this chapter, but to consider the dynamics of the subsystem of satire in the 1590s and the role of Spenser as inspiration for authors like Thomas Nashe and Tailboys Dymoke, who, though dissimilar to Spenser in political and religious outlook, found it worthwhile to use his works to help them in conveying their own meanings. In the next chapter, I will look at Thomas Middleton in 1599 and 1604 as a young writer who appreciated Spenser not only poetically but also politically, and thus used allusions to Spenser to convey his own affiliation with the ideas about government and religions associated with the more famous poet.

5

Thomas Middleton's satires before and after the Bishops' Ban

Among the books burned by order of the Bishops' Ban on June 4, 1599, was nineteen-year-old Thomas Middleton's *Micro-Cynicon: Sixe Snarling Satyres*, a collection of verse satires. T.M. the young satirist would of course soon become Thomas Middleton the seasoned dramatist, and criticism of Middleton's work has not surprisingly focused primarily on his more mature work for the theater. Nevertheless, early satires such as *Micro-Cynicon* and *Father Hubburds Tales; or, The Ant and the Nightingale* (1604) repay scrutiny, not only for what they can tell us about Middleton's youthful political views but also for what we can learn about the understanding of Spenser's importance as a satirist during this time period. In these two works, we see a young writer trying to demonstrate his political and religious allegiance to the ideas and positions associated with Spenser without getting into trouble.[1] This goal—to be critical but not too critical, to be understood by some while not incurring censorship from others—says much about the connections between politics, religion, and satire in the 1590s.

Examining Thomas Middleton's indebtedness to Spenser in 1599 and 1604 can deepen our understanding of Spenser's role in the literary system of satire in the 1590s and the first decade of the seventeenth century. Most critics who have discussed Middleton as a satirist have discussed his work in drama, especially *A Game at Chess*, paying scant attention to the satires

---

1 Middleton's other important early satire, *The Blacke Booke*, clearly imitates the satires of Thomas Nashe and thus is tangential to the focus of this study. Margot Heinemann has ably demonstrated *The Blacke Booke*'s stylistic debts to Nashe (*Puritanism and Theatre*, 52–57), and Neil Rhodes discusses both *The Blacke Booke* and *Father Hubburds Tales* with reference to Nashe (*Elizabethan Grotesque*, 60–61). Heinemann notes that, whereas Middleton follows Nashe stylistically, the ideas he expresses both in *The Blacke Booke* and in *Father Hubburds Tales* align him politically with the Spenserian "tradition of Elizabethan Puritan satire … against the court and Church establishment—and thus on the opposite side from Nashe" (57).

in prose and poetry that he wrote as a young man, in part because artificial period and genre divisions create a tendency for scholars of early modern English literature to study works of the sixteenth century *or* the seventeenth century, to study drama *or* poetry. Obviously, this sometimes makes it harder to perceive connections and continuities in authors who straddle the turn of the century or write in multiple genres, such as Thomas Middleton. We can find in Middleton's early poetry cautious efforts to express the kinds of political and religious perspectives that he would more boldly and clearly express in later dramas.

The purpose of this chapter is to consider the ways that Spenser's meaning to other satirists changed after his own death, after the Bishops' Ban, and after the change of monarchs in 1603. Although I focus on changing literary uses of Spenserian indirect satire—for example, the inflection of nostalgia that attaches to Spenserianism in the early seventeenth century—I begin the chapter with an overview of Middleton's religious and political sympathies over the course of his life. I argue that, despite the variety of his literary output and the multiplicity of sources and influences to which he was indebted, Middleton uses these varied means to express what is a remarkably stable set of religious and political orientations.

Middleton's early political and religious sympathies

In examining Middleton's political and religious ideas, we see consistency over his lifetime in his commitment to reformist Protestantism; what changes is the way he expresses this mindset. Middleton enters the print scene in the 1590s, and his praise of aristocrats such as the Earl of Essex and Lord Compton—as well as his blame of the Cecils—aligns him with writers like Spenser. The connections between Middleton's politico-religious orientations and those of Spenser appear clear in the 1590s, but the accession of James I in 1603 changed the terms by which writers expressed these same ideas. Spenser posthumously would play a role in offering opposition writers ways of signaling their dissatisfaction with the current regime, and the "Spenserian" rhetorical strategy for expressing discontent develops in parallel with the choice of some writers to align themselves with the City instead of the court. I argue that Middleton avails himself of both rhetorical strategies in defining himself as an oppositional writer.[2]

---

2 O'Callaghan discusses the ways that the Spenserian poets positioned themselves as oppositional poets; Margot Heinemann argues in *Puritanism and Theatre* for Middleton as an opposition writer.

Middleton's most notorious expression of political and religious attitudes appears in *A Game at Chess* (1624).[3] The anti-Spanish, anti-Catholic satirical play was licensed by the Master of the Revels on June 12, 1624 and enjoyed a wildly popular run of nine consecutive days in August 1624 before being shut down in response to complaints to the government from the Spanish ambassador Don Carlos de Coloma. Manuscripts of the play proliferated in the following months, and the play was eventually printed, without being licensed by the Stationers' Company, after James I's death in 1625. In this play, as Andrew McRae observes, Middleton employs a strongly Protestant worldview to explore the moral questions raised within the play; further, as Paul Yachnin argues, although the offensive portrayals of Spaniards, especially the ambassador Count Gondomar, were what led to the closing of the play, Middleton's satire also takes aim at James I for his gullible susceptibility to the plots of Catholic foreigners (McRae, *Literature, Satire*, 148–49; Yachnin, "*Game*," 117–18).

In *A Game at Chess*, we see the mature version of Middleton's nationalist and Protestant sympathies; from his early works and alliances, however, we learn that Middleton had a lifelong sympathy for this reform-minded Protestantism. In the 1590s, this Protestant orientation appears through Middleton's use of objects of praise (Robert Devereux, Second Earl of Essex) and blame (William Cecil, Lord Burghley, and his son Robert Cecil) similar to those emphasized in the poetry of Edmund Spenser. By 1604, following the execution of Essex, the death of Queen Elizabeth, and the accession of King James I, the cultural expression of this religious and political alignment appears instead through connections to the City of London, as opposed to court connections, as evidenced by Middleton's literary collaborators, patronage relationships, and pageants.

Middleton's first publication, *The Wisdom of Solomon, Paraphrased* (1597), seems an appropriate choice for a Puritan-leaning young man (Middleton was seventeen) to present his intellectual gifts to the world. His dedication of such a strongly Protestant work to Robert Devereux, Second Earl of Essex, suggests that Middleton may have been one of the many who saw Essex as the successor to Robert Dudley, Earl of Leicester, as the great hope for the international triumph of English Protestantism. Spenser himself provides an illustration of this shift in the 1590s, when

---

3 Numerous critics have discussed the political and personal allusions in the play and have connected it to the situation between England and Spain in 1624. For helpful overviews of the play and the circumstances of its performances and printing, see Patterson, *Censorship and Interpretation*, 17; Yachnin, "*Game*"; Prescott, "Housing chessmen," 222–29; Clegg, *Press Censorship Jacobean*, 187–89; and McRae, *Literature, Satire*, 145–52.

the bids for recognition as a member of the Leicester faction of his early career give way in 1596 to the fulsome praise of Essex in *Prothalamion* (see Prescott, "Laurel and myrtle," 70, for a discussion of this as a careerist move). Although we do not know the extent of the patronage relationship between Spenser and Essex during the lifetime of the former, Essex paid the funeral expenses of Spenser, indicating some patronage connection. We see in Middleton's dedicatory epistle to Essex a youthful optimism regarding the poet–patron relationship that turns to cynicism or outright hostility for the next decade and a half, until it returns, matured, in his dedication of the pageant *The Triumphs of Truth* to the Lord Mayor of London, Sir Thomas Middleton, in 1613. The extended metaphor of sowing and harvesting and the humility with which Middleton addresses Essex suggest an unironic endorsement of the idealized relationship between poet and patron that Spenser had imagined in such works as *The Teares of the Muses* and *The Ruines of Time* (see Martines [*Society*, 59] for an analysis of this idealized view of patronage). Middleton writes:

> The summer's harvest, right honourable, is long since reaped, and now it is sowing time again. Behold, I have scattered a few seeds upon the young ground of unskilfulness. If it bear fruit, my labour is well bestowed, but if it be barren, I shall have less joy to set more. The husbandman observes the courses of the moon, I the forces of your favour; he desireth sunshine, I cheerful countenance, which once obtained, my harvest of joy will soon be ripened. My seeds as yet lodge in the bosom of the earth like infants upon the lap of a favourite, wanting the budding springtime of their growth, not knowing the east of their glory, the west of their quietness, the south of their summer, the north of their winter. But if the beams of your aspects lighten the small moiety of a smaller implanting, I shall have an everyday harvest, a fruition of content, a branch of felicity.
> Your Honour's, addicted in all observance, Thomas Middleton
> (Middleton, *Wisdom*, 1919)

The image of poet as husbandman will appear again later in his career, when the ant-ploughman of *Father Hubburds Tales* will turn out to be Oliver Hubburd and therefore the putative "author" of the piece. But there, the satirical epistle dedicatory to the fictional "Sir Christopher Clutch-Fist," a "pinching patron, and the muses' bad paymaster," stands in stark contrast to Essex as dedicatee here (Middleton, *Father Hubburd's*, 164). The distance, both literal and metaphorical, between a husbandman and the sun and moon emphasizes the studied abjection of the young poet seeking patronage. Additionally, however, the image of Essex as the sun who nourishes the Protestant seeds sown here by

Middleton—given that Biblical translation is by definition at this time a Protestant act—recalls the religious significance attributed to Essex's military successes against Catholic foes. Another sincere dedication further connects Middleton with the patronage relationships established by Spenser. In 1600, Middleton dedicates *The Ghost of Lucrece* to William, Second Baron Compton, the stepson of Lady Compton and Mounteagle, to whom Spenser had dedicated *Mother Hubberds Tale* in 1591 (Lady Compton, born Anne Spencer, was one of the Spencers of Althorp with whom Spenser claimed kin several times in his work).[4]

Following these two sincere dedications to Essex and Compton, Middleton appears to enter a period of disillusionment with patronage, judging from his subsequent publications—*News from Gravesend: Sent to Nobody* (1604; cowritten with Thomas Dekker) begins with an epistle dedicatory to "Sir Nicholas Nemo, alias Nobody," which, in its length and Nashean rhetorical excesses, seems determined to break the rules of decorum governing the complaints of poets—what Anne Lake Prescott calls the "poetics of artistic dejection"—thus crossing into the territory of satire. Additionally, he opens the second edition of *Father Hubburds Tales* with the aforementioned address to Sir Christopher Clutch-Fist, who Adrian Weiss hypothesizes in the notes to *Father Hubburds Tales* may satirize Lord Compton (164). Thus, we can learn little about Middleton's alliances in this period from dedications, but his partners in literary collaboration evidence an alignment with the City of London and its merchants—generally seen as Puritan-leaning—more so than with the court of James I and James's favored writer, Ben Jonson. Middleton's playwriting connections with the Thomas Dekker syndicate starting in 1602 suggest sympathy for the religious and political outlooks that were beginning to coalesce into an oppositional poetic practice, imaginatively centered, for the Spenserian poets at least, on the memory and values of Spenser.[5] One of the Spenserian poets, Michael Drayton, collaborated with Middleton and others on Middleton's first play, the now-lost *Caesar's Fall; or, Two Shapes* (Ornstein, "Dates," 63). Neil Carson identifies and analyzes some of the groups that wrote plays collaboratively during this period, including evidence of Middleton's work with Dekker's group (Carson, "Collaborative Playwriting"). Gary Taylor notes that "by

---

4 For more on the development of the patronage relationships among Spenser and members of the Spencer family, see Hile, "Auto/biographical fantasies."
5 See Grundy, *Spenserian Poets*; O'Callaghan, *Shepheards Nation*. Whereas Grundy focuses on the poetic connections that tied this group to one another and to the memory of Spenser, O'Callaghan interests herself in the political implications of these poetic alliances.

collaborating with Dekker, he aligned himself against Jonson, and that alignment soured relations between Jonson and Middleton for the next quarter-century" ("Thomas Middleton," 38). Drayton also was publicly at odds with Jonson (Norbrook, *Poetry and Politics*, 174–75); indeed, Jonson may be the best route to connect the religious and political sympathies of Middleton, studied primarily by specialists in Renaissance drama, with those of Spenser and the Spenserian poets, whom scholars seldom analyze with reference to contemporary drama. David Norbrook summarizes the political and religious significance of the opposition between Jonson and other poets and dramatists: "the reason Jonson enjoyed such high favour, especially in the earlier parts of James's reign, was at least partly ideological: as a Catholic, and then a high-church Anglican, he had no sympathy with the tradition of low-church Protestantism with which Spenser was associated" (Norbrook, *Poetry and Politics*, 176).

Jonson's preeminence in court masques during the Jacobean period serves as a further example of this ideological and religious divide, as dramatists with allegiance to Puritan-leaning Protestantism tended to contribute to civic pageantry instead of to court-centered theatricals. Middleton firmly allied himself with this group through his seven mayoral pageants and his work, beginning in 1620, as official Chronologer of the City of London (Bergeron, *English Civic Pageantry*, 179). Margot Heinemann adduces Middleton's 1620 dedication of *The Marriage of the Old and New Testament, or God's Parliament House* to Richard Fishbourne and John Browne, two Puritan-leaning London merchants, as evidence of his connections with "Parliamentarian and Puritan patrons, as well as Puritan and Calvinist views" (Heinemann, *Puritanism and Theatre*, 126). Norbrook connects Middleton to the Spenserian poet William Browne through their shared friendship with Fishbourne (Norbrook, "The Masque of Truth," 109n68); and Heinemann, in a lengthy appendix on "Middleton's Parliamentary Puritan Patrons," argues that "Middleton is unusual in the closeness of his links with the City and with circles which must be considered as definitely Puritan" (Heinemann, *Puritanism and Theatre*, 258).

Given that the City paid for Middleton's civic pageants, it comes as no surprise that Middleton devotes much praise to the City itself in his first Lord Mayor's Show, *The Triumphs of Truth* (1613), and he frequently uses Spenserian ideas and imagery to convey this praise. David Bergeron notes Middleton's debts to Spenser's allegorical logic in his own depiction of Error in the pageant and concludes that "No other pageant-dramatist, nor Ben Jonson in the masque for that matter, gives greater evidence of understanding the traditional iconographical presentation of allegorical figures" (Bergeron, *English Civic Pageantry*, 181, 182). Middleton's use of the iconography of the mother goddess Cybele creates a complex web of meaning that connects the pageant to Spenser's earlier use of the goddess to glorify London. Middleton builds his description of the personification of London—"attired like a reverend mother, a long white hair naturally flowing on either side of her; on her head a model of steeples and turrets" (Middleton, *Triumphs of Truth*, 969)—upon the attributes of the mother goddess Cybele, best known iconographically by her crown of turrets and other city buildings.[6]

In doing so, Middleton reifies the allegorical connection between Cybele and London that Spenser had asserted in the Thames–Medway marriage canto of *The Faerie Queene*, in which the Thames wears "a Coronet / .... / In which were many towres and castels set" (4.11.27.6, 8). Spenser then compares Thames's crown explicitly to that of Cybele:

> Like as the mother of the Gods, they say,
>   In her great iron charet wonts to ride,
>   When to *Ioues* pallace she doth take her way;
>   Old *Cybele*, arayd with pompous pride,
>   Wearing a Diademe embattild wide
>   With hundred turrets, like a Turribant.
>   With such an one was Thamis beautifide;
>   That was to weet the famous Troynouant,
> In which her kingdomes throne is chiefly resiant.
>
> (4.11.28)

Through his own use of Cybele, Spenser connects London to the idealized cities of Troy and Rome: "Riding on the crest of the famous rivers and gods of the pagan East, Cybele brings to Albion the riches of other times and cities, uniting within herself both the fecundity of nature and the dynamic of historical succession" (Hawkins, "From mythography," 58). The westward movement of Cybele, who resides in the city most favored by Fortune at any given moment, appears, as Lawrence Manley argues, "in epic movement toward Troynovant. As the major focus of this

---

6 In her earlier form in Anatolia, Phrygia, and early Greece, she wore a *polos*, a high cylindrical hat, but, by the time of the Romans, the *polos* became conflated with the mural crown of Tyche, the deity who governed the fortunes of a city (perhaps through a misreading of *polos* as *polis*, city). This conflation of iconography of Cybele and Tyche presumably played a role in the conflation of the goddesses themselves, such that Cybele, formerly a goddess of fertility akin to Ceres, became associated with power, city-building, and the fortunes that cause cities to rise and fall (Roller, *In Search of God the Mother*).

epic movement, the city symbolically embodies historic destiny" (Manley, "Spenser and the city," 218). The London/Troynovant connection was of course a commonplace (see, e.g., Federico, *New Troy*; Hadfield, *Shakespeare, Spenser*), but, by following Spenser's use of Cybele to make the connection, Middleton both connects himself ideologically with Spenser and compliments the patrons of his pageant by deploying this myth of the magnificence of London.

My goal in thinking about Middleton's politics and religion over the course of decades, and across the division from sixteenth to seventeenth century, is to think about the ways that a fairly stable political orientation can manifest differently in different circumstances. A poet who introduces himself to the world with a version of the Book of Proverbs dedicated to the Earl of Essex is the same poet who, two years later, uses subtle allusions to Spenser to sharpen the force of his satire of Lord Burghley and his son. Five years later, he uses more overt Spenserianism, in the form of an insect and bird satire whose title alludes directly to Spenser, and the rhetoric of nostalgia to criticize the direction Jacobean England is beginning to take. In his youth, Middleton uses Spenserianism to clarify and communicate his values; as a mature artist, he forges his own path, but in order to express the same basic political and religious values.

The politics of satire and the burning of Middleton's *Micro-Cynicon* (1599)

Cyndia Clegg has documented the unsystematic, arbitrary way that the Elizabethan authorities undertook censorship, and Annabel Patterson explores the psychological impact of such unpredictability on writers, the psychic effects of "subtle intersections of state censorship with self-censorship, as fear shades into caution, caution into prudence, and prudence into more self-serving emotions and motives" (Clegg, *Press Censorship Elizabethan*; Patterson, *Censorship and Interpretation*, 17). In Chapter 4, I discussed the congeniality of Spenserian indirect satire to Thomas Nashe and Tailboys Dymoke, who used similar strategies to create satirical meanings and subtly imitated two poems of Spenser: "March" and *Muiopotmos*, respectively. I want to emphasize, though, that just as Spenser developed his style of indirect satire in response to concerns about censorship—fears raised most directly, one presumes, by the temporal proximity of John Stubbs's censorship experience to the publication of Spenser's first major work, *The Shepheardes Calender*—other writers' own fears of censorship affected the extent to which they could directly model their satirical works on those of Spenser during the 1590s. A censorship system that depends on absolute power exercised arbitrarily creates fear and uncertainty in writers and publishers, and they respond with careful attention to moment-by-moment shifts in the censorship environment, with incremental assays at daring becoming more or less bold depending on the reception of previous efforts.

When looking at how other authors responded to Spenser's satirical works in the 1590s and the early 1600s, a storyline emerges: Whereas *The Shepheardes Calender* includes a number of satirical moments, as noted in Chapter 2, Spenser's satirical credibility was enhanced by the government response to *Complaints*, and Spenser's references to foxes and his antagonism to Lord Burghley became the simplified version of "Spenserian satire." But no writer was foolish enough to directly imitate Spenser's most inflammatory satirical work, *Mother Hubberds Tale*, in the period after *Complaints* was called in. Instead, some writers imitated his indirect satirical methods and alluded to his other works in creating their own satirical poetry. The calling-in of *Mother Hubberds Tale* definitely had a chilling effect on beast fables: although a few beast fables appeared in print in the 1590s, satirical writers mostly channeled their energies into formal verse satires. After the Bishops' Ban, and after the death of Queen Elizabeth, poets reversed this strategy, so that cautiously Spenserian animal fables featuring insects and birds begin to appear in the early seventeenth century. We cannot determine how much the increase in animal fables owes to the Bishops' Ban's explicit references to specific instances of formal verse satire and how much to the deaths of two people who had been part of the censorship of *Complaints*: Lord Burghley's death in 1598 and Queen Elizabeth's death in 1603. All we know is that the dearth of published animal fables in the 1590s corresponds neatly to the scarcity of formal verse satires in the first years of the seventeenth century, suggesting that Spenser's censorship episode, by virtue of having occurred eight years farther in the past than the Bishops' Ban, was less of a deterrent after 1599 to writers considering satirical meaning-making.

As I argued in Chapter 3, Spenser's prominence and meaning in the literary system of the 1590s gave him disproportionate influence over other writers during the period. What "Spenser" stood for was characterized by a certain doubleness, in Michelle O'Callaghan's words: "he was simultaneously the laureate poet gloriously serving his monarch and the oppositional poet, the persecuted critic of the corrupted times" (*Shepheards Nation*, 1). O'Callaghan argues that this double view of Spenser emerged after his death, but I believe that this view of him developed in the literary imaginary in the early 1590s: the first installment of *The Faerie Queene* in 1590 celebrated his queen, while the 1591 *Complaints* criticized that queen's chief advisor; Faeryland allegorically complimented England, but works such as *Colin Clouts Come Home Againe*, and even *Amoretti* and *Epithalamion*, emphasized Spenser's place at the periphery, politically and in terms of courtiership. I argued in Chapter 3 that the young Joseph Hall in his satires seems to be reacting against the towering figure of the "decorous" Spenser, that side of Spenser's public persona that led to Marx calling him, centuries later, "Elizabeth's arse-kissing poet" (qtd. in Riley, "Marx & Spenser," 457). But other young satirists, including Thomas Middleton, responded to and were inspired by the figure of the "opposition" Spenser.

The limited critical attention to *Micro-Cynicon* has tended to assess it as a mostly unremarkable iteration of Juvenalian verse satire, notable for the ways in which the future dramatist sometimes shifts from the discursive satirical approach characteristic of the genre to semi-dramatic character sketches that aim for more realism than one generally finds in formal verse satires (see, e.g., McCaw, *Middleton's Protest*, 10–12; Barker, *Thomas Middleton*, 30; Holmes, *Art*, 7). As discussed in Chapter 1, numerous critics have offered hypotheses for what led to the Bishops' Ban, with some asserting that the bishops were motivated by moral concerns, others arguing that politics drove the decision to ban these books, and still others seeking ways around the erotica/politics dichotomy created by earlier scholars. I believe that *Micro-Cynicon* was singled out to be among the satires specifically named in the Bishops' Ban and burned because the offense it gave was clearer and more specific than has been recognized. In the literary-political climate of 1599, because the genre of formal verse satire cued readers to look for topical, political allusions, the apparently general nature of Middleton's satire in *Micro-Cynicon* was not enough to spare it from scrutiny. The first two satires in the collection, focusing on "Insatiate Cron" and his son, "Prodigal Zodon," were likely read as referring to William and Robert Cecil. Middleton's use of imagery and ideas associated with Lord Burghley, most notably by Spenser in *Mother Hubberds Tale*, increases the likelihood that contemporary readers would read Cron as a satire on the Lord Treasurer. Given this association, the repeated references to Cron's death (and the unflattering observation that Cron has "fled to hell") would presumably be particularly offensive, given that Lord Burghley had died less than a year earlier.

The general obscurity in which *Micro-Cynicon* languishes means that few critics who have considered the Bishops' Ban have paid specific attention to what Middleton's work might have done to merit being recalled and burned, but the two hypotheses that have been put forth address both sides of the erotica/politics split in critical opinion regarding the motivations of the ban. John Peter, arguing that *Micro-Cynicon* offended the morals of the censors, calls the author "deliberately offensive" and notes that "in the fifth satire, 'Ingling Pyander,' besides what appear to be dark references to pederasty, there are several touches of unpleasantness where Marston's influence may be suspected" (Peter, *Complaint and Satire*, 147). Peter's allusions to "dark references to pederasty" are of a piece with his own moral repugnance at the style and method of the satirists who followed Marston's lead, but he is certainly correct that Middleton's fifth satire contains a titillating situation that leads to moral corruption of the satiric speaker—and thus perhaps of the reader as well. The speaker "loved Pyander well" before he realized that Pyander, "Whose rolling eye sets gazers' hearts on fire, / Whose cherry lip, black brow and smiles procure / Lust-burning buzzards to the tempting lure," was in fact "a pale chequered black hermaphrodite" (Middleton, *Microcynicon*, 5.42, 5.36–38, 5.24). Proving the relevance of Bruce Smith's assertion that, with late Elizabethan verse satire, "scourgers could be seduced by their sexual subjects and ... the seducers could turn into scourgers of moral authority" (Smith, *Homosexual Desire*, 164), part of the speaker's desire to expose Pyander stems from his own shame at being deceived ("shall I then procure eternal blame / By secret cloaking of Pyander's shame, / And he not blush?" [5.53–55]), and the rest from his vexation that he spent his money in vain ("Fair words I had, for store of coin I gave, / But not enjoyed the fruit I thought to have" [5.82–83]).

Cyndia Clegg, on the other hand, explains *Micro-Cynicon*'s inclusion in the named works of the Bishops' Ban as stemming from political, not moral, offensiveness in its second satire, which mocks "Prodigal Zodon." According to Clegg, because of the heightened political tensions in England at the time of publication surrounding the Earl of Essex's Irish expedition and concerns regarding his loyalty to the Queen, instead of appearing to be "a general satire of pretension and vanity," "Zodon looks like Essex, a man who indulged in luxuries though beset by debts" (Clegg, *Press Censorship Elizabethan*, 213). She comments that phrases such as "glorious on his progress day" and "Two days encaged at least in strongest hold" (Middleton, *Microcynicon*, 2.26, 2.29) might have seemed extremely topical if the book had been published after Essex's departure for Ireland. Clegg does not argue strenuously for Middleton's authorial intention to criticize Essex (Middleton's dedication of *The Wisdom of*

Solomon, Paraphrased [1597] to Essex only two years earlier would make this a problematic assertion). Instead, she believes that Whitgift, because of his warm friendship with Essex, responded to Essex's concerns about John Hayward's *The First Part of the Life and Raigne of King Henrie the IIII* (1599) with such zeal that he also identified and banned several other books that he saw as giving bad press to Essex, including *Micro-Cynicon*.

The bishops' silence regarding their motivations, coupled with the varied and complex cultural and political meanings of the genre of verse satire in the late 1590s, mean that we cannot definitively identify a single unifying offense committed by all of the named works, or even by Middleton's *Micro-Cynicon* alone. Instead, we can look at the ways that a single work may have given offense for multiple reasons, which, taken together, constituted grounds for censorship. As religious leaders, the bishops may have been shocked not only by Pyander's cross-dressing but also by the speaker's frank desire for Pyander. As a friend of Essex, Whitgift may have zealously attempted to protect his friend's political interests. Likewise, however, Whitgift and Bancroft, as part of what was after all a *state* church, may have taken action on behalf of both Robert Cecil and the memory of his recently deceased father, William Cecil, Lord Burghley, both extremely high-ranking advisors to Queen Elizabeth. Richard McCabe notes that both Whitgift and Bancroft "were in constant correspondence with Robert Cecil on the issue of the press" and that their letters indicate a commitment to politically motivated censorship (McCabe, "Elizabethan satire," 189).

In *Micro-Cynicon*, Middleton uses facts and images strongly associated with the Cecils and with Spenser's satire on them: calling Cron a fox; emphasizing the father–son relationship between these two satirical characters (and emphasizing their power by making this dyad's initials correspond to that other rapacious and power-hungry father and son, Chronos and Zeus);[7] referring to a "fardel at his [Cron's] back" in the satire on Zodon; and creating the name Zodon itself, which derives from the Greek *zodion* for "little animal." With these clues or "entry codes"— the allegorization of the father–son dyad and the allusions to animals and hunchbacks—a searching reader, such as Whitgift or Bancroft, could perceive the indirect satire on the Cecil father and son.

Middleton refers to a fox only once, in a dense passage (editor Wendy Wall calls it "obscure") that seems allusive in part because the nature and animal images seem incongruous with the rest of the poem. The overall

---

7 I am indebted to Anne Lake Prescott for this observation.

message of the passage seems to be that desire (presumably lascivious) would be preferable to the "gain insatiate" that "this hoar-agèd peasant deems his bliss":

> O that desire might hunt amongst that fur!
> It should go hard but he would loose a cur
> To rouse the fox hid in a bramble bush,
> Who frighteth conscience with a wry-mouthed "Push!"
> (Middleton, *Microcynicon*, 1.17–22)

The image of desire using a dog to hunt for a fox hidden, confusingly, in both fur and in a bramble bush—shifting the poem temporarily to allegory and beast fable—surely would remind a sixteenth-century reader of Spenser's known satirical methods. Additionally, though, this difficult passage becomes much more comprehensible if we read it with the popular image of the aged, censorious Burghley in mind. Though none of the words in this passage describes an old man, the fur suggests someone wealthy, especially in proximity to the word "fox," as fox fur served symbolically to identify usurers.[8] Further, the descriptor "wry-mouthed" calls to mind an old man expressing his disdain with the interjection "push" (obsolete, now "pish"); ingenious readers might find support for importing the idea of Burghley through the similarity of a "bramble" to a "burr." This passage, which differs in tone from the rest of the satire, calls attention to the possibility of a reading influenced by the concerns of *Mother Hubberds Tale*, as does Middleton's emphasis on the father–son relationship between Cron and Zodon.

One way that Spenser had identified Lord Burghley as a target of the satire in *Mother Hubberds Tale* was by criticizing the Fox's preferential treatment of his cubs:

> He fed his cubs with fat of all the soyle,
> ....
> And loded them with lordships and with might,
> So much as they were able well to beare,
> That with the weight their backs nigh broken were.
> (lines 1151, 1156–58)

---

8 See, for example, discussion of examples from Shakespeare, Thomas Nashe, Robert Greene, and Thomas Dekker associating usurers with fox-fur garments in H.C. Hart's edition of Shakespeare's *Measure for Measure* (Hart, "Commentary," 77n7). An anti-Cecilian libel written after the fall of Essex refers to either Robert Cecil or his brother Thomas (Lord Burghley after the death of William Cecil) as wearing a fox-furred cloak: "Little Cecil trips up and down / He rules both court and crown / With his brother Burghley clown / In his great fox furred gown" (qtd. in Croft, "Reputation," 47).

Significantly, Catholic apologist Richard Verstegan, in an unlicensed tract against Lord Burghley smuggled into England, describes *Mother Hubberds Tale* using only the detail that it concerns "the false fox and his crooked cubbes," indicating that contemporary readers saw the father–son(s) relationship as crucial in identifying the real-world targets of Spenser's satire (Verstegan, *A Declaration*, 68; see Chapter 1 for fuller discussion).

Clegg's argument identifying Zodon with Essex fails to convince not only because of Middleton's public warmth for Essex in his dedication of *The Wisdom of Solomon, Paraphrased*, but also because it doesn't take account of the significance of the father–son dyad in Middleton's creation of these characters. Numerous details of Cron and Zodon line up neatly with the biographical details of Cecil *père et fils*, who were without a doubt the most hated and powerful father–son pair of late Elizabethan England. Like Lord Burghley, Cron has recently died, bequeathing his fabulous wealth to his corrupt son: "And scraping Cron hath got a world of wealth. / Now what of that? Cron's dead. Where's all his pelf? / Bequeathèd to young Prodigal. That's well: / His god hath left him, and he's fled to hell" (Middleton, *Microcynicon*, 2.49–52). Lord Burghley had died August 4, 1598, ten months before the burning of *Micro-Cynicon*.[9] Additionally, the satire's references to Cron's base birth and facetious references to London as "Troynovant" call to mind Lord Burghley's pretensions in claiming ancient genealogical connections (see, e.g., Alford, *Burghley*, 6, 349n8). Mockery of these pretensions appears most freely in unlicensed pro-Catholic propaganda tracts; for example, Catholic apologist Robert Parsons in 1592 states that Burghley first claimed descent from the Caecilius Claudius described by Pliny, before later connecting himself with the ancient Welsh Sitsilt family. Parsons asks, if this were true, if it were likely that Burghley's grandfather

> would keepe an Inne in Sta[m]ford as diuers vvorshipfull yet aliue or lately dead haue affirmed to haue layen in the same; also how it is possible that his sonne the Treasures father, named also Dauid Cecil (if I forget not) should be onely groome of the vvardrobe, & so plaine, and meane a man, as thousandes yet can testifie that he was? & how finally VVilliam Cecil their child now Treasurer could be so poore, and meanely brought vp, as to get parte of his mayntenance by ringing the morning bel at his beginning in S. Ihons colledge in Cambridge as commonly yet in that vniuersitie is reported. (Parsons, *An Aduertisement*, 39–40)

---

9 *Micro-Cynicon* was not entered into the Stationers' Register (see Clegg, *Press Censorship Elizabethan*, 286n52), so the *terminus a quo* for the book's publication is January 1, 1599.

Parsons closes his withering analysis of Burghley's pretensions to status by noting that, instead of lions for his coat of arms, "a good fatt capon, or a rosted pigg seemeth a fitter cognisaunce for an Inneholders grandchild as this man affirmeth, seing that those things are more commonly to be founde in Innes, and Osteries then are Lyons" (Parsons, *An Aduertisement*, 40). Verstegan also makes reference to Burghley's father's relatively low-ranking post of groom of the wardrobe, noting that to Burghley's "wylinesse was joined a wonderfull ambition," even though he was "by birth but of meane degree," and warning of the possibility "whereby England may happen to haue a King *Cecill* the first, that is suddainly metamorphosed from a grome of the wardrobe, to the wearing of the best robe within the wardrobe" (Verstegan, *A Declaration*, 9, 55–56).

Middleton of course is more circumspect than these illicit publications, but Cron's exaggeratedly abject poverty in his youth, coupled with the reference to Troynovant, which facetiously implies how very, very far back Cron's pedigree extends, echo the criticisms made of Burghley in unlicensed works and in works such as Spenser's that were censored. Cron's son Zodon is a "mounted beggar" (Middleton, *Microcynicon*, 2.31),

> A base-born issue of a baser sire,
> Bred in a cottage, wand'ring in the mire
> With nailèd shoes and whipstaff in his hand,
> Who with a "hey and ree" the beasts command,
> And being seven years practised in that trade,
> At seven years' end by Tom a journey's made
> Unto the city of fair Troynovant,
> Where through extremity of need and want
> He's forced to trot with fardel at his back
> From house to house, demanding if they lack
> A poor young man that's willing to take pain
> And mickle labour, though for little gain.
>
> (2.33–44)

The narrative of these two satires together—the story of a poor young man who becomes wealthy and powerful, hoards his wealth, and then bequeaths it at his death to his undeserving and corrupt son—allegorizes (in exaggerated form, of course) the actual biographies of the two most powerful men in England in the 1590s. Middleton emphasizes the connection with the reference to the "fardel at his back" (2.41); the syntax is cloudy, and the fardel could be on the back of either father or son, but anything reminiscent of a hunchback at this time served to point the allusion to Robert Cecil, whose back was crooked (see Croft, "Reputation").

The "fardel" calls to mind Spenser's fox cubs with backs "nigh broken" (Spenser, *Mother Hubberds*, line 1158), and both are part of the mean-spirited shorthand from the 1590s up to Robert Cecil's death in 1612 and beyond that used language of deformity and subhumanness to refer to Cecil because of his crooked back and short stature. Pauline Croft has analyzed Cecil's reputation by studying the libels written against him both after the fall of the Earl of Essex and following Cecil's death, finding that "The themes which emerged most insistently and savagely were those of [Robert Cecil, Earl of] Salisbury's crooked back and his sexual appetites" (Croft, "Reputation," 54). Animal imagery abounds to highlight these themes, with fox, ape, dolphin, and spider imagery used to refer to him (Bellany and McRae, "Early Stuart libels"). Middleton's sly use of a fardel on a back to allude to Cecil's crooked back is echoed by other anti-Cecil writers. Writing in 1592, Verstegan jests that Robert Cecil's father should have helped him to a job as "writer vnder some clerck or officier of the courte," because "he was fittest for such purpose, for that he caried his deske on his back" (Verstegan, *A Declaration*, 71). Twenty years later, following the Earl of Salisbury's death in 1612, a libelist describes him as "a Ciciliane monster beegott of a fox / some caulde him crookebacke & some litle Robbin / hee bore on his backe a packe like ower Dobbin" (Anonymous libel, 1612).

Another way that Middleton subtly connects this satire to Spenser's work is through the unusual name of Zodon. A search of Early English Books Online for the word "Zodon" yields only Middleton's *Micro-Cynicon*, but a search for the Greek word *zodion* indicates that the etymological connection between this word and the English "zodiac" (which tangentially connects Zodon's name to Zeus through the mythological reference) was well known. All occurrences of the word *zodion* appear in the context of providing an etymology for "zodiac." In three instances (Richard Eden's translation of Martín Cortés, 1589; Thomas Blundeville, 1594; and Thomas Hill, 1599), the author translates *zodion* simply as "beast," but Philemon Holland's 1609 translation of Ammianus Marcellinus retains the sense of the word as a diminutive (especially fitting for the short and hunchbacked Robert Cecil): "*Zodiak*, of *Zodion* in Greeke, a little living creature" (Marcellinus, *Annotations*, C4v). As I have argued, the beast fable was in the 1590s the satire that dared not speak its name, but Middleton finds ingenious ways of referring to animal satire in general and to Spenser's infamous *Mother Hubberds Tale* in particular.

These allusions to Spenser's methods of satirizing William and Robert Cecil—reference to a fox, emphasis on a corrupt father–son dynasty, subtle allusions to physical deformity, and an animal reference in Zodon's name—served to teach contemporary readers how to understand the satire by suggesting the likelihood that Middleton shared the political and religious ideas associated in the public mind with Spenser. Identifying the nature of Middleton's offense in this work is important for what it tells us about Middleton—about his politics in the late 1590s, for example, and also his ideological alignment with Edmund Spenser and others whose satirical toolboxes the young poet raided to create this early work. Identifying the possible source of the decision to censor Middleton's work is also important for what it tells us about the political significance of the genre of formal verse satire in the 1590s. To a present-day reader, the references to the Cecils in the first two satires of *Micro-Cynicon* may appear tenuous and circuitous. And yet the reader of a formal verse satire in the 1590s came to the text not only with a wealth of contextual information about animal nicknames, popular criticisms of leading political figures, and the like, but also with a desire, inspired by the social meaning of the genre itself, to find secrets hidden within the text. In this rhetorical situation, readerly ingenuity met authorial intention to create topical interpretations.

Spenser's satiric influence on Middleton's *Father Hubburds Tales*

Being an oppositional writer in a time of repressive censorship is a dangerous business; having learned his lesson in 1599, Middleton in *Father Hubburds Tales* (1604) aimed to convey a satirical message, but more safely. He blunts the force of the satire by making *Father Hubburds Tales* quite different in form from the verse satires of the 1590s and by creating extremely general satiric targets. At the same time, he calls attention to the fact that there is indeed a satirical message by making insistent reference to Spenser. Andrew McRae argues that, rather than forcing satire "underground," the Bishops' Ban instead "contributed to a dispersal or diffusion of the mode, which subsequently informed a wide range of texts" (McRae, *Literature, Satire*, 90). Middleton, because of the 1599 burning of *Micro-Cynicon*, was presumably highly motivated in 1604 to vent his satirical ire in non-incendiary ways. In *Father Hubburds Tales; or, The Ant and the Nightingale*, Middleton responds to the danger of censorship and/or punishment by hiding his meanings in typically Spenserian fashion.[10] As Spenser did in his *Complaints* volume, Middleton creates

10 The first edition of the work was titled *The Ant, and the Nightingale, or Father Hubburds Tales*; the second edition, which like the first appeared in 1604, was titled *Father*

formal and stylistic parallels with the medieval complaints tradition, thus distancing himself from the problematic, classically inspired formal verse satire even as he deploys nostalgia as a tool for political critique of Jacobean England. Second, in creating an "insect fable" akin to Spenser's *Virgils Gnat* and *Muiopotmos*, Middleton invites readers to use the same interpretive strategies they had applied to Spenser's *Prosopopoia; or, Mother Hubberds Tale* and to the fox imagery in *Micro-Cynicon* to understand the satirical message. By adapting these strategies from Spenser, and by insistently reminding readers of Spenser's infamous satire, Middleton places himself both politically and artistically within the camp of the Spenserian poets of the early seventeenth century.

Father Hubburds Tales, differentiated in multiple ways from *Micro-Cynicon*, appears innocuous. Ovid's Philomel, in her nightingale form, catches an ant, but he persuades her not to eat him. Instead, he tells of his past—like her, he used to be a human, and he reports his experiences as a ploughman, as a soldier, and as a scholar. Middleton distinguishes this satire formally from the clearly Juvenalian mode of *Micro-Cynicon* by using the mixed verse and prose associated with Menippean satire (the ant's stories are in prose, whereas the conversations between the ant and Philomel are in verse) and thematically by means of the fable-like use of animals as characters. To complicate these classical satiric models with reference to the native English tradition, we might also say that the plot and concerns of *Father Hubburds Tales*—the unfair treatment of ploughmen by rack-renting aristocrats, the lack of public care for a soldier wounded in battle, and the declining appreciation of poets and scholars—seem more akin to the medieval complaint than to early modern satire per se. Additionally, the work engages with the estates satire tradition, but Middleton modifies the typically inclusive estates satire model by focusing *only* on poor characters. George Gascoigne had connected Philomel with satire in *The Steele Glas* (1576), a work that also includes passages of estates satire, and so we can see Middleton's work referencing an entirely different literary genealogy than *Micro-Cynicon* and the other verse satires of the 1590s, with debts to Ovid, Menippus, Gascoigne, and English complaint in sharp contrast to the 1590s poems' allegiance to Juvenal. Yet whereas Middleton in *Micro-Cynicon* makes no overt reference to Spenser and does not model the form on Spenser but uses Spenser's indirect satirical strategies to criticize the Cecils, in

---

Hubburds Tales, or the Ant, and the Nightingale. See Shaaber, "The ant," and Kaplan, "Printer's copy," for a more detailed explication of bibliographic issues related to the two editions of the work.

Father Hubburds Tales he references Spenser insistently, both explicitly and through formal and stylistic parallels.

Presumably these references to Spenser serve to counteract the danger that, because of the vagueness regarding specific targets in *Father Hubburds Tales,* Middleton risks blunting entirely the satiric force of his work. Calling attention repeatedly to Spenser's *Mother Hubberds Tale* reminds Middleton's audience to read carefully to interpret his meaning. Whereas the first edition uses "Father Hubburds Tales" as the subtitle, the second edition foregrounds the allusion by making that the main title of the work. Middleton alludes to Spenser's work again in the address to the reader: "Why I call these *Father Hubburd's Tales* is not to have them called in again, as the *Tale of Mother Hubburd*: the world would show little judgment in that, i'faith, and I should say then *plena stultorum omnia,* for I entreat here neither of ragged bears or apes, no, nor the lamentable downfall of the old wife's platters" (Middleton, *Father Hubburd's,* lines 62–67). Of course *Mother Hubberds Tale* does not include an old wife's platters; perhaps Middleton had not read Spenser's controversial satire, or perhaps he purposefully introduced an erroneous plot point in order to imply his own lack of familiarity with Spenser's work, given that it was a banned book. Despite this effort at deniability, Middleton's reference to the title reminds his audience of it, and the reference to animals would call to many readers' minds the fact that topical interpretations of the animal characters in that work were what led to its censoring.

This reminder to read attentively, and especially to think about the cultural meanings of the animal characters, would prime Middleton's audience to read this work with the same searching ingenuity that they brought to Spenser's *Mother Hubberds Tale* and to the formal verse satires of the 1590s. The work repays such a reading. Plot parallels with Spenser's translation of the pseudo-Virgilian *Culex,* titled *Virgils Gnat,* remind readers of Spenser's ideal of poetry as a guide and teacher for those in political power. References to monkey and marmoset characters and the frequent description of the ant-ploughman's young lord as an ape or baboon echo the fox and ape villains in the beast fable of *Mother Hubberds Tale,* as does the use of estates satire. Additionally, the use of a passage from Proverbs and a tale from Ovid as intertexts for the work suggests Middleton's reasons for using an ant as the protagonist and leads to a potentially antiroyalist interpretation of the satire.

The use of an insect protagonist would surely call to readers' minds Spenser's use of a gnat character in *Virgils Gnat* and a butterfly in *Muiopotmos; or, The Fate of the Butterflie* (both published in 1591 in

Complaints) or the bumblebee protagonist of Dymoke's very Spenserian *Caltha Poetarum*, one of the poems named in the 1599 Bishops' Ban, as discussed in Chapter 4. Confirmation of contemporary understanding that *Virgils Gnat* refers to poets' attempts to reform their social superiors appears in Thomas Scot's 1616 comment that "If *Spencer* now were liuing," "The Ghost of *Virgils Gnat* would now sting so, / That great Men durst not in the Citie goe" (Scot, *Philomythie*, B1r–B1v). As Spenser does in *Virgils Gnat*, Middleton plays up the contrast between his insect protagonist and the more powerful figure he seeks to influence. The ant tells Philomel, "I am a little emmet [ant] born to work" and "Why seeks your gentleness a poor worm's end? / … . / I come to wonder, not to work offence: / There is no glory to spoil innocence" (Middleton, *Father Hubburd's*, lines 174, 164, 166–67). The subtly anti-Jacobean didactic focus of *Father Hubburds Tales* appears in Philomel's merciful response to the ant. Philomel, presumably a type of Queen Elizabeth, models the kindness to inferiors presented as proper to royalty; she releases the ant from her hold, saying, "I give thee life and way. / The worthy will not prey on yielding things. / Pity's enfeoffed to the blood of kings!" (lines 183–85). The use of "enfeoff," a feudal term, further emphasizes the sense of nostalgia, as Elizabeth through Philomel becomes associated with an idealized view of the feudal ties that connected people in earlier days.

As a satirist, Spenser was best known for his *Mother Hubberds Tale*, and Middleton, as he had done in *Micro-Cynicon*, uses beast fable imagery in "The Ant's Tale when he was a Ploughman" to connect this work to Spenser's famous satire. Each of the ant's tales focuses on the unfair treatment that a poor man endures at the hands of the wealthy and powerful, but the first tale, that of the ant-ploughman, is by far the longest and most thoroughly developed. The ant tells what happened to him and his fellow ploughmen when his wise, prudent, and hospitable landlord died, leaving the estate to his son, who was "accustomed to wild and unfruitful company about the court and London" (Middleton, *Father Hubburd's*, lines 320–21). After his father's death, the son engages a monkey and a marmoset as servants, further identified as a "French page and Italianate servingman," respectively, and then himself becomes "so metamorphosed into the shape of a French puppet that, at the first, we [i.e., the ploughmen] started and thought one of the baboons had marched in in man's apparel" (lines 330, 374–76). References to these animals abound in the rest of the tale. The son quickly signs away his patrimony to a merchant and a mercer in order to have ready cash. The ant-ploughman describes the son's profligacy in detail, but he also pays brief attention to how life changed for the ploughmen: "what a sad Christmas we all kept in the country without either carols, wassail-bowls, dancing of Sellinger's Round in moonshine nights about maypoles, shoeing the mare, hoodman-blind, hot-cockles, or any of our old Christmas gambols; no, not so much as choosing king and queen on Twelfth Night" (lines 638–42). Again, we here see nostalgia for an earlier era, when landlords understood that their social position conferred upon them the obligation of hospitality, especially at Christmas-time, toward social inferiors (Heal, *Hospitality*; Palmer, *Hospitable Performances*, 27–31).

The wide variety of animal characters hearkens to *Virgils Gnat*, *Muiopotmos*, and *Mother Hubberds Tale*; in addition, Middleton's unusual use of the ant alludes both to Proverbs and to Ovid's *Metamorphoses* 7, creating an intertextual web of ideas about ants that coalesces into a message against the oppression of the poor. Ants' industriousness is, quite literally, proverbial, appearing notably in Proverbs, 6:6–9, which Middleton paraphrases in *Father Hubburds Tales* just before Philomel catches the ant:

> There was a bed of busy, toiling ants,
> That in their summer, winter's comfort got,
> Teaching poor men how to shun after-wants;
>   Whose rules if sluggards could be learned to keep,
>   They should not starve awake, lie cold asleep.
>   (Middleton, *Father Hubburd's*, lines 121–25)

Using an ant to represent the lives of a ploughman, a soldier, and a scholar reminds the reader of the laboriousness of all of these endeavors, and lends them as well the aura of virtue that attaches to the ant's work in cultural references to the ant's industry. Dignifying the work of these unglamorous characters certainly serves a polemical purpose, but I believe the work supports an even more radical interpretation.

Let us compare Middleton's paraphrase of the passage from Proverbs with the Geneva Bible version:

> 6 Go to the pismire [ant], O sluggard: behold her ways, and be wise.
> 7 For she having no guide, governor, nor ruler,
> 8 Prepareth her meat in the summer, and gathereth her food in harvest.
> 9 How long wilt thou sleep, O sluggard? when wilt thou arise out of thy sleep? (*Proverbs of Solomon*, 6:6–9)

We see that in *Father Hubburds Tales*, Middleton left out one verse – Proverbs, 6:7 – about how the ant has "no guide, governor, nor ruler." One can certainly read the Proverbs passage as favoring political hierarchy, as William Burton does in a 1595 sermon:

> And what a shame is this to the slouthful person (if he be not past shame) that hath both guides, and gouernours, and rulers, both to teach him, and keep him in order, besides the benefite of reason and vnderstanding: and yet for all these meanes and helpes, which the Pismire wanteth, is carelesse of his owne good? (Burton, *Rowsing*, 10–11)

In Burton's reading, guides, governors, and rulers are unambiguously good. Yet, Middleton's ant-ploughman, ant-soldier, and ant-scholar are human laborers who would be better off *without* the oppression and corruption of their "natural betters." In this regard, both the missing Proverbs, 6:7 and the plot points—such as, for example, the unfair treatment of the ploughmen through the legal machinations of the young heir to the estate and the disregard of needs of the disabled soldier, whose captain and commanders cheat him of his pay, granting him only "a passport to beg in all countries" (Middleton, *Father Hubburd's*, lines 951–52)—will remind the audience that, to the extent they buy the connection between English laborers and the virtuous, foresightful, and industrious ant, perhaps those ant-people would also be better off without the guides, governors, and rulers who oppress them.

The industrious ants of Proverbs, of course, remain ants, but Middleton surely had in mind as well a tale in which ants crawling up and down the length of a tree *do* become human. In Book 7 of *Metamorphoses*, King Aeacus, heartbroken over the death of his subjects from a plague, prays to Jupiter to have his city filled with people again. Aeacus relates, "And Jupiter sent omens—lightning followed by confirming thunder.... I happened to be standing beside an oak.... On this tree we saw a long line of ants carrying bits of grain, huge burdens for their tiny mouths.... Marveling at how many there were, I said, 'Father, highest of the gods, grant to me the same number of citizens to fill my empty city!'" (Ovid, *Metamorphoses*, 122). He sleeps and dreams of the ants, who "appeared to grow and to become larger and to raise themselves from the ground, stand upright, shed their thin bodies, their many legs, and their black color, and take on human form" (122–23). He wakes and goes outside to find the ant-men of his dream, whom he names the Myrmidons, hailing him as king. He notes to his companion that "they still have the character they had before: a frugal, hardworking race, holding on to what they've acquired and storing it up for the future. All the same age and equal in courage, they will go off to war with you as soon as the wind blowing from the east ... changes around to the south" (123).

Middleton's Philomel sings not in an oak tree, but "On a green hawthorn, from the thunder blest" (line 109); the thunder blessing may connect this tree to Jupiter's blessing in *Metamorphoses*. Although an oak tree would connect these images more firmly to the Ovidian text, the hawthorn in the early seventeenth century was seen as the usual perch for the nightingale.[11] Additionally, the use of the hawthorn tree, traditionally associated with fairies, serves to connect Philomel to Queen Elizabeth, the "Faery Queen" of early modern English literature (Spence, *Fairy Tradition*, 321–22; Henderson and Cowan, *Scottish Fairy Belief*). Of the "bed of busy, toiling ants" in *Father Hubburds Tales*, only one actually transforms to a human, but the allusions to the tale of King Aeacus serve to remind the reader that those who look like ants—ploughmen, poor soldiers, and scholars—might rise up and become, like the Myrmidons, a warlike people.

Nostalgia for the past permeates this satire, from the black-letter type used for the ant's tales, to the use of the medieval forms of beast fable and estates satire, to the references to Edmund Spenser's satirical work.[12] Middleton uses this nostalgia to imply—circuitously, of course—that England under James was in decline from an idealized time represented by Elizabeth. Some references to James seem laudatory, such as "there's a manly lion now can roar, / Thunder more dreaded than the lioness; / Of him let simple beasts his aid implore, / For he conceives more than they can express" (lines 222–25). In the same section, however, he implies that the English have already forgotten Elizabeth ("They that forget a queen, soothe with a king" [line 200]) and that even more "curs ... fawn" over Robert Cecil under James's rule than flattered his father in Elizabeth's time ("Else would not soothing glossers oil the son, / Who, while his father lived, his acts did hate" [lines 214, 216–17]).[13] In this way, Middleton seems strongly to suggest that James—and his luxury-seeking, spendthrift ways—bears some responsibility for the decline in care for the poor evidenced in the ant's tales.

11 For example, "the Nightingale vpon the hawthoren singeth" (Carlton, *Madrigals*, B2v) and "The Nitingale vpon the hawthorne brire / And all the wingd Musitions in a Quire, / Do with their notes rebuke dull lazie men" (Chettle, *Englands Mourning*, F3r).
12 According to Zachary Lesser, "one of the dominant meanings of black letter in this period ... was the powerful combination of Englishness (the 'English letter') and pastness (the 'antiquated' appearance of black letter by the seventeenth century) that I call typographic nostalgia. It is this combination that allows black letter to evoke the traditional English community" ("Typographic nostalgia," 107). Note that Spenser himself had used black-letter type to activate both nostalgic and nationalistic feelings in his *Shepheardes Calender* (see Galbraith, "English").
13 Although Curtis Perry argues ("Citizen politics") that Elizabethanism was not a fully developed rhetorical strategy of protest during the first decade of James's reign, his discussion of Dekker's use in *The Whore of Babylon* (1607) of explicit praise of James coupled with implicit critique seems germane to the similar strategy discussed here.

Conclusion; or, "So what?"

Under conditions of censorship both violent and capricious, authors had to consider the possibility of offending not only with *what* they said but also with *how they said it*. I believe that writers in the 1590s saw Spenser's *Mother Hubberds Tale* as an unsafe stylistic model for satire, but that the Bishops' Ban—by censoring primarily works modeled on either Juvenal or the railing satirical style exemplified by Thomas Nashe's contributions to his book war with Gabriel Harvey—made Spenser's indirect satires seem a more acceptable model for satires written after the ban. These stylistic tendencies were strong enough to become a trend or fad, as we can see from comparing Middleton's work in satire during this time period with that of John Donne, that is, his *Satires* of the 1590s and his *Metempsychosis; Poêma Satyricon* (1601; published 1633).

These two writers came to satire after 1599 from very different positions, in terms of both censorship risk and ideology. Middleton, who printed his works and whose *Micro-Cynicon* was named and burned, had much more to fear from government oversight after 1599 than did Donne, whose poetry circulated only in manuscript. Thus, in Middleton we must read the poetry as the author's negotiation between what he wants to say and what he can safely say; for this reason, the Spenserianism of his satires, whether he writes in the Juvenalian vein before the ban, as in *Micro-Cynicon*, or the Menippean after the ban, as in *Father Hubburds Tales*, suggests an ideological commitment to the religious and political ideas associated by him and his contemporaries with Spenser, and this fits with what we know of Middleton's lifelong sympathy for the reform-minded Protestantism associated with the Leicester faction and celebrated by Spenser, as discussed in the first section of this chapter.

On the other hand, we would not expect the sometimes Catholic, sometimes Anglican Donne to use Spenserianism as a covert means of signaling Puritan dissent—he sympathized with neither the ideas nor the forms favored by Spenser and the Spenserian poets (Norbrook, *Poetry and Politics*, 177). However, unconcerned with outright censorship, the manuscript poet Donne has the freedom simply to explore contemporary trends in satirical writing; the Spenserianism of *Metempsychosis*, coupled with the absence of same from his *Satires* of the 1590s, suggests that he may simply be following a fad.[14] In the supposedly unfinished *Metempsychosis*, Donne narrates the transmigration of a single soul from the apple

---

14 For critical comments noting Spenserian elements in Donne's *Metempsychosis*, see Smith, "John Donne's"; Corthell, "Donne's," 98–99.

that Adam and Eve ate to a mandrake, a sparrow, two fishes, a whale, a mouse, a wolf, the wolf's half-wolf/half-dog offspring, an ape, and finally, at the point where the poem ends, a human: Themech, the wife of Cain. Donne never arrives at the revelation he promises in the "Epistle," that he will "deliver you by her relation all her passages from her first making when she was that apple which Eve eat, to this time when she is he, whose life you shall find in the end of this book" (Donne, *Progress of the Soul*, 177). Probably intentionally, however, the apparently unfinished state of the poem has not prevented efforts to identify the target of the satire, with, for example, M. van Wyk Smith arguing that the poem satirizes Robert Cecil ("John Donne's," 142–43).

Donne's subtitle, *Poêma Satyricon*, tells us how to approach reading, but the poem clearly differs importantly from his satires of the 1590s. Janel Mueller, arguing against reading *Metempsychosis* as a satire, succeeds in describing, though not explaining, the important shift that took place in satirical writing in England after the Bishops' Ban. She writes:

> [T]he prosodic, thematic, and tonal differences between the *Metempsychosis* and Donne's undoubted five satires have been almost entirely lost to view. The *Metempsychosis* confronts the scholar and critic with a number of distinctive characteristics—a rapid and continuous narrative sequence, a commitment to myth, the dominant themes of change and gradation into evil rather than achieved and assailable vice, a strong narrative presence which is subject to wide variations of tone and mood, and a full-blown epic framework. None of these can be matched, except intermittently, by Donne's satires. (Mueller, "Donne's," 113)

Despite the stylistic and generic differences, the *Satires* and *Metempsychosis* are certainly both satires, and I believe that closer attention to the government's interventions into the literary field in both 1591 and 1599 can help to explain the differences in works of satire by Middleton, Donne, and others before and after the Bishops' Ban.

Writers in the first decade of the seventeenth century wrote under demonstrably different conditions than those writing in the 1590s: whereas censorship of a beast fable in 1591 had led to the near-absence of this form in printed works of the 1590s, censorship of formal verse satires led to their decline, and a concomitant increase in pastorals and animal satires in the next decade. Additionally, the change of monarch in 1603 meant not only the need to determine, very carefully, the attitudes of a different person toward public criticism and censorship of same, but it also meant the development of new complaints, new things that annoyed English subjects about court and Crown. Spenserianism became a safer and also inherently nostalgic way of expressing some of these new complaints. The freer imitations of Spenser, rather than the allusions to Spenser that had predominated in the 1590s, will be the subject of the next chapter.

6

After the Bishops' Ban: imitation of Spenserian satire

Spenser's death in 1599, the promulgation of the Bishops' Ban in 1599, and the death of Queen Elizabeth in 1603—each of these could be expected to affect the writing of poetry in England, with Spenser's influence becoming modified by nostalgia, authors trying to interpret the text of the Bishops' Ban to determine how to respond to its directive "That noe Satyres or Epigramms be printed hereafter" (qtd. in McCabe, "Elizabethan satire," 188), and everyone watching to see what degree of oversight of the press would characterize King James's reign. The previous chapter speculated on the impact of these three events by comparing two works by Thomas Middleton from 1599 and 1604, to see the extent to which Middleton's consistent political and religious sympathy with attitudes and values associated with Spenser showed up as stylistic "Spenserianism" in these two satirical poetic works. In this chapter, I will focus on the early seventeenth century, with close attention to several works by a few members of the loose alliance generally referred to as "Spenserian poets": Michael Drayton, William Browne, and George Wither.

A poet who wished to write satirical verse in 1600 might rightly conclude from the named works in the Bishops' Ban that formal verse satire was an unsafe mode for expressing satirical meanings. The additional knowledge that the still-living Queen Elizabeth or the still-powerful Robert Cecil, son of Spenser's enemy Lord Burghley, might continue to take exception to satirical beast fables certainly combined to create a chilling effect on the production of satirical poetry in the first years of the seventeenth century. With the accession of James I to the English throne, we see authors cautiously working to find the line of satirical safety without crossing it. Certainly, beast fables did not immediately become "safe" in 1599 or in 1603. During the 1590s, beast fables were clearly seen as potentially hazardous: other than Nashe's interpolation of a short beast fable into *Pierce Penilesse His Svpplication to the Diuell*

(1592), the only other published example I know of is Tailboys Dymoke's insect-and-flower fable *Caltha Poetarum*, discussed in Chapter 4, which was published pseudonymously and almost immediately censored in 1599.

One can perceive, in authors' decisions regarding which works to publish and which to keep in manuscript, a hierarchy of "animal fable safety," with authors clearly hoping that birds and insects would be perceived as less objectionable figures to populate an animal fable than foxes, apes, and lions: as already discussed in Chapter 5, Middleton published an insect-and-bird poem, *Father Hubburds Tales*, in 1604. In the same year, Michael Drayton published a bird fable, *The Owle*, which I will discuss more fully in the first part of this chapter. In 1605, Peter Woodhouse published *Democritus His Dreame; or, The Contention between the Elephant and the Flea*, which attempted to forestall the possibility of topical readings by insisting that the animal story was the dream of Democritus, which Democritus narrated within the narrator's own dream:

> A Shadowe of a shadowe thus you see,
> Alas what substance in it then can bee?
> If any thing herein amisse doe seeme:
> Consider 'twas a dreame, dreamt of a dreame.
>
> (Woodhouse, *The Flea*, E2r)[1]

Whether one agrees with Hoyt Hudson that the tale is humorous rather than satirical, or with A.B. Grosart and Arthur Sherbo that the characters do in fact glance at real people, Woodhouse (or "Woodhouse," since all we know about him is that he *may* have been a friend of Thomas Nashe; see Sherbo) takes no chances by repeatedly making the point that there is no matter here, only a dream (Hudson, "John Hepwith's," 59; Grosart qtd. in Hudson, 61; Sherbo, "Tommaso," 427).

In keeping with this idea of a hierarchy or continuum of "safer" animals to fabulize, we can gain some sense of the distance seventeenth-century readers might have perceived between a bird fable and a beast fable by the fact that just two years later, in 1607, Richard Niccols wrote two satires: he published the bird satire *The Cuckow*, but his notably derivative Spenserian beast fable, *The Beggers Ape*, remained unpublished until after his death. John Hepwith (possibly a pseudonym; see Hudson, "John Hepwith's," 40) wrote *The Caledonian Forest*, a beast fable satirizing the Duke of Buckingham, in 1628, but the poem was not published until 1641. Thus, it appears that, in the first decade of the seventeenth century,

---

1 Note that the title page title differs from the in-text and running text title.

English satirists considered *Mother Hubberds Tale* and beast satires in general to remain potentially dangerous satirical forms for imitation or allusion. In this chapter, I will consider the continuing relevance of Spenserian indirection in English satirical poetry—especially animal fables and pastoral satire—in the early years of the seventeenth century.

"Spenserianism" in the early seventeenth century: the Spenserian poets

Many scholars have observed that, in the early seventeenth century, "Spenserianism" became more than a matter of poetic style, becoming instead a means of expressing a reasonably clear set of values through poetry. Decades ago, Joan Grundy, in *The Spenserian Poets*, identified the mindset of these poets as "deeply and positively conservative: they looked back to the past with a conscious and aggressive nostalgia... . [They] were aware of themselves as, in part at least, outsiders," and they valued "patriotism, the English countryside, and the cult of pure beauty" (Grundy, *Spenserian Poets*, 7). Grundy's characterization avoids explicit discussion of politics while still glancing at what are clearly political divisions. David Norbrook addresses the politics of these poets directly, but with the caution that "it is misleading to speak of a formal 'opposition' based on a coherent ideology [because] there might be opposing factions at court but they were often motivated by personal rather than political disagreements." This comment complicates Norbrook's characterization of the group as "alienated from the court and sometimes us[ing] the traditional symbolism of Protestant pastoral to voice their discontent," because they did not all have the same reasons for feeling alienated from the court (Norbrook, *Poetry and Politics*, 175).

Still, it is useful to think of these poets as a group, and Michelle O'Callaghan analyzes the Spenserians in ways that emphasize them as a loose coalition of like-minded individuals rather than a group of same-thinking ideologues. They "engaged with Spenser in order to define their own identities and, just as importantly, to define a community" (O'Callaghan, *Shepheards Nation*, 1). Thinking about what poets signal in the early seventeenth century by adopting a Spenserian style or ethos can help us to see how they used Spenser to connect political and religious affiliations of the late sixteenth century to those of the early seventeenth century. Thinking in this way—that is, analyzing the links between what the Spenserian poets admired or missed from the sixteenth century and what they deplored in the seventeenth, and considering how Spenserianism serves as an shorthand way of making these links visible—allows us to see a throughline connecting Spenser's world with the changed world of the new century, in which different players—a new monarch, a new Cecil, new favorites, new powerful noblemen—often played anew situations that Spenser had observed in his time. In this sense, although Norbrook is right to caution us against seeking "a formal 'opposition' based on a coherent ideology," we can, by thinking diachronically across the turn of the century and the turn of the monarch, see the similarities that connect the Spenserian poets, where synchronic analysis emphasizes their differences.

A few questions and answers—which, I admit, are oversimplifications—will suffice to create an overview of my argument about how diachronic thinking can help to focus some of the concerns of these poets. Who is the Protestant hero who will fight for the English Protestant cause? The Earl of Leicester → Philip Sidney → the Earl of Essex → the new King James (briefly and hopefully, before the character of his reign became apparent) → Prince Henry. Who is the enemy to be vanquished? Not surprisingly, political and religious animosities combine to create two powerful enemies: France and Spain, both Catholic, both shifting over the course of the period under discussion in terms of which seemed the greater threat. Because of how each nation was imagined, with the French danger stemming from their supposed affectedness and luxuriousness and the Spanish danger arising from their military strength and general wiliness, Spain generally had the primary place in the English imaginary of the enemy. Where do virtue and vice reside? Perhaps the question of "where," though answered by the poets, is not as important as calling attention to the fact that they were asking it at all. Although Spenser was hesitant to criticize his queen directly, his responses to this question in such texts as *Mother Hubberds Tale* and *Colin Clouts Come Home Againe*, as well as to some extent in *The Faerie Queene*, show his own awareness of the moral emptiness of some corners of the English royal court, though he balances his satirical criticisms in both *Mother Hubberd* and *Colin Clout* with high praise of some members of the court. Spenserian poets of the seventeenth century, nostalgic for Queen Elizabeth and inspired by Spenser's willingness to criticize, found little to admire in the court, finding virtue instead in the country. (As mentioned in Chapter 5, Thomas Middleton also aligned himself against the court, but with greater allegiance to the city instead of the country.)

Thus, in this chapter I will examine the ways that these early seventeenth-century poets use Spenser and Spenserian indirection to connect their complaints of the new century, the new monarch, the new court, and the new favorites with the ideas and ideals explored by Spenser in the previous century.

Michael Drayton's *The Owle*: the rhetoric of nostalgia and poetic genealogy

By all accounts, Michael Drayton suffered a great disappointment in 1603, when his poetic celebration of the new king, *To the Maiestie of King James: A gratulatorie poem by Michaell Drayton*, failed to garner any positive attention from James. This disappointment presumably led to his anticourt satire, *The Owle*, which he published the following year, although he created deniability that the poem commented in any way upon contemporary events by asserting that he had finished the poem a year earlier but had not yet published it because he had interrupted his work to write a congratulatory poem for the new king: "(it gaue place by my inforcement) vndertaking then in the generall joye of the Kingdome, and my zeale to his Highnesse, to write his Majesties descent in a Poeme gratulatorie" (Drayton, "To the reader," A4r).[2]

Drayton himself blamed his lack of success gaining patronage from King James on his "forward pen," and the apparent corroboration of this interpretation by Henry Chettle, who chides Drayton in *Englands Mourning Garment* for celebrating James before he mourned Elizabeth, has led numerous editors and critics to accept this interpretation.[3] Jean R. Brink argues against this story by noting that other authors, including Chettle, rushed into print immediately after Elizabeth's death; that other authors failed to mourn Elizabeth poetically, with no apparent damage to their ability to gain royal patronage; and that Ben Jonson not only did not mourn Elizabeth before praising James but actually disparaged her in order to flatter Queen Anne. Brink posits that James may have objected to Drayton's somewhat officious advice that he banish "The foole, the Pandar, and the Parasite" from his court, or that—because Drayton had already lost the patronage of Lucy, Countess of Bedford—James may never have seen the poem at all (Brink, *Michael Drayton*, 14–18; Drayton, *To the Maiestie*, line 168).

---

2 Drayton excised this reference to the celebration of King James's accession in the revised version that he published in 1619.
3 See Newdigate, *Michael Drayton*, 125–26, for this interpretation, including quotations from Drayton and Chettle. Grundy (*Spenserian Poets*, 10) and Hardin (*Michael Drayton*, 77) follow Newdigate.

If James did see it, he might have been offended as much by Drayton's tactless references to his parentage as by the advice on how to order his court. James's sensitivity regarding the treatment of his mother is well known to Spenserians from his banning of *The Faerie Queene* in Scotland and his unsuccessful attempts to have Spenser punished for his allegorical treatment of James's mother, Mary, Queen of Scots, in Book 5 of *The Faerie Queene*. Richard McCabe argues that James's efforts to control the message about his mother stemmed not from filial affection but from concern for his own claims to the English throne (McCabe, "Masks," 224), and presumably this sensitivity would be heightened in the period between Elizabeth's death in March 1603 and James's coronation in July of the same year, during which time Drayton published his "gratulatory poem." Cyndia Clegg analyzes James's "Achilles' heel—his sensitivity about his mother, Scotland, and his own security," noting that these issues motivated "most of the acts of personal censorship he performed as King of England" (*Press Censorship Jacobean,* 94); true, Drayton received no official condemnation for his poem, but James did not appreciate or reward it, and Drayton's treatment of James's mother may explain why.

Just as Spenser could easily have chosen to make his treatment of Mary, Queen of Scots, less inflammatory by not naming her allegorized version "Duessa," as McCabe notes, Drayton could have chosen, as John Fenton did, to skirt around references to James's parents. Like Drayton, Fenton chose to highlight James's genealogy and claims to the throne in his *King Iames, His Welcome to England*, but, most tactfully, he skips over two generations of the family tree in order to avoid direct reference to Mary and her disastrous, murderous marriage to James's father, Henry Stuart, Lord Darnley:

> In time of which, this worthy *Richmonds* Earle,
> Had two young Princes, and one Princely gerle.
> *Margret* by name, from out whose lineall race
> Thou didst discend, and iustly claim'st thy place.
> (Fenton, *King Iames*, B1v)

In contrast, Drayton not only provides much fuller details of James's parents' and grandmother's marriages in the poem itself, he also includes an image of James's family tree that, in its tortured efforts to illustrate how Margaret Tudor was one of James's great-grandmothers on both his mother's and his father's sides, serves to represent visually the unusualness of the marital alliances of James's immediate forebears.

Drayton's poem connects James to the royal line of Scotland by referring to James V: "The fifth of that Name, *Scotlands* lawfull King, / Father to *Mary* (long in *England* seene) / The *Daulphins* dowager, the late *Scottish* Queene" and helpfully notes in the margin that Mary was "Maried whilst he was Daulphin," referring to her marriage to James Hepburn, Fourth Earl of Bothwell, the presumed murderer of her second husband (and James's father), Lord Darnley (lines 100–2). Of course the reason Mary was "long in England seene" was that she was the prisoner (or "guest") of Elizabeth for two decades before her execution in 1586. Drayton's attention to James's paternal line creates equally awkward thoughts in a reader's mind:

> But now to *Margarite* backe againe to come,
> From whose so fruitfull, and most blessed wombe
> We bring our full joy, *James* her husband dead,
> Tooke gallant *Anguish* to a second bed,
> To whom ere long she bare a princely gerle,
> Maried to *Lenox,* that brave-issued Earle,
> This beautious *Dowglasse,* as the powers imply,
> Brought that Prince *Henry,* Duke of *Albany,*
> Who in the prime of strength, in youths sum'd pride
> Maried the Scotch Queene on the other side,
> Whose happy bed to that sweet Lord did bring,
> This Brittaine hope, *James* our undoubted King,
> In true succession, as the first of other
> Of *Henries* line by Father, and by Mother.
>
> (lines 103–16)

Marginal notes to lines 106, 109, and 110 identify "Archibald Dowglasse Earle of Anguish," "The Countesse of Lenox," and "Henry Lord Darly [*sic*]," respectively, just in case some less perspicuous readers should lose track of the real people among the poetry. What reasonably well-informed person could read this in 1603 and not think, upon reading of the "happy bed" of Mary and Lord Darnley, of Lord Darnley's eventual murder, less than two years after his ill-fortuned wedding?

Did Drayton have reservations about the new king (such reservations as McCabe thinks motivated Spenser's portrait of Mary in *The Faerie Queene*) and thus wanted to remind readers of James's embarrassing family history? Did he describe his pen as "forward" not because it was too early, but because it was too "forward" in the sense of aggressive (i.e., the opposite of "froward") when he "taught [James's] title to this Ile in rime," that is, the genealogical details of his title to the throne? (Drayton,

To Master George Sandys, lines 20, 22). Did he *accidentally* write a poem that James might have found embarrassing? These questions are unanswerable, but at any rate, the pique that led Drayton to compose the bird satire *The Owle* was presumably at least partly created by James's lack of appreciation for his congratulatory verse of the previous year.

I have already discussed Middleton's *Father Hubburds Tales* as a cautiously yet clearly Spenserian poem that suggests a preference to avoid formal verse satire after the Bishops' Ban targeted his *Micro-Cynicon* and that tested the waters of Jacobean censorship while launching some early critiques of courtly culture under James. That poem, entered into the Stationers' Register on January 3, 1604, was followed shortly thereafter by Drayton's *The Owle* on February 8: another Spenser-inspired animal fable that avoided the animal characters that had gotten Spenser into trouble, sticking to different neighborhoods in the animal kingdom, in this case the birds. The more obviously derivative Spenserian beast fables, which were not published until considerably later in James's reign (and considerably later than their actual times of composition)—Niccols's *The Beggers Ape* and Hepwith's *The Caledonian Forest*—do not interest me as much as these early attempts to "bring back" Spenserian animal-themed satire under the reign of a new king.[4]

I argue here that, in *The Owle*, Drayton contextualizes his satire through allusions that, by and large, "skip a generation" by referencing not Spenser but Spenser's own stated poetic forebears, especially Chaucer and Skelton, but also, in passing, Mantuan. Drayton draws on late medieval bird satires, especially as developed by John Skelton's *Speke Parott*, to allude to Spenser without referencing him too directly. Dense networks of allusions characterize almost all Renaissance literature, and poets use these allusions, especially at times of anxiety, to create or clarify where they are in the literary field, where they stand in, in Bourdieu's phrase, that "space of positions" (Bourdieu, "Field of Cultural," 30). For example, part of the "New Poet" Spenser's self-introduction in 1579 with *The Shepheardes Calender* involved connecting himself with significant predecessors, and so he mimicked medievalism in general, especially Chaucer, and also alluded specifically to Skelton by naming his poetic alter ego Colin Clout. As I've already noted, 1604 was, at least potentially, a more promising time to publish an animal satire than previous years, but that didn't mean it was an entirely safe project. Deniability is essential for the satirist in conditions of harsh censorship, but too much deniability will

---

4 For a full discussion of the Niccols and Hepwith poems, see Hoyt Hudson's discussion of the topical satire contained therein ("John Hepwith's").

blunt the force of the satire. For Drayton, positioning himself through allusions—to Spenser, to Skelton, to the medieval tradition of bird-themed complaints—allows him to steer a middle course between these two possibilities.

In *Spenser's Famous Flight*, Patrick Cheney builds an argument about Spenser's career path upon the widespread use of bird metaphors for poetry, providing a series of examples of avian imagery for poets ranging from the ancient Greeks up to the Renaissance (Cheney, *Spenser's Famous Flight*, 10–11). Cheney does not address the *Complaints* volume, and he generally gives satire a wide berth, but this work on the poet as bird provides valuable context for the medieval bird satires that Drayton draws upon. The three late medieval or early Renaissance bird poems that I will discuss here were all available in print in the second half of the sixteenth century: John Lydgate's *The Churl and the Bird* was republished in 1565, as was the anonymous *Parliament of Birds*; Skelton's *Speke Parott* appeared in an edition for Thomas Marsh in 1568. All of these draw on the poet-bird connections elucidated by Cheney to create satire and social criticism, and Drayton builds upon these as well, combining elements from each of these bird satires to create a thoroughly Spenserian poem without directly alluding to Spenser.

I will briefly discuss these three earlier bird poems before moving into a more detailed discussion of Drayton's poem and how it builds upon themes and motifs from the earlier poems. Lydgate's *The Churl and the Bird* allegorizes the experience of the poet through the tale of a churl who catches a bird singing in a laurel tree and places her in a cage in his house. The bird's location in the laurel tree helps us to identify her as a poet, and the following comment early in the poem cues the reader to seek an allegorical reading:

> And semblably poetes laureate,
>   Bi dirk parables ful convenyent
> Feyne that briddis & bestis of estat—
>   As roial eglis & leones …
>   (Lydgate, *The Churl and the Bird*, lines 15–18)

Upon being caged, the bird tells the churl that she will not sing; the churl threatens to eat her; she replies that she won't make much of a meal, but that if he will release her, she will reward him. He does so, and she proceeds to mock him, boasting of the magic jacinth jewel she has inside her body ("iagounce," line 232), the virtues of which sound like an idealized list of the benefits conferred by poetry: the jacinth not only gives men victory in battle but makes the bearer rich and beloved, brings happiness to all, and so forth (lines 236–49). The poem as a whole presents a satirical message through animal fable; the bird represents a poet but not specifically a satirist, except perhaps in her mockery of the churl for releasing her.

The anonymous *Parliament of Birds* (not to be confused with Chaucer's *Parliament of Fowls*) uses a fairly straightforward animal fable to allegorize the social order. Small birds, such as the robin and the wren, represent "the commons," and they complain to the Eagle-King about two injustices: the king asked all the birds to donate feathers to the Crow; thus enriched by others, the Crow changed from a "knave" to a "knight," but now the birds want their feathers back. More troubling are the rapacity and overreaching of the Hawk, who speaks more than any other character, downplaying the justice of the commons' claims to the King and, indeed, arguing that they should not speak at all (Patterson, *Fables*, 50). The Eagle-King sets both situations to right, and the poem closes with a disclaimer of allegorical intent that nevertheless serves as a reminder to read allegorically:

> Loke thy fethers and wrytyng be dene—
> What they saye and what they mene.
> For here is none other thynge
> But fowles, fethers, and wrytyng.
>
> (*Parliament of Birds*, lines 307–10)

This is of course a satire, but the satirical voice is the narrator's voice, not that of a particular bird speaker.

The most influential example of a bird satirist comes in Skelton's *Speke, Parrott*, and Skelton is certainly aware of the ways that he follows and revises these earlier bird-themed satires. In his insistent repetition of "let Parrot have lyberte to speke," which occurs, with minor variations of wording, three times (Skelton, *Speke Parott*, lines 98, 141, 210), Skelton references the disagreement in *The Parliament of Birds* about which birds have the right to speak to the king. Skelton alludes more directly to Lydgate's *The Churl and the Bird* in his notice to the reader of satirical intent:

> For trowthe in parabyll ye wantonlye pronounce,
> Langagys divers; yet undyr that dothe reste
> Maters more precious than the ryche jacounce.
>
> (lines 364–66)

The "jacounce" or jacinth stone was, of course, the metaphor that Lydgate's bird used to tell the churl about the riches conferred by poetry.

But whereas neither of these other two bird-themed satires had a bird satirist, Skelton's satirical narrative voice is the parrot. It is as though Skelton pondered the bird–poet connections demonstrated by Cheney and illustrated in these other satires and asked himself what kind of bird would represent a satirist. If it's obvious that the eagle will be the king and the wrens will be the commons, who will the satirist be? His answer is the parrot, a mimic and wiseacre whose comprehensive knowledge appears in his ability to speak in multiple languages but who can nevertheless deny that he truly understands what he says: this allegorizes perfectly the pose adopted by many satirists under conditions of oppressive censorship.

In *The Owle*, Drayton alludes to all of these medieval bird satires, demonstrating his "Spenserianism" not through direct reference to Spenser but rather by connecting himself to Spenser's poetic predecessors. By placing his poem within the tradition of bird satires most thoroughly exemplified by Spenser's poetic forebear Skelton, Drayton highlights the imagined poetic genealogy that Spenser created for himself in *The Shepheardes Calender*, connecting himself explicitly to poets two generations back in order to connect himself implicitly to Spenser, his more proximate inspiration for animal-themed indirect satire (on poetic genealogies in general, see Falco, *Conceived Presences*, especially his brief discussion of the genealogy "lead[ing] backward from Spenser's Colin Clout to Skelton to Chaucer," 51).

Spenser had claimed literary and satirical kinship with Skelton by naming his poetic alter ego Colin Clout; during the 1590s and beyond, poetic allusions to Spenser used this pseudonym at least as frequently as his real name, as I have already discussed. Paul McLane has analyzed the significance of Spenser's connecting himself to Skelton in *The Shepheardes Calender*, arguing in particular that Skelton's well-known animosity toward Cardinal Wolsey sharpened the force of Spenser's critiques of Lord Burghley ("Skelton's *Colyn Clout*"). I argue here that contemporaries' close association of Spenser and Skelton through the name Colin meant that Drayton could signal satirical kinship with Spenser by alluding to Skelton. As I already mentioned, bird satires were apparently seen as less inflammatory and potentially dangerous in the first decade of the seventeenth century than beast satires; Drayton also avoids the danger of connecting himself too closely to Skelton by choosing another satirical bird speaker, the owl, while still referencing Skelton's narrator by including his own multilingual parrot: this one a spy who, like Skelton's parrot, knows a *lot* about the goings-on of this bird community. Drayton's "prattling *Parrot*" spies on both his peers and the Spanish; he "had a

Tongue for every Language fit, / A cheverell Conscience, and a searching Wit" (Drayton, *The Owle*, lines 466, 469–70).

In addition to the similarities with Skelton's parrot, we can see connections as well between Drayton and the other bird satires I have discussed. Like the *Parliament of Birds*, *The Owle* engages with questions of freedom of speech, with the Eagle-King granting to the Owl "libertie of speech" and eagerly desiring to hear those things that "all the rest through negligence or feare / Smothred in silence" (lines 325, 322–23). Like Lydgate in *The Churl and the Bird*, Drayton makes it clear that his bird-speaker represents a poet. In the dedicatory epistle to his patron, Sir Walter Aston, Drayton writes,

> The Wreathe is *Ivie* that ingirts our browes
> Wherein this Nights-Bird harb'reth all the day:
> We dare not look at other crowning Boughes,
> But leave the *Lawrell* unto them that may.
> (Drayton, *The Owle*, "To the Honourable Knight, Sir Walter Aston," lines 9–12)

Richard Hardin describes the Owl as "partly the voice of wisdom, partly that of Drayton himself fulfilling what he believed to be one of the sacred roles of the poet" (*Michael Drayton*, 79). By self-consciously referencing the three medieval bird satires already discussed and also making the Owl in some sense a mouthpiece for himself, Drayton illustrates the poet–bird connections studied by Patrick Cheney.

Setting himself up as a bird-poet uses medieval tropes to prime the reader to look for allegorical meanings, but Drayton also circuitously alludes to Spenser twice. In the address "To the Reader," Drayton continues the epistle by excusing himself for writing an animal fable, noting that "the greatest Masters in this Art ... haue written upon as slight matter. As the Princes of the *Greekes* and *Latines*, the first of the Frogs Warre, the latter of a poore Gnat: and VIDA very wittily of the Chest-play and Silke-worme; Besides many other that I could recite of the like kind" (Drayton, *The Owle*, 479). Given that Spenser had written a very famous, much more recent beast satire (in addition to translating *Virgils Gnat*), Drayton's calling attention to unnamed beast satirists calls Spenser to mind. Similarly, he connects himself to Spenser by elegizing Philip Sidney, who, as "the Cocke," receives sixteen lines of fulsome praise and mourning (for identifications of the Cock with Sidney, see Hardin, *Michael Drayton*, 113; Buxton, "Notes," 294n1281; Brink, *Michael Drayton*, 71–72). Drayton avoids Spenser's ambivalent, almost judgmental attitude toward Sidney's death (as discussed in Falco, *Conceived Presences*, 88; Klein, "Spenser's *Astrophel*," 52; Steinberg, "Spenser, Sidney," 194) while still developing one of the key emphases found in Spenser's *Astrophel*: Sidney's excellence as both a warrior *and* a poet. In Spenser's description, Astrophel "both in deeds and words ... nourtred was, / Both wise and hardie" (*Astrophel*, lines 71–72). Drayton precedes the remembrance of the Cock with a lengthy discussion of the virtue of joining words and deeds. The general statement "Vertue, whose chiefe prayse in the Act doth stand, / Could wish the Tongue still coupled with the Hand" leads immediately into the section on the Cock: "But in the *Cocke* which death untimely wrackt, / In him was both the Elegance and Act" (Drayton, *The Owle*, lines 1279–82). Drayton thus links himself to Spenser by noting that he writes the kinds of works that Spenser did: beast fables and elegies for Philip Sidney.

Implied criticism of James and implied kinship with Spenser prime the reader to seek—and find—allegorical identifications of the bird characters in the poem. Though the twenty-first-century reader is at too great a disadvantage to make many hypotheses, an identification of one of the characters with Robert Cecil would be unsurprising in a poet who allied himself with Spenser, the antagonist of Cecil's father, Lord Burghley. Buxton, deciphering an annotated contemporary text, identifies the Vulture as Cecil (Buxton, "Notes," 292n444), but I think it more likely that the Cuckoo represents Cecil. The Cuckoo, like Cecil, is criticized for being corrupt as well as sexually immoral, but those facts are of course too vague to enable a positive identification. Such identification comes from a jest at the expense of Lord Burghley and his anxious attention to matters of genealogy (Alford, *Burghley*, 6, 349n8). In introducing the Cuckoo, Drayton pauses to describe at length the bird's distinguished lineage, including the following lines:

> And since the *Romans* from the *Asian* Broyles,
> Return'd with Conquest and victorious Spoyles.
> The *Cuci* heere continually have beene,
> As by their ancient Evidence is seene.
> Of Consull *Cuccus*, from whose mighty name,
> These liuing Cuccos lineally came.
> (Drayton, *The Owle*, lines 975–80)

My goal here is not to interpret the historical allegory of this poem—John Buxton demonstrates that the allegory was difficult even for contemporaries by noting that, in Beaumont and Fletcher's *The Scornefull Ladie*, "the disappointed Roger asks whether he had gone to all the trouble of expounding the Owl only to be jilted" (*Michael Drayton*, 291–92), and

Richard Hardin argues that for "the uninitiated reader (which class includes all of us)," the general complaints about social ills in the seventeenth century form a sufficiently coherent message of nostalgia for the past, even without adequate understanding of the allegory.[5] Instead, I have aimed to analyze the ways that Drayton uses allusions to a century's worth of bird-themed political satire in order to connect himself with Spenser and thus to signal to his reader the presence of allegory. Drayton hides these connections in plain sight by means of the complex network of subtle allusions to earlier satiric works, creating a branch for himself in the family tree of medieval and Renaissance satirists.

The making of a Spenserian satirist: George Wither, 1613–15

A decade later, it was still dangerous to write satire, and allusions to Spenser still worked in the second decade of the seventeenth century to situate a work in the literary field of satire. This section will explore the ways that George Wither used Spenserianism at the beginning of what would become a very long writing career in order to fashion himself as a bold writer who was, like Spenser, unafraid to speak the truth to those in power. Four works—Wither's *Abuses, Stript and Whipt* (1613); William Browne and collaborators' *Shepherds Pipe* (1614), which included two eclogues by Wither; Wither's *A Satyre Dedicated to His Most Excellent Majestie* (1614); and Wither's *Shepheards Hunting* (1615), which includes Wither's poems from the Browne collection among its five eclogues—together create a story arc of Wither's self-fashioning as a Spenserian satirist.

George Wither's *Abuses, Stript and Whipt* (1613), a collection of formal verse satires that was allusively Spenserian in a similar vein to Middleton's *Micro-Cynicon* (see Chapter 5), landed him in prison for four months in 1614, presumably because Henry Howard, Earl of Northampton, thought the collection criticized him with its reference to the "man-like Monster" who abuses power yet duplicitously escapes detection by the king (Pritchard, "Abuses"). Others have considered the reasons for the delay in punishment, with Pritchard noting the evidence that Princess Elizabeth had shielded Wither from punishment immediately after the work's publication (it was registered with the stationers on January 16, 1613) (Pritchard, "Abuses," 344) and David Norbrook hypothesizing that

---

5 Interested readers should consult Buxton's notes, which include annotations from two seventeenth-century copies of the poem, one from a copy of the poem presented by Drayton to his friend Richard Butcher (Buxton, *Michael Drayton*, 291–94).

Northampton's anxieties in spring 1614 about the upcoming Parliament (what would become the "Addled" Parliament) once again aroused his wrath about Wither's satires and made imprisoning their author seem expedient (*Poetry and Politics*, 188).

The warrant for Wither's arrest was issued from Northampton's house, and Wither remained in prison from March 20 through July 26, 1614 (O'Callaghan, *Shepheards Nation*, 173). Two important events occurred during Wither's imprisonment: the publication of *Shepherds Pipe* and the death of Northampton on June 15. Wither's contributions to *Shepherds Pipe* represent a conciliatory gesture, an attempt to soften Wither's authorial persona and to downplay the offense of *Abuses*, presumably in order to secure his release from prison. The death of Northampton, however, leads to an about-face in Wither's strategies of authorial self-fashioning, with Wither reminding his audience of the boldness of *Abuses*'s "man-like Monster" by referring to monsters in both of the works published after Northampton's death and his own release from prison: *A Satyre* and *Shepheards Hunting*. Whatever threats Northampton posed had died with him in June, and Wither's imprisonment had ended by the time he published both works (though *A Satyre*, entered in the Stationers' Register less than two weeks after Wither's release from prison, was therefore likely composed in part during his imprisonment), so the boldness of the *Satyre* and *Shepheards Hunting* seems somewhat inflated, a strategy of authorial self-representation more than a real satiric intervention into the world of politics. Throughout this story of the young George Wither's development of a public authorial persona, the importance of Spenserianism remains a touchstone, a concept and set of values that inform Wither's work in both formal verse satire and pastoral and that he uses to help him define himself as an author to his readers.

Although Joan Grundy classifies Wither as a Spenserian poet because of his personality and values, not his poetry, asserting that his satires "are not Spenserian at all" (*Spenserian Poets*, 161–62), I disagree. Just as Middleton, amid the numerous entirely un-Spenserian formal verse satires of his contemporaries in the 1590s, evidences an affinity for Spenser through allusion in *Micro-Cynicon*, Wither likewise repeatedly alludes to both Spenser and "Spenserianism" in *Abuses, Stript and Whipt* by his insistent attention to virtues (as Grundy notes, *Spenserian Poets*, 162) and by his sustained use of the beastliness of Man as a metaphoric touchstone for the work as a whole. If one can be "Spenserian" through allusion, not only through imitation, then Wither's *Abuses, Stript and Whipt* meets the criterion. Initially, Wither creates a connection with

Spenser in the same way that satirists of his day often call attention to the presence of allegorical satirical meanings in a work: by arguing that no such connection exists. In apologizing for the "honest plain matter" that he presents, he tells his readers "doe not looke for *Spencers* or *Daniels* well-composed numbers" (Wither, *Abuses*, 17). Here, just as Joseph Hall had done in *Virgidemiarum* (as discussed in Chapter 3), Wither distinguishes the rough style appropriate for satire from the smooth decorum of Spenser's non-satiric works; by doing so, however, he also alludes to Spenser more generally.

Although this is the only reference to Spenser by name, allusions and patterns of animal imagery serve to "activate" Spenser in the mind of his readers. Even twenty-five years after the publication and calling-in of *Mother Hubberds Tale*, animal fables were still very much associated with Spenser, with animal allegory serving to suggest the presence of satire. For example, Thomas Scot, in *Philomythie* (1616), complaining of the hyper-vigilance of his "wondrous witty age" in reading potentially topical allegories, writes, "If Spencer now were living, to report / His Mother Hubberts tale, there would be sport / .... / I dare not for my life in my tale, / Use any English Bird, Beaste, Worme, or Snaile" (qtd. in Clegg, *Press Censorship Jacobean*, 115). George Wither makes the human–animal divide an ordering concept for his exploration of human vices and virtues. His speaker argues in the "Introduction" for the ease with which we can know the natures of various animals:

> The Elephant much loue to Man will show.
> The Tygers, Wolues, and Lyons, we doe finde,
> Are rauenous, fierce, and cruell euen by kinde.
> We know at carryon we shall finde the Crowes,
> And that the Cock the time of midnight knowes.
>
> (Wither, *Abuses*, 43)

He then contrasts the difficulty of understanding the nature of the "Creature called *Man*," who, because of human inconsistency and mutability, is not "*semper idem* in his will, / Nor stands on *this* or *that opinion* still, / But varies" (43, 44). Man is thus *worse* than the beasts, who are at least true to their natures, whereas humans, through their own fault, degenerated from their original state, "made by God; iust and vpright by nature. / ... in his likenesse fram'd," into the collection of vices that Wither will spend the rest of the work detailing and decrying (Wither, *Abuses*, 49). This sense that each of the vices to which Wither devotes an individual satire should be understood as making humans worse than animals becomes a foundational comparison for the work as a whole, and Wither's repeated references and allusions to animals, too numerous to detail fully here, keep this comparison ever in the mind of the reader.

Wither's style in these formal verse satires tends more toward prolixity than aggression, but he occasionally does become more biting. Among the frequent animal imagery, one example stands out, because it does something similar to what I describe in Chapter 3 with Joseph Hall, who alludes to Spenser's *Faerie Queene* several times in *Virgidemiarum*, but with the twist of rendering the Spenserian imagery disgusting in order to fit the antidecorum of satire. I discuss briefly in Chapter 1 Spenser's lines from *Ruines of Time* that lament the ascendancy of Lord Burghley following the death of the Earl of Leicester: "He now is gone, the whiles the Foxe is crept / Into the hole, the which the Badger swept" (*Ruines*, lines 216–17). Wither alludes to these lines, transferring the allegory to a university setting, where older, bachelor scholars, unable to marry, engage in even more shameful acts than the younger scholars, whose vices are mere "mischiefes" in comparison:

> Thence springs it that the Townesmen are reputed,
> Thus by a common voice to be *Cornuted*.
> For I haue known that such haue dayly beene
> Where younger scholers neuer durst be seene.
> And all (vnlesse that they haue eyes like Moles)
> May see those Foxes vse the Badgers holes.
>
> (Wither, *Abuses*, 206)

Both through the university setting and through making the imagery clearly sexual, Wither pushes the anthropomorphism farther than Spenser does. The specifically sexual sense of this animal allegory, with the townsmen in the role of clean badgers being cuckolded by the foxy scholars, adds an extra frisson of disgust to the already rather gross behavior of actual foxes described by Topsell: "The wily Foxe neuer maketh a Denne for himselfe, but finding a badgers caue, in her absence, layeth his excrement at the hole of the denne, the which when the Gray returneth, if she smell (as the sauour is strong) she forbeareth to enter as noisome, and so leaueth her elaborate house to the Fox" (Topsell, *Historie*, 34).

Abuses, Stript and Whipt is obviously not a Spenserian imitation, but although he does not employ prosopopoia to create talking animals that blur the boundaries between human and animal, Wither nevertheless uses his formal verse satires to accomplish the same goal that prosopopoietic animal satires do: highlight and analyze human vice by comparing humans with animals. Book 1, satire 5, "Of Revenge," for example, calls vengeance

> a signe of *Brutish* wildenesse,
> Not fitting any but the *Tyger, Beare,*
> Or such like creatures that remorslesse teare
> What ere they light on. Cast it from you then,
> Be in condition, as in shape y'are *Men.*
>
> (Wither, *Abuses*, 89)

As in Bedell's *Shepherds Tale of the Pouder-Plott*, discussed in Chapter 3, to be "in shape" a human but "in condition" a beast creates uncomfortable classification problems. Similarly, Book 1, satire 14, "Of Cruelty," also questions the assumption that animals are more vicious than humans. All men agree, the narrator asserts, that cruelty is an *"inhumane hellish wickednesse. / A monstrous Passion, so vnfitt to rest / Or harbour in a reasonable brest"* (Wither, *Abuses*, 162). "Inhumane," "monstrous," and the lack of a "reasonable brest" all reference the division between human and animal, and yet "beasts, in whom it rather should remaine, / Doe for the greatest part the same refraine," while the vice appears frequently in humans (Wither, *Abuses*, 162). Over and over again, Wither considers that dividing line and the ways that humans descend into beastliness, thus going against their original and God-given nature, but no one more so than the "man-like Monster" presumed to be the source of the work's offensiveness, leading to Wither's imprisonment:

> The *Picture* of a Beast in *Humane* shape;
> 'Tis neither *Monkey*, nor *Baboone*, nor *Ape*,
> Though neere condition'd. I haue not sought it
> In *Affrick* Deserts, neither haue I brought it
> Out of *Ignota terrà*, those wilde Lands
> Beyond the farthest *Megalanick* strands
> Yeeld not the like; the Fiend liues in this *Ile*,
> And I much mus'd thou spi'dst not all this while
> That man-like *Monster*.
>
> (Wither, *Abuses*, 349–50)

The passage goes on to detail this man's offenses in the court—he appears "meeke, demure / Deuout, chaste, honest, innocent, and pure" when in the presence of the king but shows his true self to "meaner eyes" (Wither, *Abuses*, 350). I am interested here, though, in how Wither dwells upon the human–animal divide. The manlike monster is a "Beast in *Humane* shape," and the references to specific primates and to exotic new lands— where racism blinkered Europeans from recognizing fully their fellow humans—serve as a collage of images to meditate upon the troubling overlap early modern Europeans saw between human and beast. Wither thus attempts and succeeds at an interesting experiment: creating a formal verse satire with significant debts to Spenser and to the rhetorical tropes of animal satire in general.

Allen Pritchard argued in 1963 that Wither owed his imprisonment to the machinations of Henry Howard, Earl of Northampton, but most critics both before and after Pritchard have agreed that Wither's offense was mild, perhaps even unintentional (see especially Clegg, *Press Censorship Jacobean*, 113–16). Pritchard thus writes of "the enthusiasm of admirers who persisted in reading personal satire on Northampton into *Abuses*" (Pritchard, "*Abuses*," 345), and Clegg imagines him as a "political pawn" in Northampton's efforts to ensure the failure of the Addled Parliament of 1614 (*Press Censorship Jacobean*, 115). Michelle O'Callaghan reinforces the idea of Northampton as particularly sensitive to the possibility of print criticism by analyzing the numerous cases of defamation, or *scandalum magnatum*, that he brought to the Star Chamber between 1612 and 1614 (O'Callaghan, *Shepheards Nation*, 172–73; O'Callaghan, "Taking liberties," 156–61). In general, these analyses find two principal offenses offered by Wither's *Abuses*: explicitly anti-Spanish comments, which would have aroused the anger of Northampton, who was crypto-Catholic religiously and pro-Spain politically, and the allegory of the "man-like Monster," presumed to be Northampton.

Yet it seems to me that scholars who believe that Wither offended only unintentionally give too much credence to the claims of his lack of malicious intent put forth by himself and his friends in *Shepherds Pipe, A Satyre*, and *Shepheards Hunting*. I believe this primarily because the shift from the appeasement strategy of *Shepherds Pipe* to the more provoking tone in *A Satyre* and *Shepheards Hunting* can best be explained by the death of Northampton in June 1614. The possibility that Wither's self-presentation as an unusually bold and courageous author contains an element of self-aggrandizement seems particularly likely with *Shepheards Hunting*, which was entered in the Stationers' Register on October 8, 1614, but not published until the following spring (Doelman, "Introduction and notes," 14), by which time Wither had to feel fairly safe (for the moment at least—his pen would get him into trouble again in 1621, when he published *Wither's Motto*).

But in the spring of 1614, when Wither was in prison and Northampton still lived, the work that he and his friends did in *The Shepherds Pipe* to create an image of him as unjustly persecuted gives us a sense of how unsafe he felt then. William Browne and collaborators' *The Shepherds Pipe* is a fairly traditional set of eclogues that use Spenser's *Shepheardes*

Calender as a model for using pastoral to comment on contemporary politics, but the collection also subtly works to create an image of Wither as an inoffensive Spenserian pastoral poet, whose *Abuses, Stript and Whipt* was unjustly interpreted as pointed, specific satire. As a collection of pastorals by multiple poets, *The Shepherds Pipe* creates a sense of a poetic community, as O'Callaghan notes (*Shepheards Nation*, 33–35, 50–51, 61), but this also means that the collection's characterization of Wither as wronged by the justice system communicates group support. The Spenserian rhetoric of the later eclogues, and the specific real-world situations on which they comment, have been well documented by others (see, e.g., Norbrook, *Poetry and Politics*, 186–87; Doelman, "Introduction and notes," *passim*; O'Callaghan, *Shepheards Nation*, chapter 1). I will focus on the ways in which Browne "activates" Spenser in the first eclogue, in which Wither appears as the character Roget, before turning to a consideration of how Wither's own eclogues in the collection create an image of him as a wronged and misunderstood poet who has done nothing to deserve the punishment he receives (in true pastoral style, the Marshalsea Prison becomes, in the eclogues of *Shepherds Pipe* and *Shepheards Hunting*, a cave).

The first eclogue in *The Shepherds Pipe* highlights the importance of Wither's situation by presenting a dialogue between Willy, Browne's alter ego, and Roget, the fictionalized Wither character, who complains of how others misinterpret his poetry, reading topical satire where he intends none. In this eclogue, written by Browne, the character of Roget presents a fictionalized, pastoralized version of the woes that beset Wither before his imprisonment (Willie and Roget meet "upon a greeny Ley" in this eclogue, according to the "Argument," not in the cave that will later serve as his prison). Roget complains, "If I chance to name [an] ass / In my song, it comes to pass, / One or other sure will take it / As his proper name" (Browne, *Shepherds Pipe*, 31). Roget's efforts to enjoy a pastoral *otium*, keeping his "harmless flock of sheep" safe "from wolves and foxes" are all "in vain," because of the "Wicked swains" who work against him with mischiefs such as "break[ing] my lambkins' legs / Or unhang[ing] my wether's bell" (Browne, *Shepherds Pipe*, 32). Having thus characterized Roget as a well-meaning but persecuted shepherd, Browne then moves to connect this poem to the Spenserian tradition, but in an oddly indirect way.

Willy suggests that they pass the time with poetry, and Roget complies by reciting the extremely long tale of Ionathas and Fellicula. The poem was written by Thomas Hoccleve, a contemporary of Chaucer, as Browne informs the reader at the end of the eclogue: "THOMAS HOCCLEVE, one of the privy seal, composed first this tale, and was never till now imprinted... . He wrote in Chaucer's time" (Browne, *Shepherds Pipe*, 54). However, in the hundreds of lines before this revelation, Browne subtly leads the reader to believe that Roget's story is an interpolation of a Spenserian poem by repeated allusions to Spenser both before and after the recitation of the tale.

Willy, in asking Roget to "Make the woods and vallies ring," tells him that "on knap of yonder hill / Some sweet shepherd tune[s] his quill, / And the maidens in a round / Sit (to hear him) on the ground" (Browne, *Shepherds Pipe*, 33), thus alluding to the Mount Acidale episode in Book 6, canto 10 of *The Faerie Queene*, when Colin Clout sings while surrounded by beautiful maidens. Roget agrees to sing a song, telling Willy that he learned the song "Long agon in Janiveere / Of a skillful aged sire, / As we toasted by the fire" (Browne, *Shepherds Pipe*, 33). The reference to the month and to an old shepherd who taught him (though of course Colin Clout is an old man in December, not January) here reminds the reader of Spenser, specifically *The Shepheardes Calender*.

After Roget finishes reciting the story, Willy offers to give him "the best Cosset in my fold, / And a Mazor for a fee" if Roget will teach him the song (Browne, *Shepherds Pipe*, 51), calling to mind the "mazer ywrought of the Maple warre" and "yonder spotted Lambe" that Willy and Perigot pledge as part of their poetic battle in "August" of *The Shepheardes Calender* (lines 26, 37). Roget once again references the Mount Acidale episode by telling Willy that the first singer of the lay "Many times ... hath been seen / With the fairies on the green, / And to them his pipe did sound, / Whilst they dancèd in a round" (Browne, *Shepherds Pipe*, 52). Before the end of the eclogue, when Browne finally identifies the author of the story as Hoccleve, not Spenser, Roget alludes one last time to Spenser by telling Willy that the author was "Scholar unto Tityrus, / Tityrus, the bravest swain / Ever livèd on the plain" (Browne, *Shepherds Pipe*, 53). This allusion serves as a bridge between the contemporary reader's probable expectation that the author is Spenser and Browne's identification of the author as Hoccleve a few lines later: whereas Hoccleve was acquainted with the living Chaucer, Spenser, who was the first to call Chaucer "Tityrus," in *Shepheardes Calender*, presents himself, and was understood by his contemporaries as, a student of Chaucer. Thus here Browne does something quite similar to what Drayton does in *The Owle*; that is, he "skips a generation" in terms of allusions, connecting himself to a forebear of Spenser in order to signal that his readers ought to view the poem as Spenserian, and thus to bring the same reading strategies to this text that they would bring to an example of Spenser's own indirect satire.

Alluding both before and after the tale both to *The Shepheardes Calender* and to Colin Clout's experience on Mount Acidale serves to "activate" Spenser for the text as a whole, so that readers will bring the same reading strategies to this text that they brought to the eclogues of *The Shepheardes Calender*. The text repays such attentive reading, because, in the other eclogues in the collection, we find methods similar to Spenser's in *The Shepheardes Calender* for signaling to his reader to look for allegory or allusion. As with *Shepheardes Calender*, we are not able at this remove to identify with certainty all of the references to contemporary persons or events, but we can nevertheless feel confident that, for example, the very strange name "Weptol" in the second eclogue is supposed to be recognized as strange, and that the reader is to pay attention (Michelle O'Callaghan suggests that the name is an anagram for John Powlet; *Shepheards Nation*, 42). The seventh eclogue, in which Palinode tries to persuade his friend Hobbinoll not to marry the unchaste Phillis, should likely be read as a satire on the wedding of Frances Howard and Robert Carr, Earl of Somerset, as many have noted (see, e.g., Norbrook, *Poetry and Politics*, 186). Palinode reminds Hobbinoll of the time when, hunting filberts, he happened upon Phillis "Like to a new-struck *doe* from out the bushes, / Lacing herself, and red with gamesome blushes" and trying to avoid being seen, but his advice does not alter Hobbinoll's intentions (Browne, *Shepherds Pipe*, 96).

Significantly, though, activating Spenser in this way also creates an association between Roget, Wither's alter ego, and Spenser, as Roget is the one who "Make[s] the woods and vallies ring" with the story that Browne leads the reader to believe is Spenser's. Wither strengthens the association in his own contributions to the collection, Eclogue 9 and Eclogue 11 (which will appear in Wither's *Shepheards Hunting* as, respectively, Eclogue 5 and Eclogue 4). Both eclogues address the question of whether or not to write poetry, rehearsing concerns familiar to any reader of Spenser's "October" and using imagery that also calls to mind Colin Clout and the ladies of Mount Acidale. In each, the Wither character (Thirsis in Eclogue 9, who will become Roget when the eclogue is republished in *Shepheards Hunting*, and Roget in Eclogue 11) encourages his interlocutor to follow his muse with reference to that image: Thirsis tells Alexis that if he sings while shepherding, "Thy sheep to listen will more near thee feed, / The wolves will shun them, birds above thee sing, / And lambkins dance about thee in a ring" (Wither in Browne, *Shepherds Pipe*, 114). In Eclogue 11, Roget reminds Willie of his merit by describing what happened when he sang the previous year at "our last year's revelling": "I saw the lasses cling / Round about thee in a ring" (Wither in Browne, *Shepherds Pipe*, 142).

Wither thus extends the work Browne had already done in the first eclogue to depict him as a Spenserian poet. He does not defend himself strenuously in his poems in *The Shepherds Pipe*; instead, he presents himself as a true poet and puts his only direct words of self-defense into the mouth of Alexis, in a lengthy speech:

> I must confess that long
> In one thing I did do thy nature wrong:
> For, till I marked the aim thy Satyres had
> I thought them overbold and Thirsis mad,
> But since I did more nearly on thee look
> I soon perceived that I had all mistook;
> I saw that of a cynic thou madst show,
> Where since I find that thou wert nothing so,
> And that of many thou much blame hadst got
> When as thy innocence deserved it not.
>   (Wither in Browne, *Shepherds Pipe*, 110–11)

Where other poems in the collection clearly have pointed topical significance, the poems connected with Wither—Browne's Eclogue 1 and Wither's Eclogues 9 and 11—give a wide berth to contemporary England, staying safely in the past or in the world of pastoral to create an image of Wither as a dedicated poet above all else. After the death of Northampton and his release from prison, however, Wither abandons this conciliatory tone and begins the process of representing himself as another kind of Spenserian poet: the fearless poet committed to speaking the truth, even if doing so endangers him.

Wither published his *Satyre Dedicated to His Most Excellent Majestie* in early August 1614, almost immediately after his July 26 release from prison. The conciliatory voice of Wither's *Shepherds Pipe* eclogues is gone, replaced by the stridency and pugnacity that had characterized *Abuses, Stript and Whipt* (O'Callaghan, *Shepheards Nation*, 176; McRae, *Literature, Satire*, 94):

> But know I'me he that entred once the list,
> Gainst all the world to play the *Satyrist*:
> Twas I, that made my measures rough, and rude,
> Daunce arm'd with whips, amid'st the multitude,

> And vnappalled with my charmed *Scrowles*,
> Teaz'd angry *Monsters* in their lurking holes.
>
> (Wither, *Satyre*, B2v)

This reference to a monster early in the poem would likely remind readers of the "man-like Monster" of *Abuses*. This passage clearly depicts Wither's speaker as an intentional teaser of monsters, which surely colors reception of his next reference to monsters, when he claims to have been misunderstood by his "foe," who "doth mis-conster / That which I haue enstil'd a *Man-like Monster*, / To meane some priuate person in the state" (Wither, *Satyre*, B5r). He defends his innocence but also claims for himself the liberty to speak directly to the king, sometimes through allusive references to the same Aesopian rhetoric discussed in the first part of this chapter, as with the numerous uses of animal fable to make a point (e.g., the lion and the "horned beasts," B7v; the mouse and the lion, E8r).

As with *Abuses*, Wither includes a number of allusions that would call Spenser to his reader's mind, most significantly near the end, when he offers King James a poetic work in praise of his daughter, Princess Elizabeth, and abruptly shifts at this point to pastoral language and imagery. He knows how "to tune an Oaten pipe," and so his song in praise of the princess "shall last as long / As there is either *Riuer, Groue*, or *Spring*, / Or *Downe*, for *Sheepe*, or *Shepheards Lad* to sing" (Wither, *Satyre*, F1v). If the song does not please the court, then he will seclude himself on a mountain or in a grove, and "There to my fellow *Shepheards* will I sing, / Tuning my *Reed*, vnto some dancing *Spring*, / .... / Till the *Hilles* answere, and the *Woods* redouble it" (Wither, *Satyre*, F2v). For the Spenserian poets, the echoing woods of Spenser's *Epithalamion* (even though the Virgilian image did not originate with Spenser), along with the image of ladies (or "lambkins," as in Browne's first eclogue of *The Shepherds Pipe*) circling a shepherd-poet, and references to "wolves and foxes," serve frequently to allude to Spenser. Echoing woods appeared in Browne's first eclogue of *The Shepherds Pipe*, and the image will recur in Wither's second eclogue of *The Shepheards Hunting*, when the "loud-loud *Ecchoes*" of his hunting-dog satyres "teare the Wood" (Wither, *Shepheards Hunting*, 2.166). As in *Abuses*, Wither creates in his *Satyre to His ... Majestie* a hybrid voice that combines the harsh language of the typical satirist with characteristic Spenserian allusions to animal fables and pastoral. Presumably written during Wither's imprisonment, the work focuses on Wither's desire for freedom, but the boastful emphasis on his commitment to truth, and his two references to "monsters," suggest that the death of Northampton has already freed Wither somewhat from the fears of censorship and further punishment that must have contributed to his playing it safe in his contributions to *The Shepherds Pipe*.

In *The Shepheards Hunting*, we see Wither out of danger and working to consolidate the events and literary works of the previous two years to create a stable authorial persona as a Spenserian satirist. He presents three new poems (Eclogues 1–3), as well as his two eclogues from Browne's *Shepherds Pipe*, only slightly edited except for the addition of a long passage added to the end of the fifth eclogue of *Shepheards Hunting* that allows Wither to close the collection with Roget reiterating his talent (he has made his cave-prison "Eccho forth delights") and his courage ("And I'le fulfill what my *Muse* drawes mee to, / Maugre all *Jayles*, and *Purgatories* to") (Wither, *Shepheards Hunting*, 5.216, 223–24).[6]

Although Wither's alter ego, Roget, makes some weak references to being misconstrued ("what we speake is tooke as *others* please"; Wither, *Shepheards Hunting*, 1.136), he is generally much more direct here than his character was in *Shepherds Pipe* about being a satirist and intentionally offensive, in part, it seems, because his imprisonment has enhanced his reputation among his peers. Wither's previous works had of course also been published to contribute to his career path, but with other motives as well: *Abuses* aimed at critique, *Shepherds Pipe* at mollifying Northampton, and *Satyre* at gaining Wither's release from prison. Here, however, career interests become paramount: Wither makes frequent references to fame, and he allegorically narrates the events of the previous two years of his life using an inventive combination of elements of beast satire and pastoral that firmly aligns him with the Spenserian tradition of satire. The work as a whole forms a loose narrative. The first eclogue places the work within the same fictional community of *The Shepherds Pipe*; Eclogues 2 and 3 provide an allegorized version of the story of Wither's offense, arrest, and imprisonment; and Eclogues 4 and 5, republished from *Shepherds Pipe*, create an image of Roget/Wither as a poetic leader of his community—a proponent of Spenserian poetic values and an encourager of his friends' poetic efforts.

Eclogue 1 sets the scene in Roget's cave-prison, where Willie (still representing William Browne, as in *Shepherds Pipe*) visits him to share

---

6   Quotations from Wither's *Shepheards Hunting* will be cited parenthetically in the text by eclogue and line numbers. Note that William B. Hunter Jr., the editor of the edition of *Shepheards Hunting* cited here, uses the 1622 republication of the poem in Wither's *Juvenilia* as the copy-text. In the 1622 version, Wither changed the name of his poetic alter ego, Roget, to Philarete ("lover of virtue"), the poetic cognomen that replaced Roget in Wither's later work. Because the name Roget was intended to create a link with the poems in Browne's *Shepherds Pipe*, I continue to refer to this poetic speaker as Roget.

news and commiserate with him about his plight. Roget reassures him that his knowledge of his own innocence makes his imprisonment less painful, and he promises that, if Willie will return the next day, he will tell his whole story. In the second eclogue, Roget fulfills his promise, sharing with Willie and Cuddy an allegorized version of Wither's own story: before his present troubles, Roget's special gift as a shepherd was not shepherding proper but "hunting *Foxes, Wolves,* and *Beasts of Prey*: / That spoyle our *Foulds,* and beare our *Lambs* away" (*Shepheards Hunting,* 2.61–62). He lists his "ten couple" dogs, "Whom by the name of *Satyres* I doe call" (2.181, 182)—he names them all, so that the reader realizes he calls his dogs "Satyres" because each one is named for one of the satires included in *Abuses, Stript and Whipt*—and then describes taking them out to hunt "monsters" (that is, the foxes and wolves that harm the sheep). Roget interrupts his tale, because his jail-keeper calls to him, but he promises to continue the story later if Willie and Cuddy will return.

Eclogue 3 continues the story, with a new friend in attendance, Alexis, who will be Roget's interlocutor in the fifth eclogue (Eclogue 9 from *Shepherds Pipe*). Roget finishes his story, telling of a hunt that sounds similar to Calidore's pursuit of the Blatant Beast into the countryside in Book 6, canto 9, of *The Faerie Queene*:

> Nor crost we onely Ditches, Hedges, Furrowes,
> But Hamlets, Tithings, Parishes, and Burrowes:
> They followed where so ev'r the game did go,
> Through Kitchin, Parlor, Hall, and Chamber to.
> And, as they pass'd the *City,* and the *Court,*
> My *Prince* look'd out, and daign'd to view my sport.
> Which then (although I suffer for it now)
> (If some say true) he liking did allow.
>
> (Wither, *Shepheards Hunting,* 3.52–59)

The dogs hunt so well that soon "every field lay strew'd / With *Monsters,* hurt and slaine," including one "viler, and more subtile then the rest" (3.123–25).[7] To Roget's chagrin, however, the monsters "laide aside their *Foxe* and *Wolvish shapes*" and disguised themselves "in the skinnes of harmlesse Sheepe" in order to gain pity for themselves by showing their wounds to passers-by and blaming Roget and his dogs (3.135, 136). These deluded

---

7 Line 3.125 in Hunter's 1622 copy-text reads "More subtile, and more noysome then the rest." I have substituted "viler, and more subtile then the rest" from the original 1615 publication, because this version makes it clearer in this line and the preceding line that the beast that is "viler and more subtle" than the other monsters is himself a monster, and thus likely the "man-like Monster" that appears in *Abuses, Stript and Whipt* and in *A Satyre to His … Majestie* (Wither, *The Shepherds Hunting, Being, Certaine Eglogs,* D5v).

observers, along with others who "[keep] such *Monsters* tame / … . / … Foxes, Beares, & Wolves, as some great treasure" (3.143, 145), bring about Roget's imprisonment, despite his innocence.

The final two eclogues in the collection have little to say about Roget's present plight; instead, they work together to strengthen the sense of Roget/Wither as a poetic follower of Spenser, as Roget gives wise counsel to his friends, encouraging Willie to continue to compose poetry despite his fear of criticism (Eclogue 4) and advising Alexis on how to integrate a poetic vocation into his active life of shepherding (Eclogue 5). These eclogues' general themes of the value of the poetic vocation are highly reminiscent of Spenser's frequent comments on the topic, especially in "October." Wither highlights the similarity of topics by encouraging the reader to connect the two poems, through the similarity to Spenser's Cuddie's loss of decorum in "October," at which E.K. drily comments, "He seemeth here to be ravished with a Poetical furie. For … the numbers rise so ful, and the verse groweth so big, that it seemeth he hath forgot the meanenesse of shepheards state and stile" ("October," 182n110). Wither calls "October" to the reader's mind by having Willie call Roget back from his flight of poetic fancy in a similar moment of self-consciousness of decorum:

> I doe feare thou wilt be gon,
> Quite above my reach anon.
> The kinde flames of Poesie
> Have now borne thy thoughts so high,
> That they up in Heaven be,
> And have quite forgotten me.
> Call thy selfe to minde againe,
> Are these Raptures for a Swaine,
> That attends on lowly Sheepe,
> And with simple Heards doth keepe?
> (Wither, *Shepheards Hunting*, 4.417–26)

These few examples are only a selection of details that illustrate the pervasive Spenserianism of the collection as a whole, bringing together beast fable and pastoral to create a hybrid form that alludes insistently and originally to Spenser. Whereas we have seen debts to Spenser in satirical poetry downplayed or obfuscated, Wither here seems comfortable paying obvious homage to Spenser in a clearly satirical work. I believe this confidence derives from the fame Wither had achieved through his recent experiences, fame that he references over and over again in *Shepheards Hunting*. Through enduring imprisonment for *Abuses*; keeping his plight before the public through his contributions to *Shepherds Pipe*; and publishing the bold *Satyre to His ... Majestie*, proclaiming his commitment to telling the truth in his poetry, regardless of the consequences (a show of bravery presumably made considerably easier by the death of Wither's enemy, Northampton, two months before the publication of the *Satyre*), Wither had earned the respect and admiration of his peers.

In his own person, Wither alludes to this newfound fame in his "Postscript to the Reader," commenting, "It is very true (I know not by what chance) that I have of late been so highly beholding to *Opinion*, that I wonder how I crept so much into her favour" (Wither, *Shepheards Hunting*, 188). Within the fictional world of the eclogues, the shepherds wax even more effusive about Roget's new fame. In the second eclogue, Cuddy tells Roget, "at all meetings where our *Shepheards* bee, / Now the maine Newes that's extant, is of thee," which leads Roget to acknowledge the fact that if he had not been imprisoned, but rather had stayed on a mountain keeping his sheep, "My *name* should in obscuritie have slept" (Wither, *Shepheards Hunting*, 2.15–16, 19). When Roget finishes his story, in Eclogue 3, his friends project his fame into the future. Cuddy declares, "Beleeve it, heere's a *Tale* will suten well, / For *Shepheards* in another *Age* to tell," and Willie elaborates: "thou shalt be remembred with delight, / By this, hereafter, many a *Winters night*. / For, of this sport another *Age* will ring; / Yea, *Nymphes* that are unborne thereof shall sing" (Wither, *Shepheards Hunting*, 3.162–67).

The boldness that Wither showed both in publishing *Abuses, Stript and Whipt* and in keeping his name, and his story, before the reading public as an example of a true poet unjustly punished for his work served him well by bringing him public fame at a young age (as he mentions several time in *Shepheards Hunting*). His fame in 1615, coupled with his relative safety after the death of Northampton, gave him the freedom to do what the other satirical writers discussed in this book dared not do—to create a clear claim to be recognized by his audience as not just a Spenserian poet but a Spenserian satirist.

Conclusion

In Chapter 1, I offered a contemporary theory of how indirect satire works, focusing on the social process of meaning-making required by this type of satirical work with reference to other recent theoretical works that emphasize the social functions of satire. To conclude, I would like to reverse my chronology to consider the theories and values underlying indirect forms of satire in the late sixteenth and early seventeenth centuries. In developing this argument, we cannot take satirical poets at their word regarding their intentions or methods because of the repeated assertions during this time period—many of which I have quoted in this book—advising the reader against reading allegorically and claiming that only general criticisms are intended.

Early modern literary theory does not shed much light on indirect satire because the connections that, for example, George Puttenham and Philip Sidney make between satire and comedy thus emphasize more aggressive, direct forms of satire. Sidney's brief description asserts that satire will "make a man laugh at folly, and (at length ashamed) to laugh at himself" and that it "giveth us to feel how many headaches a passionate life bringeth us to" (Sidney, *Defence*, 128). Like Sidney, Puttenham emphasizes what George A. Test would refer to as the "laughter" trait in satire by linking it explicitly to dramatic comedies. In Puttenham's version of the history of generic forms, he claims that satire's "most bitter invective against vice and vicious men" gave way over time to dramatic comedy of two types: the first kind—the so-called Old Comedy of the Greeks— "was somewhat sharp and bitter after the nature of the satire, openly and by express names taxing men more maliciously and impudently than became"; over time, this became the less bitter New Comedy, "more civil and pleasant a great deal and not touching any man by name, but in a certain generality glancing at every abuse" (Puttenham, *Art*, 120, 121, 122). Here Puttenham, although explicitly discussing dramatic comedy, describes the contrast between what I referred to in Chapter 1 as direct satire and general satire.

Puttenham and Sidney do not discuss what I call "indirect satire" in their passages about satire. Rather, we see this type of writing described in their passages on pastoral, as already quoted in Chapter 2 (in pastoral, Puttenham writes, poets use "rude speeches to insinuate and glance at greater matters"; *Art*, 128; and according to Sidney, poets "under the pretty tales of wolves and sheep" sometimes "include the whole considerations of wrongdoing and patience"; *Defence*, 127). Certainly all of the writers discussed in this book had a clear understanding of how literary works could subversively speak to sensitive political topics, but it was not expedient to analyze this process or to call attention to it in works of literary theory.

Given the emphasis on willful obfuscation and deniability that we find in satiric poetry of this time period, it is not surprising that one of the fullest treatments of what satire is and does appears as an allegory in George Gascoigne's *Steele Glas* (1576), in which the story of the twins Poesys and Satyra (born to Plain Dealing and Simplicity) follows the plot of the myth of Procne and Philomela, with Satyra the sister raped and disfigured by her sister's cruel husband, Vain Delight. Gascoigne's myth of origin explains Satyra's ability to speak against vice: "the mighty gods" "have ... deignd ... / That with the stumps of my reproved tong, / I may sometimes, *Reprovers* deedes reprove, / And sing a verse, to make them see themselves" (*Steele Glas*, lines 132, 135–38). These two sisters, both children of Plain Dealing and Simplicity, represent allegorically the poetry of praise and blame deriving from the theory of epideictic literature (see, e.g., Hardison, *Enduring Monument*). Not surprisingly, both sisters are vulnerable to Vain Delight, but their shared allegorical parentage indicates that both are valuable. Gascoigne presents the remainder of the work, a formal verse satire that castigates various abuses, as the song of the raped and wounded Satyra. Gascoigne's allegory fits with Spenser's consistently expressed opinions about poetry, exemplified in *Mother Hubberds Tale* in the statement that poets' "onely pride / Is virtue to advaunce, and vice deride" (lines 811–12).

Thus, there exists no early modern English theory of indirect satire, and indeed, the theory of satire in general in this time period is confused and incomplete, in part no doubt because of the sense that it was safer not to speak too clearly about the ways that poets could and did criticize those in power. We can see this emphasis on discretion in Thomas Nashe's abuse of Gabriel Harvey for criticizing Spenser's malcontentedness in *Mother Hubberds Tale*: "If any man were vndeseruedly toucht in it, thou hast reuiued his disgrace that was so toucht in it, by renaming it, when it was worn out of al mens mouths and minds" (Nashe, *Strange Newes*, 282). There is a lack of theory and also a lack of continuity in the tradition, which, as I mentioned in the Introduction, gave way to more direct satire by the eighteenth century, presumably because writers came to feel more safe from censorship and prosecution.

But there is no lack of evidence for a *practice* of indirect satire in the late sixteenth and early seventeenth centuries in England, and Edmund Spenser, a towering figure in more canonical genres of poetry by the 1590s, became for English satirists in this time period a touchstone: his personal fame and his well-understood values and political and religious opinions meant that other poets could succinctly telegraph a whole set of values just by alluding to him. His own (in)famous works in the vein of indirect satire built upon previous work by authors such as Chaucer, Skelton, and others to create certain key images and ideas that could signal an oppositional stance or a satirical approach to a topic. Most importantly, his expertise with allegorical meaning-making made him remarkably inventive when using allegorical tools such as allusion, symbol, and analogy to create satirical meanings through allegorical projection, and this clearly inspired some of the inventiveness in others' satirical poetry analyzed in this book.

Spenser did not invent indirect satire, and the waning of the particular tradition of Spenserian indirect satire in England did not mean the end of indirection in satire. Writers in oppressive cultures with strict censorship will use the same tools—allusion, symbol, and analogy—to prompt their readers to project allegorical meaning from the text to the real world. Within each such culture, though, artists must create a shared set of ideas, images, and symbols in order to develop the kind of linked network of satirical writing that I describe here as a "tradition," but that I could also call a "system," in Itamar Even-Zohar's sense of one coherent part of a literary polysystem (see Chapter 3).

For the writers discussed in this book, Spenser's supremacy in the overall literary polysystem of late sixteenth-century England enabled the shared ideas signaled by "Spenser" and Spenserianism to provide coherence to a certain approach to politically engaged poetry—Spenserian indirect satire. I hope that other scholars will use these ideas as lenses to explore other works from this tradition and to look at other times and places to see how oppressive conditions result in indirect satire elsewhere. Recent work by satire theorists has focused on the social work that satire performs; in this book I have aimed to build upon this work to explore the impact of the social world on satire—from the way that social conditions can inhibit or promote certain approaches to satire to the necessity of shared ideas, images, and symbols between author and reader in order for the reader to correctly project allegorical meanings. Most importantly, though, I have argued that for his contemporaries, the name "Spenser" meant more than it does to us now, four hundred years later, when we think of his reputation as resting primarily on his work in epic and pastoral. In Philippe Codde's terms (see Chapter 3), Spenser in the 1590s was so "canonized" as an author that even his work in noncanonized genres such as satire became "central" and influential for other poets (Codde, "Polysystem theory," 104n18). He was in his time a complete poet, and his reputation for and influence on satirical poetry should become part of our understanding of what Spenser meant to his contemporaries.

Bibliography

Primary works

Anonymous libel, 1612. *Newsletters from the Archpresbyterate of George Birkhead* 193 (from Archives of the Archdiocese of Westminster, Series A, AAW A XI, no. 136, pp. 369–72). Available at: www.earlystuartlibels.net/htdocs/cecil_section/D16.html.

Bedell, William. *A Protestant Memorial; or, The Shepherd's Tale of the Pouder-Plott: A Poem in Spenser's Style.* London: 1713. Accessed through Eighteenth-Century Collections Online.

Bellany, Alastair, and Andrew McRae, eds., "Early Stuart Libels: an edition of poetry from manuscript sources." *Early Modern Literary Studies,* Text Series I (2005). Available at: www.earlystuartlibels.net/htdocs/index.html.

Bion. "Fragment XIII." *Bion of Smyrna: The Fragments and the* Adonis. Ed. J.D. Reed. Cambridge: Cambridge University Press, 1997. 117–19.

Browne, William. *The Shepherds Pipe. Early Stuart Pastoral: The Shepherds Pipe by William Browne and Others and The Shepherd's Hunting by George Wither.* Ed. James Doelman. Toronto: Centre for Reformation and Renaissance Studies Publications, 1999. 21–151.

Burnet, Gilbert. *The Life of William Bedell, D.D., Lord Bishop of Kilmore in Ireland.* London: John Southby, 1685. Accessed through Early English Books Online.

Burton, William. *The Rowsing of the Sluggard, in 7. Sermons.* London: 1595. Accessed through Early English Books Online.

Carlton, Richard. *Madrigals to Fiue Voyces.* London: 1601. Accessed through Early English Books Online.

Catullus. *The Poems of Gaius Valerius Catullus.* Trans. F.W. Cornish. *Catullus, Tibullus, and Pervigilium Veneris.* Loeb Classical Library. Cambridge, MA: Harvard University Press, 1962. 1–183.

Chaucer, Geoffrey. *The Book of the Duchess. The Riverside Chaucer.* 3rd ed. Ed. Larry D. Benson. Boston: Houghton Mifflin, 1987. 329–46.

Chaucer, Geoffrey. *General Prologue. The Canterbury Tales. The Riverside Chaucer.* 3rd ed. Ed. Larry D. Benson. Boston: Houghton Mifflin, 1987. 23–36.

Chaucer, Geoffrey. *The Nun's Priest's Tale. The Canterbury Tales. The Riverside*

Chaucer. 3rd ed. Ed. Larry D. Benson. Boston: Houghton Mifflin, 1987. 253–61.

Chaucer, Geoffrey. *The Pardoner's Tale*. *The Canterbury Tales*. *The Riverside Chaucer*. 3rd ed. Ed. Larry D. Benson. Boston: Houghton Mifflin, 1987. 193–202.

Chettle, Henry. *Englands Mourning Garment*. London: 1603. Accessed through Early English Books Online.

Churchyard, Thomas. "If slouth and tract of time." John Skelton, *Pithy Pleasaunt and Profitable Works of Maister Skelton, Poete Laureate*. London: Thomas Marsh, 1568. A3r–A5r. Accessed through Early English Books Online.

Clogie, Alexander. *Speculum Episcoporum; or, The Apostolick Bishop. Two Biographies of William Bedell, Bishop of Kilmore, with a Selection of His Letters and an Unpublished Treatise*. Ed. E.S. Shuckburgh. Cambridge: Cambridge University Press, 1902. 76–213. Accessed through Google Books.

Copland, Robert. *The Kalender of Shepardes*. London: 1570. Accessed through Early English Books Online.

de la Primaudaye, Pierre. *The Third Volume of the French Academie*. London: George Bishop, 1601. Accessed through Early English Books Online.

Dodoens, Rembert. *A Nievve Herball, or Historie of Plantes*. Trans. Henry Lyte. London: Gerard Dewes, 1578. Accessed through Early English Books Online.

Donne, John. *The Progress of the Soul (Metempsychosis)*. *John Donne: The Complete English Poems*. Ed. A.J. Smith. Harmondsworth: Penguin Books, 1971. 176–93.

Drayton, Michael. *The Owle*. *The Works of Michael Drayton, Vol. 2*. Ed. J. William Hebel. Oxford: Basil Blackwell, 1961. 477–514.

Drayton, Michael. *To Master George Sandys*. *The Works of Michael Drayton, Vol. 3*. Ed. J. William Hebel. Oxford: Basil Blackwell, 1961. 206–8.

Drayton, Michael. *To the Maiestie of King James: A Gratulatorie Poem by Michaell Drayton*. *The Works of Michael Drayton, Vol. 1*. Ed. J. William Hebel. Oxford: Basil Blackwell, 1961. 469–77.

Drayton, Michael. "To the reader." *The Owle*. London: 1604. A4r. Accessed through Early English Books Online.

Dymoke, Tailboys [Thomas Cutwode]. *Caltha Poetarum; or, The Bumble Bee*. London: Thomas Creede, for Richard Olive, 1599. Accessed through Early English Books Online.

Fenton, John. *King Iames, His Welcome to England*. London: 1603. Accessed through Early English Books Online.

Fletcher, Phineas. *The Purple Island, or, The Isle of Man Together with Piscatorie Eclogs and Other Poeticall Miscellanies*. Cambridge: Printers to the University of Cambridge, 1633. Accessed through Early English Books Online.

Foxe, John. *The First Volume of the Ecclesiasticall History... [Actes and Monuments]*. London: John Day, 1576. Accessed through Early English Books Online.

Gascoigne, George. "The author to the reader." *The Steele Glas*. *George Gascoigne's The Steele Glas and The Complainte of Phylomene*. Ed. William L. Wallace. Salzburg: Institut für Englische Sprache und Literatur, Universität Salzburg, 1975. 92–93.

Gascoigne, George. *The Steele Glas. George Gascoigne's* The Steele Glas *and* The Complainte of Phylomene. Ed. William L. Wallace. Salzburg: Institut für Englische Sprache und Literatur, Universität Salzburg, 1975. 86–138.
Guilpin, Everard. "Satyre Preludium." *Skialetheia, or, A Shadowe of Truth, in Certaine Epigrams and Satyres.* Ed. D. Allen Carroll. Chapel Hill: University of North Carolina Press, 1974.
Hall, Joseph. *Virgidemiae. The Poems of Joseph Hall, Bishop of Exeter and Norwich.* Ed. Arnold Davenport. Liverpool: Liverpool University Press, 1969; originally published 1949. 5–99.
Harvey, Gabriel. *Fovre Letters and Certeine Sonnets ..., 1592.* Ed. G.B. Harrison. New York: Barnes & Noble, 1966.
Harvey, Gabriel. "Letter V." *The Works of Edmund Spenser. A Variorum Edition. The Prose Works.* Ed. Rudolf Gottfried. Baltimore: The Johns Hopkins Press, 1949. 463–77.
Harvey, Gabriel. *Pierces Supererogation, or, A New Prayse of the Olde Asse.* London: 1593. Accessed through Early English Books Online.
Harvey, John. *A Discoursiue Probleme Concerning Prophesies ...* London: 1588. Accessed through Early English Books Online.
Jewel, John. *A Replie vnto M. Hardinges Ansvveare ...* London: 1565. Accessed through Early English Books Online.
Jones, T. Wharton, ed. *A True Relation of the Life and Death of the Right Reverend Father in God William Bedell.* London: Camden Society, 1872. Accessed through Google Books.
Juvenal. "Satire 3." *Juvenal and Persius.* Ed and trans. Susanna Morton Braund. Loeb Classical Library 91. Cambridge, MA: Harvard University Press, 2004. 164–93.
Lydgate, John. *The Churl and the Bird. The Minor Poems of John Lydgate: Part II: Secular Poems.* Ed. Henry Noble MacCracken. Early English Text Society, Vol. 192. London: Oxford University Press, 1934; repr. 1961. 468–85.
Marcellinus, Ammianus. *Annotations and Conjectures. The Roman Historie.* Trans. Philemon Holland. London: Adam Jslip, 1609. Accessed through Early English Books Online.
Marprelate, Martin [pseud.]. *The Epistle. The Martin Marprelate Tracts: A Modernized and Annotated Edition.* Ed. Joseph Black. Cambridge: Cambridge University Press, 2008. 1–45.
Marston, John. "In lectores." *The Scourge of Villainy. John Marston: The Works, Vol. III.* Ed. A.H. Bullen. New York: Georg Olms Verlag, 1970. 295–382.
Marvell, Andrew. "Second Song." *Miscellaneous Poems.* London: R. Boulter, 1681. 138–39. Accessed through Early English Books Online.
Middleton, Thomas. *Microcynicon: Six Snarling Satires.* Ed. Wendy Wall. *Thomas Middleton: The Collected Works.* Ed. Gary Taylor and John Lavagnino. Oxford: Clarendon Press, 2007. 1970–84.
Middleton, Thomas. *The Nightingale and the Ant* and *Father Hubburd's Tales.* Ed. Adrian Weiss. *Thomas Middleton: The Collected Works.* Ed. Gary Taylor and

John Lavagnino. Oxford: Clarendon Press, 2007. 149–82.
Middleton, Thomas. *The Triumphs of Truth.* Ed. David M. Bergeron. *Thomas Middleton: The Collected Works.* Ed. Gary Taylor and John Lavagnino. Oxford: Clarendon Press, 2007. 963–76.
Middleton, Thomas. *The Wisdom of Solomon Paraphrased.* Ed. G. B. Shand. *Thomas Middleton: The Collected Works.* Ed. Gary Taylor and John Lavagnino. Oxford: Clarendon Press, 2007. 1915–69.
Nashe, Thomas. *The Choise of Valentines. The Works of Thomas Nashe, Vol. III.* Ed. Ronald B. McKerrow. New York: Barnes & Noble, 1965. 397–416.
Nashe, Thomas. "Somewhat to read for them that list." *Syr P.S. His Astrophel and Stella.* London: Thomas Newman, 1591. Accessed through Early English Books Online.
Nashe, Thomas. *Strange Newes. The Works of Thomas Nashe, Vol. I.* Ed. Ronald B. McKerrow. New York: Barnes & Noble, 1965. 247–335.
Ovid. *The Metamorphoses of Ovid.* Trans. Michael Simpson. Amherst: University of Massachusetts Press, 2001.
Paris, Matthew. *Matthaei Paris, monachi Albanensis, Angli, historia maior.* London: 1571. Accessed through Early English Books Online.
The Parliament of Birds. Two Early Renaissance Bird Poems. Ed. Malcolm Andrew. Cranbury, NJ: Associated University Presses, 1984. 59–68.
Parsons, Robert. *An Aduertisement Written to a Secretarie of My L. Treasurers of Ingland ...* Antwerp, 1592. Accessed through Early English Books Online.
A Pastoral Occasion'd by the Arrival of His Royal Highness Prince George of Denmark ... London: N. Thompson, 1683. Accessed through Early English Books Online.
The Proverbs of Solomon [Geneva Bible]. Available at: www.genevabible.org/files/Geneva_Bible/Old_Testament/Proverbs.pdf.
Puttenham, George. *The Art of English Poesy.* Ed. Frank Whigham and Wayne A. Rebhorn. Ithaca: Cornell University Press, 2007.
Raynarde the Foxe [*Here beginneth the booke of Raynarde the Foxe, etc.*]. London: Thomas Gaultier, 1550. Accessed through Early English Books Online.
Ronsard, Pierre de. "L'amour oyseau." *Ronsard: Œuvres completes.* Ed. Jean Céard, Daniel Ménager, and Michel Simonin. Paris: Editions Gallimard, 1993. I.290–91.
Sackville, Thomas. "Sackville's induction." *The Mirror for Magistrates.* Ed. Lily B. Campbell. Cambridge: Cambridge University Press, 1938. 298–317.
Scot, Thomas. *Philomythie ...* London: 1616. Accessed through Early English Books Online.
Shakespeare, William. "Sonnet 130." *The Norton Shakespeare.* Ed. Stephen Greenblatt et al. New York: W.W. Norton, 1997. 1967.
Shakespeare, William. *Venus and Adonis. The Norton Shakespeare.* Ed. Stephen Greenblatt et al. New York: W.W. Norton, 1997. 601–34.
Sidney, Philip. *The Defence of Poesy. Sir Philip Sidney: Selected Prose and Poetry.* 2nd ed. Ed. Robert Kimbrough. Madison: University of Wisconsin Press, 1983. 97–158.

Sidney, Philip. "Sonnet 12." *Astrophil and Stella*. *Sir Philip Sidney: Selected Prose and Poetry.* 2nd ed. Ed. Robert Kimbrough. Madison: University of Wisconsin Press, 1983. 169-70.
Skelton, John. *Agenst Garnesche*. *John Skelton: The Complete English Poems*. Ed. John Scattergood. New Haven: Yale University Press, 1983. 121-34.
Skelton, John. *Collyn Cloute*. *John Skelton: The Complete English Poems*. Ed. John Scattergood. New Haven: Yale University Press, 1983. 246-78.
Skelton, John. *Garlande or Chapelet of Laurell*. *John Skelton: The Complete English Poems*. Ed. John Scattergood. New Haven: Yale University Press, 1983. 312-58.
Skelton, John. *A Replycacion Agaynst Certayne Yong Scolers Abjured of Late*. *John Skelton: The Complete English Poems*. Ed. John Scattergood. New Haven: Yale University Press, 1983. 373-86.
Skelton, John. *Speke Parott*. *John Skelton: The Complete English Poems*. Ed. John Scattergood. New Haven: Yale University Press, 1983. 230-46.
Spenser, Edmund. *Astrophel and The Doleful Lay of Clorinda*. *The Yale Edition of the Shorter Poems of Edmund Spenser*. Ed. William A. Oram et al. New Haven: Yale University Press, 1989. 563-81.
Spenser, Edmund. *Colin Clouts Come Home Againe*. *The Yale Edition of the Shorter Poems of Edmund Spenser*. Ed. William A. Oram et al. New Haven: Yale University Press, 1989. 517-62.
Spenser, Edmund. *Complaints*. *The Yale Edition of the Shorter Poems of Edmund Spenser*. Ed. William A. Oram et al. New Haven: Yale University Press, 1989. 215-457.
Spenser, Edmund. *Daphnaïda*. *The Yale Edition of the Shorter Poems of Edmund Spenser*. Ed. William A. Oram et al. New Haven: Yale University Press, 1989. 485-515.
Spenser, Edmund. *The Faerie Queene*. Ed. A. C. Hamilton, text ed. Hiroshi Yamashita and Toshiyuki Suzuki. Harlow: Pearson Education, 2001.
Spenser, Edmund. *Muiopotmos; or, The Fate of the Butterflie*. *Complaints*. *The Yale Edition of the Shorter Poems of Edmund Spenser*. Ed. William A. Oram et al. New Haven: Yale University Press, 1989. 406-30.
Spenser, Edmund. *Prosopopoia; or, Mother Hubberds Tale*. *Complaints*. *The Yale Edition of the Shorter Poems of Edmund Spenser*. Ed. William A. Oram et al. New Haven: Yale University Press, 1989. 327-79.
Spenser, Edmund. *The Shepheardes Calender*. *The Yale Edition of the Shorter Poems of Edmund Spenser*. Ed. William A. Oram et al. New Haven: Yale University Press, 1989. 1-213.
Spenser, Edmund. *The Ruines of Time*. *Complaints*. *The Yale Edition of the Shorter Poems of Edmund Spenser*. Ed. William A. Oram et al. New Haven: Yale University Press, 1989. 225-61.
Spenser, Edmund. "Sonnet XXXVII." *Amoretti*. *The Yale Edition of the Shorter Poems of Edmund Spenser*. Ed. William A. Oram et al. New Haven: Yale University Press, 1989. 622.
Spenser, Edmund. *The Teares of the Muses*. *Complaints*. *The Yale Edition of the*

Shorter Poems of Edmund Spenser. Ed. William A. Oram et al. New Haven: Yale University Press, 1989. 262–91.

Spenser, Edmund. *A Theatre for Worldlings. The Yale Edition of the Shorter Poems of Edmund Spenser.* Ed. William A. Oram et al. New Haven: Yale University Press, 1989. 459–84.

Threnodia in obitum D. Edouardi Lewkenor Equitis, & D. Susannae coniugis charissimae. London: Samuel Machan, 1606. Accessed through Early English Books Online.

Topsell, Edward. *The Historie of Fovre-Footed Beastes.* London: William Jaggard, 1607. Accessed through Early English Books Online.

Verstegan, Richard. *A Declaration of the True Causes 1592.* Ilkley: Scolar Press, 1977.

Verstegan, Richard. *Odes in Imitation of the Seauen Penitential Psalms ...* Antwerp: A. Conincx, 1601. Accessed through Early English Books Online.

Wadsworth, James, and William Bedell. *The Copies of Certaine Letters Which Haue Passed betweene Spaine and England in Matter of Religion.* London: William Stansby, 1624. Accessed through Early English Books Online.

Walton, Izaak. *Walton's Lives of Dr. John Donne, Sir Henry Wotton, Mr. Richard Hooker, Mr. George Herbert, and Dr. Robert Sanderson.* London: 1867. Accessed through Google Books.

Webbe, William. *A Discourse of English Poetry.* London: 1586. Accessed through Early English Books Online.

Wilkins, John. *An Alphabetical Dictionary. An Essay towards a Real Character, and a Philosophical Language.* London: Samuel Gellibrand and John Martin, 1668. Accessed through Early English Books Online.

Wither, George. *Abvses Stript and Whipt. Juvenilia: Poems by George Wither.* Manchester: Charles S. Simms, for the Spenser Society, 1871. 5–368.

Wither, George. *A Satyre Dedicated to His Most Excellent Majestie.* London: George Norton, 1614. Accessed through Early English Books Online.

Wither, George. *The Shepheards Hunting. The English Spenserians: The Poetry of Giles Fletcher, George Wither, Michael Drayton, Phineas Fletcher, and Henry More.* Ed. William B. Hunter. Salt Lake City: University of Utah Press, 1977. 135–90.

Wither, George. *The Shepherds Hunting, Being, Certaine Eglogs ... .* London: George Norton, 1615. Accessed through Early English Books Online.

Woodhouse, Peter. *The Flea: Sic parva componere magnis.* London: 1605. Accessed through Early English Books Online.

Secondary works

Adams, Simon. "Dudley, Sir Robert (1574–1649)." *Oxford Dictionary of National Biography.* Oxford: Oxford University Press, 2004. www.oxforddnb.com/view/article/8161.

Alford, Stephen. *Burghley: William Cecil at the Court of Elizabeth I.* New Haven: Yale University Press, 2008.

Allen, Don Cameron. "On Spenser's *Muiopotmos*." *Studies in Philology* 53.2 (1956): 141–58.
Allen, Don Cameron. "Three poems on Eros." *Comparative Literature* 8.3 (1956): 177–93.
Anderson, George K. *The Legend of the Wandering Jew*. Providence, RI: Brown University Press, 1965.
Anderson, George K. "The Wandering Jew returns to England." *Journal of English and Germanic Philology* 45.3 (1946): 237–50.
Anderson, Judith H. "Arthur and Argante: parodying the ideal vision." *Reading the Allegorical Intertext: Chaucer, Spenser, Shakespeare, Milton*. Judith H. Anderson. New York: Fordham University Press, 2008. 126–34.
Anderson, Judith H. "Spenser's *Muiopotmos* and Chaucer's *Nun's Priest's Tale*." *Reading the Allegorical Intertext: Chaucer, Spenser, Shakespeare, Milton*. Judith H. Anderson. New York: Fordham University Press, 2008. 109–25.
Anderson, Judith H. "*Venus and Adonis*: Spenser, Shakespeare, and the forms of desire." *Reading the Allegorical Intertext: Chaucer, Spenser, Shakespeare, Milton*. Judith H. Anderson. New York: Fordham University Press, 2008. 201–13.
Ashworth-King, Erin L. *The Ethics of Satire in Early Modern English Literature*. PhD dissertation. Chapel Hill: University of North Carolina, 2009.
Barker, Richard Hindry. *Thomas Middleton*. New York: Columbia University Press, 1958.
Beal, Peter. *Index of English Literary Manuscripts*, 4 vols. London: Mansell; New York: Bowker, 1980.
Ben-Porat, Ziva. "The poetics of literary allusion." *PTL: A Journal for Descriptive Poetics and Theory of Literature* 1 (1976): 105–28.
Bendall, Sarah, Christopher Brooke, and Patrick Collinson. *A History of Emmanuel College, Cambridge*. Woodbridge: Boydell Press, 1999.
Benson, Larry D. "Explanatory notes." *The Riverside Chaucer*. 3rd ed. Ed. Larry D. Benson. Boston: Houghton Mifflin, 1987. 795–1116.
Bergeron, David M. *English Civic Pageantry, 1558–1642*. Rev. ed. Tempe, AZ: Medieval and Renaissance Texts and Studies, 2003.
Berry, Herbert, and E.K. Timings. "Spenser's pension." *Review of English Studies* n.s. 11 (1960): 254–59.
Betts, Hannah. "'The Image of this Queene so quaynt': the pornographic blazon 1588–1603." *Dissing Elizabeth: Negative Representations of Gloriana*. Ed. Julia M. Walker. Durham, NC: Duke University Press, 1998. 153–84.
Black, Joseph. "Introduction." *The Martin Marprelate Tracts: A Modernized and Annotated Edition*. Ed. Joseph Black. Cambridge: Cambridge University Press, 2008. xv–cxi.
Blanchard, W. Scott. "Renaissance prose satire: Italy and England." *A Companion to Satire: Ancient and Modern*. Ed. Ruben Quintero. Oxford: Blackwell, 2007. 118–36.
Blevins, Jacob. *Catullan Consciousness and the Early Modern Lyric in England: From Wyatt to Donne*. Aldershot: Ashgate, 2004.

Bogel, Fredric V. *The Difference Satire Makes: Rhetoric and Reading from Jonson to Byron*. Ithaca: Cornell University Press, 2001.

Bond, Ronald B. "*Invidia* and the allegory of Spenser's 'Muiopotmos.'" *English Studies in Canada* 2 (1976): 144–55.

Boose, Lynda E. "The 1599 Bishops' Ban, Elizabethan pornography, and the sexualization of the Jacobean stage." *Enclosure Acts: Sexuality, Property, and Culture in Early Modern England*. Ed. Richard Burt and John Michael Archer. Ithaca: Cornell University Press, 1994. 185–200.

Boswell, Jackson C. *Spenser Allusions*. Special issue of *Studies in Philology* 109.2 (2012).

Bourdieu, Pierre. "The field of cultural production, or: the economic world reversed." *The Field of Cultural Production: Essays on Art and Literature*. Trans. Richard Nice. New York: Columbia University Press, 1993. 29–73.

Brink, Jean R. *Michael Drayton Revisited*. Boston: Twayne, 1990.

Brink, Jean R. "Who fashioned Edmund Spenser? The textual history of *Complaints*." *Studies in Philology* 88 (1991): 153–68.

Brinkley, Robert A. "Spenser's *Muiopotmos* and the politics of metamorphosis." *ELH* 48.4 (1981): 668–76.

Brown, Eric C. "The allegory of small things: insect eschatology in Spenser's *Muiopotmos*." *Studies in Philology* 99.3 (2002): 247–67.

Brown, Richard Danson. *The New Poet: Novelty and Tradition in Spenser's Complaints*. Liverpool: Liverpool University Press, 1999.

Bruster, Douglas. "The structural transformation of print in late Elizabethan England." *Print, Manuscript, & Performance: The Changing Relations of the Media in Early Modern England*. Ed. Arthur F. Marotti and Michael D. Bristol. Columbus: Ohio State University Press, 2000. 49–89.

Bullen, Arthur Henry. "Thomas Cutwode." *Dictionary of National Biography*. Ed. Leslie Stephen and Sidney Lee. Oxford: Oxford University Press, 1959–60. V.370–71.

Bushnell, Nelson Sherwin. "The Wandering Jew and *The Pardoners Tale*." *Studies in Philology* 28.3 (1931): 450–60.

Buxton, John. "Notes." *Poems of Michael Drayton, Vol. 1*. Cambridge, MA: Harvard University Press, 1953. 289–305.

Byrom, H. J. "Edmund Spenser's first publisher, Hugh Singleton." *The Library* 4th series 14.2 (1933): 121–56.

Camm, Bede. "Robert Dymoke." *Catholic Encyclopedia*, Vol. 12. Ed. Charles Herbermann. New York: Robert Appleton, 1913.

Carracedo, Juan Manuel Castro. "*Pium Vestrum Catullum Britannum*: the influence of Catullus' poetry on John Skelton." *SEDERI* 14 (2004): 3–16.

Carson, Neil. "Collaborative playwriting: the Chettle, Dekker, Heywood syndicate." *Theatre Research International* 14.1 (1989): 13–23.

Cheney, Donald. "Grief and creativity in Spenser's *Daphnaïda*." *Grief and Gender 700–1700*. Ed. Jennifer C. Vaught with Lynne Dickson Bruckner. New York: Palgrave Macmillan, 2003. 123–31.

Cheney, Patrick. *Shakespeare, National Poet-Playwright*. Cambridge: Cambridge University Press, 2004.
Cheney, Patrick. *Spenser's Famous Flight: A Renaissance Idea of a Literary Career*. Toronto: University of Toronto Press, 1993.
Clark, Danielle. "Writing sexual fantasy in the English Renaissance: potency, power and poetry." *Writing and Fantasy*. Ed. Ceri Sullivan and Barbara White. London: Longman, 1999. 109–21.
Clegg, Cyndia Susan. *Press Censorship in Elizabethan England*. Cambridge: Cambridge University Press, 1997.
Clegg, Cyndia Susan. *Press Censorship in Jacobean England*. Cambridge: Cambridge University Press, 2001.
Codde, Philippe. "Polysystem theory revisited: a new comparative introduction." *Poetics Today* 24.1 (2003): 91–126.
Combe, Kirk. "The new voice of political dissent: the transition from complaint to satire." *Theorizing Satire: Essays in Literary Criticism*. Ed. Brian A. Connery and Kirk Combe. New York: St. Martin's Press, 1995. 74–94.
Corthell, Ronald J. "Beginning as a satirist: Joseph Hall's *Virgidemiarum Sixe Bookes*." *SEL: Studies in English Literature, 1500–1900* 23.1 (1983): 47–60.
Corthell, Ronald J. "Donne's *Metempsychosis*: an 'alarum to truth.'" *SEL: Studies in English Literature 1500–1900* 21 (1981): 97–110.
Court, Franklin E. "The theme and structure of Spenser's *Muiopotmos*." *SEL: Studies in English Literature, 1500–1900* 10.1 (1970): 1–15.
Crewe, Jonathan V. *Unredeemed Rhetoric: Thomas Nashe and the Scandal of Authorship*. Baltimore: The Johns Hopkins University Press, 1982.
Crisp, Peter. "Allegory, blending, and possible situations." *Metaphor and Symbol* 20.2 (2005): 115–31.
Croft, Pauline. "The reputation of Robert Cecil: libels, political opinion and popular awareness in the early seventeenth century." *Transactions of the Royal Historical Society* 6th series 1 (1991): 43–69.
Cumming, W.P. "Ovid as a source for Spenser's monster-spawning mud passages." *Modern Language Notes* 45.3 (1930): 166–68.
Cummings, R.M., ed. *Spenser: The Critical Heritage*. New York: Barnes & Noble, 1971.
Danner, Bruce. *Edmund Spenser's War on Lord Burghley*. Basingstoke: Palgrave Macmillan, 2011.
Davenport, Arnold. "Commentary." *The Poems of Joseph Hall, Bishop of Exeter and Norwich*. Ed. Arnold Davenport. Liverpool: Liverpool University Press, 1969; originally published 1949. 157–277.
Davenport, Arnold. "Interfused sources in Joseph Hall's satires." *Review of English Studies* 18.70 (1942): 208–13.
Davenport, Arnold. "Introduction." *The Poems of Joseph Hall, Bishop of Exeter and Norwich*. Ed. Arnold Davenport. Liverpool: Liverpool University Press, 1969; originally published 1949. xiii–lxxxii.
Deamer, Peggy. "Branding the architectural author." *Perspecta* 27 (2005): 42–49.

Deneef, A. Leigh. *Spenser and the Motives of Metaphor.* Durham, NC: Duke University Press, 1982.

Denkinger, Emma Marshall. "Spenser's *Muiopotmos* again." *PMLA* 46.1 (1931): 272–76.

Dent, Robert William. *Proverbial Language in English Drama Exclusive of Shakespeare, 1495–1616.* Berkeley: University of California Press, 1984.

Devereux, Janice, ed. *An Edition of Luke Shepherd's Satires.* Tempe, AZ: Arizona Center for Medieval and Renaissance Studies, 2001.

Doelman, James. "Introduction and notes." *Early Stuart Pastoral: The Shepherds Pipe by William Browne and Others and The Shepherd's Hunting by George Wither.* Ed. James Doelman. Toronto: Centre for Reformation and Renaissance Studies Publications, 1999. 7–19 and *passim.*

Driver, Martha W. "When is a miscellany not miscellaneous? Making sense of the *Kalender of Shepherds.*" *Yearbook of English Studies* 33 (2003): 199–214.

Dubrow, Heather. *Captive Victors: Shakespeare's Narrative Poems and Sonnets.* Ithaca: Cornell University Press, 1987.

Duncan-Jones, Katherine. "City limits: Nashe's 'Choise of Valentines' and Jonson's 'Famous Voyage.'" *Review of English Studies* n.s. 56.224 (2005): 247–62.

Duncan-Jones, Katherine. "'Much ado with red and white': the earliest readers of Shakespeare's *Venus and Adonis* (1593)." *Review of English Studies* 44.176 (1993): 479–501.

Dundas, Judith. "*Muiopotmos*: a world of art." *Yearbook of English Studies* 5 (1975): 30–38.

Dunseath, T.K. *Spenser's Allegory of Justice in Book Five of* The Faerie Queene. Princeton: Princeton University Press, 1968.

Dutton, Richard. *Licensing, Censorship and Authorship in Early Modern England: Buggeswords.* Basingstoke: Palgrave, 2000.

Dutton, Richard. "*Volpone* and beast fable: early modern analogic reading." *Huntington Library Quarterly* 67 (2004): 347–70.

"Dymoke." *Dictionary of National Biography.* Ed. Leslie Stephen and Sidney Lee. Oxford: Oxford University Press, 1921–22. VI.294–96.

Elliott, Robert C. *The Power of Satire: Magic, Ritual, Art.* Princeton: Princeton University Press, 1960.

Escobedo, Andrew. "Daemon lovers: will, personification, and character." *Spenser Studies* 22 (2007): 202–25.

Evans, Robert C. "Nashe's 'Choise' and Chaucer's Pardoner." *ANQ: A Quarterly Journal of Short Articles, Notes, and Reviews* 9.4 (1996): 21–24.

Even-Zohar, Itamar. "Introduction." *Polysystem Studies.* Special issue of *Poetics Today* 11.1 (1990): 1–6.

Even-Zohar, Itamar. "Laws of literary interference." *Polysystem Studies.* Special issue of *Poetics Today* 11.1 (1990): 53–72.

Even-Zohar, Itamar. "The 'literary system.'" *Polysystem Studies.* Special issue of *Poetics Today* 11.1 (1990): 27–44.

Falco, Raphael. *Conceived Presences: Literary Genealogy in Renaissance England.*

Amherst: University of Massachusetts Press, 1994.
Fauconnier, Gilles, and Mark Turner. *The Way We Think: Conceptual Blending and the Mind's Hidden Complexities.* New York: Basic Books, 2002.
Federico, Sylvia. *New Troy: Fantasies of Empire in the Late Middle Ages.* Minneapolis: University of Minnesota Press, 2003.
Foucault, Michel. "What is an author?" *Language, Counter-Memory, Practice: Selected Essays and Interviews by Michel Foucault.* Ed. Donald Bouchard, trans. Donald Bouchard and Sherry Simon. Ithaca: Cornell University Press, 1977. 113–38.
Frantz, David O. "'Leud Priapians' and Renaissance pornography." *SEL: Studies in English Literature, 1500-1900* 12.1 (1971): 157–72.
Friedrich, Walter G. "The Stella of *Astrophel.*" *ELH* 3.2 (1936): 114–39.
Frushell, Richard C. *Edmund Spenser in the Early Eighteenth Century: Education, Imitation, and the Making of a Literary Model.* Pittsburgh, PA: Duquesne University Press, 1999.
Gaisser, Julia Haig. *Catullus and His Renaissance Readers.* Oxford: Clarendon Press, 1993.
Galbraith, Steven K. "'English' black-letter type and Spenser's *Shepheardes Calender.*" *Spenser Studies* 23 (2008): 13–40.
Gibson, Jonathan. "The legal context of Spenser's *Daphnaïda.*" *Review of English Studies* n.s. 55.218 (2004): 24–44.
Gill, R.B. "A purchase of glory: the persona of late Elizabethan satire." *Studies in Philology* 72.4 (1975): 408–18.
Goldberg, Jonathan. *James I and the Politics of Literature: Jonson, Shakespeare, Donne, and Their Contemporaries.* Baltimore: The Johns Hopkins University Press, 1983.
Gregerson, Linda. *The Reformation of the Subject: Spenser, Milton, and the English Protestant Epic.* New York: Cambridge University Press, 1995.
Griffin, Dustin. *Satire: A Critical Reintroduction.* Lexington: University Press of Kentucky, 1994.
Griffiths, Jane. "'An ende of an olde song': Middle English Lyric and the Skeltonic." *Review of English Studies* n.s. 60.247 (2009): 705–22.
Grundy, Joan. *The Spenserian Poets.* London: Edward Arnold, 1969.
Guibbory, Achsah. *Christian Identity, Jews, and Israel in Seventeenth-Century England.* Oxford: Oxford University Press, 2010.
Hadfield, Andrew. *Edmund Spenser: A Life.* Oxford: Oxford University Press, 2012.
Hadfield, Andrew. *Shakespeare, Spenser and the Matter of Britain.* Basingstoke: Palgrave Macmillan, 2004.
Hadfield, Andrew. "Spenser and John Stow." *Notes and Queries* 56.4 (2009): 538–40.
Halpern, Richard. *The Poetics of Primitive Accumulation.* Ithaca: Cornell University Press, 1991.
Hardin, Richard F. "The early poetry of the Gunpowder Plot: myth in the making." *English Literary Renaissance* 22.1 (1992): 62–79.

Hardin, Richard F. *Michael Drayton and the Passing of Elizabethan England*. Lawrence: University of Kansas Press, 1973.

Hardison, O.B., Jr. *The Enduring Monument: A Study of the Idea of Praise in Renaissance Literary Theory and Practice*. Chapel Hill: North Carolina University Press, 1962.

Harris, Brice. "The butterfly in Spenser's 'Muiopotmos.'" *Journal of English and Germanic Philology* 43.3 (1944): 302–16.

Harris, Duncan, and Nancy L. Steffen. "The other side of the garden: an interpretive comparison of Chaucer's *Book of the Duchess* and Spenser's *Daphnaida*." *Journal of Medieval and Renaissance Studies* 8 (1978): 17–36.

Harrison, T.P., Jr. "Spenser, Ronsard, and Bion." *Modern Language Notes* 49.3 (1934): 139–45.

Hart, H.C. "Commentary." *Measure for Measure*. William Shakespeare. London: Methuen, 1905. Accessed through Google Books.

Harwood, Ellen Aprill. "*Venus and Adonis*: Shakespeare's critique of Spenser." *The Journal of the Rutgers University Library* 39 (1977): 44–60.

Hawkins, Peter S. "From mythography to myth-making: Spenser and the *Magna Mater* Cybele." *Sixteenth-Century Journal* 12.3 (1981): 51–64.

Heal, Felicity. *Hospitality in Early Modern England*. Oxford: Clarendon Press, 1990.

Heffner, Ray, Dorothy E. Mason, and Frederick M. Padelford. *Spenser Allusions in the Sixteenth and Seventeenth Centuries*. Special issues of *Studies in Philology*. Part I: 1580–1625. 68.5 (1971); Part II: 1626–1700. 69.5 (1972).

Heinemann, Margot. *Puritanism and Theatre: Thomas Middleton and Opposition Drama under the Early Stuarts*. Cambridge: Cambridge University Press, 1980.

Helgerson, Richard. *Forms of Nationhood: The Elizabethan Writing of England*. Chicago: University of Chicago Press, 1992.

Helgerson, Richard. *Self-Crowned Laureates: Spenser, Jonson, Milton and the Literary System*. Berkeley: University of California Press, 1983.

Henderson, Lizanne, and Edward J. Cowan. *Scottish Fairy Belief: A History*. East Linton: Tuckwell Press, 2001.

Heninger, S.K., Jr. "*The Shepheardes Calender*." *The Spenser Encyclopedia*. Ed. A. C. Hamilton. Toronto: University of Toronto Press, 1990. 645–51.

Henry, Sean. "How doth the little Crocodile improve his shining Tale: contextualizing the crocodile of *Prosopopoia: Or Mother Hubberds Tale*." *Spenser Studies* 23 (2008): 153–79.

Herron, Thomas. "Plucking the Perrot: *Muiopotmos* and Irish politics." *Edmund Spenser: New and Renewed Directions*. Ed. J.B. Lethbridge. Madison, NJ: Fairleigh Dickinson University Press, 2006. 80–118.

Herron, Thomas. "Reforming the fox: Spenser's 'Mother Hubberds Tale,' the beast fables of Barnabe Riche, and Adam Loftus, Archbishop of Dublin." *Studies in Philology* 105.3 (2008): 336–87.

Hibbard, G.R. *Thomas Nashe: A Critical Introduction*. Cambridge, MA: Harvard University Press, 1962.

Hieatt, A. Kent. "The genesis of Shakespeare's *Sonnets*: Spenser's *Ruines of Rome: by Bellay.*" *PMLA* 98 (1983): 800–14; correspondence: *PMLA* 99 (1984): 244–45; *PMLA* 100 (1985): 820–22.
Hile, Rachel E. "Disabling allegories in Edmund Spenser's *Faerie Queene*." *Recovering Disability in Early Modern England.* Ed. Allison Hobgood and David Wood. Columbus: Ohio State University Press, 2013. 88–104.
Hile, Rachel E. "Edmund Spenser and auto/biographical fantasies of social status." *a/b: Auto/Biography Studies* 24.2 (2009): 169–93.
Hilliard, Stephen S. *The Singularity of Thomas Nashe.* Lincoln, NE: University of Nebraska Press, 1986.
Hollander, John. *Melodious Guile: Fictive Pattern in Poetic Language.* New Haven: Yale University Press, 1990.
Holmes, David M. *The Art of Thomas Middleton: A Critical Study.* Oxford: Clarendon Press, 1970.
Hook, Julius. *Eighteenth-Century Imitations of Spenser.* PhD dissertation. Urbana-Champaign: University of Illinois, 1941.
Hotson, Leslie. "Marigold of the poets." *Essays by Divers Hands, Being the Transactions of the Royal Society of Literature in the United Kingdom* 17 (1938): 47–68.
Hotson, Leslie. *Shakespeare's Sonnets Dated and Other Essays.* London: Rupert Hart-Davis, 1949.
Hudson, Hoyt H. "John Hepwith's Spenserian satire upon Buckingham: with some Jacobean analogues." *The Huntington Library Bulletin* 6 (1934): 39–71.
Hulbert, Viola Blackburn. "A new interpretation of Spenser's *Muiopotmos*." *Studies in Philology* 25.2 (1928): 128–48.
Hume, Anthea. *Edmund Spenser: Protestant Poet.* Cambridge: Cambridge University Press, 1984.
Jensen, Ejner J. "Hall and Marston: the role of the satirist." *Satire Newsletter* 4 (1967): 72–83.
Johnson, Lynn Staley. *The Shepheardes Calender: An Introduction.* University Park: Penn State University Press, 1990.
Jones, Mike Rodman. *Radical Pastoral, 1381–1594: Appropriation and the Writing of Religious Controversy.* Farnham: Ashgate, 2011.
Jones, William R. "The Bishops' Ban of 1599 and the ideology of English satire." *Literature Compass* 7.5 (2010): 332–46.
Kaplan, Joel H. "Printer's copy for Thomas Middleton's *The Ant and the Nightingale*." *Papers of the Bibliographical Society of America* 81 (1987): 173–75.
Kay, Dennis. *Melodious Tears: The English Funeral Elegy from Spenser to Milton.* Oxford: Clarendon Press, 1990.
Kernan, Alvin. *The Cankered Muse: Satire of the English Renaissance.* New Haven: Yale University Press, 1959.
King, John N. *Spenser's Poetry and the Reformation Tradition.* Princeton: Princeton University Press, 1990.
King, John. "Spenser's *Shepheardes Calender* and Protestant pastoral satire." *Renaissance Genres: Essays on Theory, History, and Interpretation.* Ed. Barbara

Kiefer Lewalski. Cambridge, MA: Harvard University Press, 1986. 369–98.

Klein, Lisa M. "Spenser's *Astrophel* and the Sidney legend." *Sidney Newsletter & Journal* 12.2 (1993): 42–55.

Lakoff, George, and Mark Johnson. *Metaphors We Live By*. Chicago: University of Chicago Press, 1980.

Lane, Robert. *Shepheards Devises: Edmund Spenser's* Shepheardes Calender *and the Institutions of Elizabethan Society*. Athens: University of Georgia Press, 1993.

Larkum, Eleri. "Dymoke, Tailboys [Thomas Cutwode] (*bap.* 1561, *d.* 1602/3)." *Oxford Dictionary of National Biography*. Oxford: Oxford University Press, 2004. www.oxforddnb.com/view/article/6985.

Lemmi, C.W. "The allegorical meaning of Spenser's *Muiopotmos*." *PMLA* 45.3 (1930): 732–48.

Lemmi, C.W. "Monster-spawning Nile-mud in Spenser." *Modern Language Notes* 41.4 (1926): 234–38.

Lesser, Zachary. "Typographic nostalgia: play-reading, popularity, and the meanings of black letter." *The Book of the Play: Playwrights, Stationers, and Readers in Early Modern England*. Ed. Marta Straznicky. Amherst: University of Massachusetts Press, 2006. 99–126.

Levin, Carole. *The Heart and Stomach of a King: Elizabeth I and the Politics of Sex and Power*. Philadelphia: University of Pennsylvania Press, 1994.

Leyburn, Ellen Douglass. *Satiric Allegory: Mirror of Man*. New Haven: Yale University Press, 1956.

Little, Katherine C. *Transforming Work: Early Modern Pastoral and Late Medieval Poetry*. Notre Dame: University of Notre Dame Press, 2013.

Long, Percy W. "Spenser's 'Muiopotmos.'" *Modern Language Review* 9.4 (1914): 457–62.

Losonczi, Eszter. *The Visual Patterns of the Wandering Jew in the Late Middle Ages*. MA thesis. Budapest: Central European University, 2012. Available at: www.etd.ceu.hu/2012/losonczi_eszter.pdf.

Lucas, Scott. "Diggon Davie and Davy Dicar: Edmund Spenser, Thomas Churchyard, and the poetics of public protest." *Spenser Studies* 16 (2002): 151–65.

Lynn, Richard E. "Ewe/who? recreating Spenser's March eclogue." *Spenser Studies* 26 (2011): 153–78.

Lyons, Jessie M. "Spenser's *Muiopotmos* as an allegory." *PMLA* 31.1 (1916): 90–113.

MacCaffrey, Wallace T. *Queen Elizabeth and the Making of Policy, 1572–1588*. Princeton: Princeton University Press, 1981.

Machosky, Brenda. *Structures of Appearing: Allegory and the Work of Literature*. New York: Fordham University Press, 2013.

Malone, Edmond. "The life of William Shakespeare." *The Plays and Poems of William Shakespeare*, Vol. 2. London: 1821. Accessed through Google Books.

Manley, Lawrence. "Spenser and the city: the minor poems." *Modern Language Quarterly* 43 (1982): 203–27.

Marotti, Arthur F. *Religious Ideology and Cultural Fantasy: Catholic and Anti-Catholic Discourses in Early Modern England*. Notre Dame: University of Notre Dame Press, 2005.
Martin, Ellen E. "Spenser, Chaucer, and the rhetoric of elegy." *Journal of Medieval and Renaissance Studies* 17.1 (1987): 83–109.
Martines, Lauro. *Society and History in English Renaissance Verse*. Oxford: Basil Blackwell, 1985.
Mazzola, Elizabeth. "Sidney, Spenser, and second thoughts: mythology and misgiving in *Muiopotmos*." *Sidney Journal* 18.1 (2000): 57–81.
McCabe, Richard A. "Elizabethan satire and the Bishops' Ban of 1599." *Yearbook of English Studies* 11 (1981): 188–93.
McCabe, Richard A. *Joseph Hall: A Study in Satire and Meditation*. Oxford: Clarendon Press, 1982.
McCabe, Richard A. "The masks of Duessa: Spenser, Mary Queen of Scots, and James VI." *English Literary Renaissance* 17.2 (1987): 224–42.
McCaw, Genevra Lee. *Middleton's Protest against Deceit and Luxury in His Time: An Examination of Six Satiric Plays*. PhD dissertation. New York: Columbia University, 1950.
McKerrow, R.B. "Commentary and introduction." *The Works of Thomas Nashe, Vols. IV and V*. Ed. Ronald B. McKerrow. New York: Barnes & Noble, 1965.
McLane, Paul E. "Skelton's *Colyn Clout* and Spenser's *Shepheardes Calender*." *Studies in Philology* 70.2 (1973): 141–59.
McLane, Paul E. *Spenser's* Shepheardes Calender: *A Study in Elizabethan Allegory*. Notre Dame: University of Notre Dame Press, 1961.
McPeek, James A.S. *Catullus in Strange and Distant Britain*. Cambridge, MA: Harvard University Press, 1939.
McRae, Andrew. *Literature, Satire, and the Early Stuart State*. Cambridge: Cambridge University Press, 2004.
Miller, David Lee. "Laughing at Spenser's *Daphnaida*." *Spenser Studies* 26 (2011): 241–50.
Milton, Anthony. *Catholic and Reformed: The Roman and Protestant Churches in English Protestant Thought, 1600–1640*. Cambridge: Cambridge University Press, 1995.
Moretti, Franco. "Conjectures on world literature." *New Left Review* 1 (Jan–Feb 2000): 54–68.
Moretti, Franco. "More conjectures." *New Left Review* 20 (Mar–Apr 2003): 73–81.
Moulton, Ian Frederick. *Before Pornography: Erotic Writing in Early Modern England*. Oxford: Oxford University Press, 2000.
Mounts, Charles. "Spenser and the Countess of Leicester." *ELH* 19 (1952): 191–202.
Mueller, Janel M. "Donne's epic venture in the *Metempsychosis*." *Modern Philology* 70.2 (1972): 109–37.
Nadal, Thomas William. "Spenser's *Muiopotmos* in relation to Chaucer's *Sir Thopas* and the *Nun's Priest's Tale*." *PMLA* 25.4 (1910): 640–56.

Newdigate, Bernard H. *Michael Drayton and His Circle*. Oxford: Basil Blackwell, 1961.
Nicholl, Charles. *A Cup of News: The Life of Thomas Nashe*. London: Routledge & Kegan Paul, 1984.
Nicholls, Mark. *Investigating Gunpowder Plot*. Manchester: Manchester University Press, 1991.
Nohrnberg, James. *The Analogy of* The Faerie Queene. Princeton: Princeton University Press, 1976.
Norbrook, David. "'The Masque of Truth': court entertainments and international Protestant politics in the early Stuart period." *Seventeenth Century* 1.2 (1986): 81–110.
Norbrook, David. *Poetry and Politics in the English Renaissance*. Rev. ed. Oxford: Oxford University Press, 2002.
O'Callaghan, Michelle. *The "Shepheards Nation": Jacobean Spenserians and Early Stuart Political Culture, 1612–1625*. Oxford: Clarendon Press, 2000.
O'Callaghan, Michelle, "Taking liberties: George Wither's *A Satyre*, libel and the law." *Literature, Politics and Law in Renaissance England*. Ed. Erica Sheen and Lorna Hutson. Basingstoke: Palgrave, 2005, 146–69.
O'Connell, Michael. "*Astrophel*: Spenser's double elegy." *SEL: Studies in English Literature, 1500–1900* 11.1 (1971): 27–35.
Oram, William A. "*Daphnaida* and Spenser's later poetry." *Spenser Studies* 2 (1981): 141–58.
Ornstein, Robert. "The dates of Chapman's tragedies, once more." *Modern Philology* 59 (1961): 61–64.
Palmer, Daryl W. *Hospitable Performances: Dramatic Genre and Cultural Practices in Early Modern England*. West Lafayette, IN: Purdue University Press, 1992.
Pasco, Allan H. *Allusion: A Literary Graft*. Toronto: University of Toronto Press, 1994.
Patterson, Annabel. *Censorship and Interpretation: The Conditions of Writing and Reading in Early Modern England*. Madison: University of Wisconsin Press, 1984.
Patterson, Annabel. *Fables of Power: Aesopian Writing and Political History*. Durham, NC: Duke University Press, 1991.
Patterson, Annabel. "Re-opening the green cabinet: Clément Marot and Edmund Spenser." *English Literary Renaissance* 16 (1986): 44–70.
Patterson, Annabel. "Still reading Spenser after all these years." *English Literary Renaissance* 25 (1995): 432–44.
Perry, Curtis. "The citizen politics of nostalgia: Queen Elizabeth in early Jacobean London." *Journal of Medieval and Renaissance Studies* 23.1 (1993): 89–111.
Peter, John. *Complaint and Satire in Early English Literature*. Oxford: Clarendon Press, 1956.
Peterson, Richard S. "Laurel crown and ape's tail: new light on Spenser's career from Sir Thomas Tresham." *Spenser Studies* 12 (1998): 1–35.
Petti, Anthony G. "Beasts and politics in Elizabethan literature." *Essays and Studies* 16 (1963): 68–90.
Prescott, Anne Lake. "The equinoctial boar: Venus and Adonis in Spenser's

garden, Shakespeare's epyllion, and *Richard III's* England." *Shakespeare and Spenser: Attractive Opposites*. Ed. Julian Lethbridge. Manchester: Manchester University Press, 2008. 168–86.

Prescott, Anne Lake. *French Poets and the English Renaissance*. New Haven: Yale University Press, 1978.

Prescott, Anne Lake. "Housing chessmen and bagging bishops: space and desire in Colonna, 'Rabelais,' and Middleton's *Game at Chess*." *Soundings of Things Done: Essays in Early Modern Literature in Honor of S.K. Heninger Jr*. Ed. Peter E. Medine and Joseph Wittreich. Newark: University of Delaware Press, 1997. 215–33.

Prescott, Anne Lake. "The laurel and the myrtle: Spenser and Ronsard." *Worldmaking Spenser: Explorations in the Early Modern Age*. Ed. Patrick Cheney and Lauren Silberman. Lexington: University Press of Kentucky, 2000. 63–78.

Pritchard, Allen. "*Abuses Stript and Whipt* and Wither's imprisonment." *Review of English Studies* n.s. 14.56 (1963): 337–45.

Questier, Michael C. *Conversion, Politics, and Religion, 1580–1625*. Cambridge: Cambridge University Press, 1996.

Quilligan, Maureen. *The Language of Allegory: Defining the Genre*. Ithaca: Cornell University Press, 1992.

Rabenstein, K.I. "Kirkman, Richard, Bl." *New Catholic Encyclopedia*, Vol. 8. 2nd ed. Detroit: Gale, 2003. 183. *Gale Virtual Reference Library*. Web. 11 Sep 2011.

Radcliffe, David Hill. *Edmund Spenser: A Reception History*. Columbia, SC: Camden House, 1996.

Ramachandran, Ayesha. "Clarion in the Bower of Bliss: poetry and politics in Spenser's 'Muiopotmos.'" *Spenser Studies* 20 (2005): 77–106.

Rambuss, Richard. *Spenser's Secret Career*. Cambridge: Cambridge University Press, 1993.

Randolph, Mary Claire. "The structural design of the formal verse satire." *Philological Quarterly* 21 (1942): 368–84.

Rathborne, Isabel E. "Another interpretation of *Muiopotmos*." *PMLA* 49.4 (1934): 1050–68.

Rebhorn, Wayne A. "Outlandish fears: defining decorum in Renaissance rhetoric." *Intertexts* 4.1 (2000): 3+. *Literature Resource Center*. Web. 16 June 2014.

Renwick, W.L. Commentary. *Daphnaïda and Other Poems by Edmund Spenser*. Ed. W.L. Renwick. London: Scholartis, 1929.

Reuning, Karl. "*The Shepherd's Tale of the Powder Plot*: eine Spenser-Nachahmung." *Beiträge zur Erforschung der Sprache und Kultur Englands und Nordamerikas* 4.2 (1928): 113–54.

Rhodes, Neil. *Elizabethan Grotesque*. London: Routledge & Kegan Paul, 1980.

Richards, Jennifer. *Rhetoric and Courtliness in Early Modern Literature*. Cambridge: Cambridge University Press, 2003.

Riley, Anthony W., and editors. "Marx & Spenser." *The Spenser Encyclopedia*. Ed. A.C. Hamilton. Toronto: University of Toronto Press, 1990. 457–58.

Roller, Lynn E. *In Search of God the Mother: The Cult of Anatolian Cybele*. Berkeley: University of California Press, 1999.

Rosen, Ralph M. *Making Mockery: The Poetics of Ancient Satire*. Classical Culture and Society Vol. 2. Oxford: Oxford University Press, 2007.
Røstvig, Maren-Sofie. *The Hidden Sense*. Maren-Sofie Røstvig, Arvid Losnes, Otto Reinert, and Diderik Roll-Hansen. *The Hidden Sense and Other Essays*. Oslo: Universitetsforlaget, 1963. 1–112.
Rustici, Craig. "*Muiopotmos*: Spenser's 'complaint' against aesthetics." *Spenser Studies* 13 (1999): 165–77.
Salyer, Sandford M. "Hall's satires and the Harvey–Nashe controversy." *Studies in Philology* 25.2 (1928): 149–70.
Segall, Kreg. "Skeltonic anxiety and rumination in *The Shepheardes Calender*." *SEL: Studies in English Literature, 1500–1900* 47.1 (2007): 29–56.
Shaaber, M.A. "The Ant and the Nightingale and Father Hubburds Tales." *The Library Chronicle* 14.2 (1947): 13–16.
Sherbo, Arthur. "Tommaso Garzoni, Thomas Nashe, and 'P.W.'" *Notes and Queries* 50 (248) (4) (2003): 426–27.
Shinn, Abigail. "'Extraordinary discourses of vnnecessarie matter': Spenser's *Shepheardes Calender* and the almanac tradition." *Literature and Popular Culture in Early Modern England*. Ed. Matthew Dimmock and Andrew Hadfield. Farnham: Ashgate, 2009. 137–49.
Silberman, Lauren. "Aesopian prosopopoia: making faces and playing chicken in *Mother Hubberds Tale*." *Spenser Studies* 27 (2012): 221–47.
Smith, Bruce R. *Homosexual Desire in Shakespeare's England: A Cultural Poetics*. Chicago: University of Chicago Press, 1991.
Smith, M. van Wyk. "John Donne's *Metempsychosis* (concluded)." *Review of English Studies* n.s. 24.94 (1973): 141–52.
Spence, Lewis. *The Fairy Tradition in Britain*. London: Rider, 1948.
Spitzer, Leo. "Spenser, *Shepheardes Calendar, March* ll. 61–114, and the Variorum Edition." *Studies in Philology* 47 (1950): 494–505.
Stapleton, M.L. "Nashe and the poetics of obscenity: *The Choise of Valentines*." *Classical and Modern Literature* 12.1 (1991): 29–48.
Stapleton, M.L. "A new source for Thomas Nashe's *The Choise of Valentines*." *English Language Notes* 33.2 (1995): 15–19.
Steane, J. B. "Introduction and notes." *The Unfortunate Traveler and Other Works*. Ed. J.B. Steane. Harmondsworth: Penguin, 1972. 13–44 and *passim*.
Stein, Arnold. "Joseph Hall's imitation of Juvenal." *Modern Language Review* 43.3 (1948): 315–22.
Stein, Harold. "Spenser and William Turner." *Modern Language Notes* 51 (1936): 345–51.
Stein, Harold. *Studies in Spenser's* Complaints. New York: Oxford University Press, 1934.
Steinberg, Glenn. "Idolatrous idylls: Protestant iconoclasm, Spenser's *Daphnaïda*, and Chaucer's *Book of the Duchess*." *Refiguring Chaucer in the Renaissance*. Ed. Theresa M. Krier. Gainesville: University Press of Florida, 1998. 128–43.

Steinberg, Theodore L. "Spenser, Sidney, and the myth of Astrophel." *Spenser Studies* 11 (1990): 187–201.
Strathmann, Ernest A. "The allegorical meaning of Spenser's *Muiopotmos*." *PMLA* 46.3 (1931): 940–46.
Stump, Donald V. "The two deaths of Mary Stuart: historical allegory in Spenser's Book of Justice." *Spenser Studies* 9 (1988): 81–105.
Taylor, Gary. "Thomas Middleton: lives and afterlives." *Thomas Middleton: The Collected Works*. Ed. Gary Taylor and John Lavagnino. Oxford: Clarendon Press, 2007. 25–58.
Test, George A. *Satire: Spirit and Art*. Tampa: University of South Florida Press, 1991.
Turner, Mark. *The Literary Mind*. New York: Oxford University Press, 1996.
Umunc, Himmet. "Chrysogone." *The Spenser Encyclopedia*. Ed. A. C. Hamilton. Toronto: University of Toronto Press, 1990. 153.
van den Berg, Kent T. "'The counterfeit in personation': Spenser's *Prosopopoia, or Mother Hubberds Tale*." *The Author in His Work: Essays on a Problem in Criticism*. Ed. Louis L. Martz and Aubrey Williams. New Haven: Yale University Press, 1978. 85–102.
Varty, Kenneth, ed. *Reynard the Fox: Social Engagement and Cultural Metamorphoses in the Beast Epic from the Middle Ages to the Present*. New York: Berghahn Books, 2000.
Villeponteaux, Mary. "'Not as women wonted be': Spenser's Amazon queen." *Dissing Elizabeth: Negative Representations of Gloriana*. Ed. Julia M. Walker. Durham, NC: Duke University Press, 1998. 209–25.
Wainwright, John B. "Bl. William Lacy." *Catholic Encyclopedia*, Vol. 20. Ed. Charles Herbermann. New York: Robert Appleton, 1913.
Walker, Julia M., ed. *Dissing Elizabeth: Negative Representations of Gloriana*. Durham, NC: Duke University Press, 1998.
Waters, D. Douglas. *Duessa as Theological Satire*. Columbia: University of Missouri Press, 1970.
Weiner, Andrew D. "Spenser's *Muiopotmos* and the fates of butterflies and men." *Journal of English and Germanic Philology* 84.2 (1985): 203–20.
Weiss, Adrian. "Watermark evidence and inference: new style dates of Edmund Spenser's *Complaints* and *Daphnaida*." *Studies in Bibliography* 52 (1999): 129–54.
Williams, Gordon. "Quail." *A Dictionary of Sexual Language and Imagery in Shakespearean and Stuart Literature*. London: Athlone Press, 1994. 1123–25.
Wilson-Okamura, David Scott. *Virgil in the Renaissance*. Cambridge: Cambridge University Press, 2010.
Yachnin, Paul. "*A Game at Chess*: Thomas Middleton's 'Praise of Folly.'" *Modern Language Quarterly: A Journal of Literary History* 48 (1987): 107–23.
Zurcher, Andrew. "Getting it back to front in 1590: Spenser's dedications, Nashe's insinuations, and Ralegh's equivocations." *Studies in the Literary Imagination* 38.2 (2005): 173–98.

Index

Note: Literary works can be found under authors' names. "n." after a page reference indicates the number of a note on that page.

allegorical intuition 13, 27, 28
allegory 7, 11, 12, 13, 14, 22–23, 27–28, 51, 55, 57–60, 73, 74, 76, 77, 101, 131, 133, 156, 160, 173–76
    allegorical meaning-making through allusion, symbol, and analogy 7, 12, 22, 27–30, 60, 175–76
Anderson, Judith 106n.14, 107, 110, 117–18
animal fable *see* fable
animal symbols, metaphors, and allegories 76, 137, 143
    ant 136–41
    ape 11, 13, 19, 20–21, 30, 137, 143, 162
    baboon 137–38, 162
    badger 19, 161
    bear 76–77, 162, 171
    bee 102–8, 111–15, 138
    bird 93–96, 153–58, 166
    boar 76, 116
    butterfly 106–10, 137
    cock 156–57, 160
    crow 95, 154, 160
    cuckoo 157
    dog 15, 76–77, 141, 143, 168, 170
    eagle 154–56
    elephant 160
    fish 143
    fox *see* fox symbols, metaphors, and allegories
    gnat 137
    halcyon/kingfisher 50
    hawk 154
    lion 77, 141, 160, 168
    lioness 54–55, 141
    man as beast 77–78, 143, 159–62
    marmoset 137–38
    mole 161
    monkey 137–38, 162
    mouse 143, 168
    nightingale 136, 138, 140–41
    parrot 155–56
    peacock 91–92, 95–96
    owl 92–93, 95–96, 155–56
    for Robert Cecil 134
    robin 154
    sheep 51, 73, 74, 75, 77, 164, 166–67, 170–72, 174
    spider 104, 106–8, 112
    swine 77
    tiger 77, 160, 162
    vulture 157
    whale 143
    wolf 15, 18, 51, 76–77, 143, 160, 164, 166, 168, 170–71, 174

Index

wren 154–55
Zodon 134
astronomy symbols, metaphors, and allegories
   moon 122
   planet 98
   star 56, 98
   sun 83–84, 98–99, 111, 122

beast fable *see* fable
Bedell, William 8, 65, 71–78, 87, 162
   Shepherd's Tale of the Pouder-Plott 8, 72–78, 162
Bion of Smyrna, "Fragment XIII" 91–96, 100, 115–16
Bishops' Ban (1599) 9, 24, 26, 70, 79, 81, 100–3, 105, 119–20, 127–29, 135, 138, 142, 145, 152
Bogel, Fredric 4, 7, 23, 78
Bourdieu, Pierre 65, 152
branding 65, 69–70, 72–73
Brink, Jean R. 6n.7, 34, 149, 156
Browne, William 75, 124, 145, 158, 163–69
   Shepheards Pipe, The 90, 158–59, 163–70, 172
Burghley, Lord *see* Cecil, William, Lord Burghley

Catullus 8, 39, 42–46
   neoteric or "new" poet 43
   satirical poet 43–44
Cecil, Robert, Earl of Salisbury 14, 19, 21, 35, 76, 108–9, 120–21, 126, 128, 130, 131n.8, 133–36, 141, 143, 145, 148, 157
Cecil, William, Lord Burghley 13–14, 19, 21, 24–25, 30, 34–36, 39, 40n.1, 89, 102, 109, 120–21, 126–28, 130–32, 135, 141, 145, 155, 157
   building at Theobalds estate 21n.4, 22, 30
   as fox 18–19, 21–22, 30, 131, 134, 136, 161
   interest in genealogy 132–33, 157
censorship 5, 12, 25–26, 66–67, 70, 79, 81, 86, 119, 126–27, 135, 142–43, 150, 152, 155, 168, 175
Chaucer, Geoffrey 14–15, 41, 88, 90, 152, 155, 164–65, 175
   Book of the Duchess 39, 48, 50, 53, 55–57, 60, 62
   Canterbury Tales
      General Prologue 114
      Nun's Priest's Tale 14–15, 17, 107
      Pardoner's Tale 60–62
      Sir Thopas 107
   Chaucerianism 11, 90
   as "Old Poet" 8, 39, 41
   Parliament of Fowls 90
Cheney, Patrick 8, 32, 39, 115n.20, 116, 153, 155–56
Churchyard, Thomas 6, 42
Clegg, Cyndia Susan 5, 24n.5, 26, 81, 102–3, 121n.3, 126, 129, 132, 150, 160, 163
Codde, Philippe 68–69, 176
Coleridge, Samuel Taylor 29
complaint 3, 7, 11–14, 17, 20, 22, 39, 68–69n.2, 136, 153
Compton, William, Second Baron Compton 120, 123
Crisp, Peter 27–28
Cutwode, Thomas *see* Dymoke, Tailboys [Thomas Cutwode]

Danner, Bruce 2n.1, 2n.3, 14, 19, 21, 30, 34
Dekker, Thomas 123–24, 131n.8, 141n.13
Devereux, Penelope, Lady Rich 98, 109
   as Sidney's "Stella" 98
Devereux, Robert, Second Earl of Essex 18, 81, 88, 97, 99, 102,

120–23, 126, 129–30, 132, 134, 148
  bee imagery 102–3
  sun imagery, 122
Devereux, Walter, First Earl of Essex 98
Donne, John 9, 142
  Metempsychosis; Poêma Satyricon 9, 142–43
  Satires 142–43
Drayton, Michael 75, 123–24, 145–46, 149–53, 155–58
  Owl, The 4, 9, 68n.2, 146, 149, 152, 155–58, 165
  To the Maiestie of King James 9, 149–51
Dudley, Robert, First Earl of Leicester 19, 32, 76, 90n.4, 96–98, 99, 109, 121–22, 142, 148, 161
Dymoke, Tailboys [Thomas Cutwode] 8, 86, 87, 103, 117, 126
  Caltha Poetarum 8, 79n.9, 81, 87, 100–15, 118, 138, 146
  political and religious sympathies, 105, 118

elegy 19, 46–49, 58, 60, 63, 156–57
Elizabeth I, Queen 5, 13, 18, 36, 67, 70, 121, 127, 129, 145, 149
  as Diana 100, 101, 103
  as fairy queen 117, 141
  nostalgia for 9, 120, 126, 136, 138–39, 141, 144, 148, 158
  as Philomel 138, 141
  praise of 8
  satire of 9, 87, 99, 103, 109–11, 115–16
  as Venus 99–118
"entry codes" and clues 22–23, 31, 40, 46, 87, 110, 130
Escobedo, Andrew 53, 59
Essex, Earl of *see* Devereux, Robert, Second Earl of Essex
Even-Zohar, Itamar 65–68, 70, 175

fable 11–17, 30, 136
  animal/beast fable 9–10, 30, 55, 70, 76–77, 79, 127, 131, 134, 137–38, 141, 143, 145–47, 152, 154, 156–57, 160, 168, 171
  bird fable 127, 146, 152–58
  hierarchy of "animal fable safety" 146
  insect fable 127, 136, 146
Fletcher, Phineas 90
formal verse satire 4, 9, 10, 22, 59, 63, 68n.2, 70, 127–28, 135–36, 143, 145, 158–59, 161, 163, 174
Foxe, John 34, 39, 44
fox symbols, metaphors, and allegories 16n.1, 19, 30
  in Bedell 73, 76–77
  in Browne 164, 168
  in Chaucer 14, 15, 19
  in ecclesiastical pastoral 14, 17–18, 19
  as Lord Burghley 18–19, 21–22, 30, 131, 134, 136, 161
  in Middleton 130–31, 136
  in *Reynard the Fox* 14–17
  in Spenser 7, 13–14, 30, 60, 76, 127, 134
  in Wither 170–71

Gascoigne, George, *Steele Glas* 49, 136, 174
genealogy, literary 4, 8, 38, 41, 44–45, 136, 149, 152, 155
genre 12, 14, 26, 36, 50–51, 53, 57, 60, 66–69, 107–8, 120, 135, 175–76
Gorges, Arthur 39, 47–48, 63
Griffin, Dustin 7, 23
Grundy, Joan 123n.5, 147, 149n.3, 159
Gunpowder Plot 71–78

Index

Hadfield, Andrew 22, 34, 48, 80n.10, 126
Hall, Joseph 8, 63–65, 71–73, 78–87
   attitude toward Spenser 79–80, 128
   Mundus Alter et Idem 79
   political and religious sympathies 86n.14
   Virgidemiarum Sixe Bookes 8, 64, 72, 78–86, 160–61
Harvey, Gabriel 35, 39, 69, 89, 100, 142, 174
Harvey–Nashe controversy *see* Nashe–Harvey controversy
Heinemann, Margot 119n.1, 120n.2, 124
Helgerson, Richard 8, 31–32, 39, 67
Henry, Prince of Wales 148
Hepwith, John, *Caledonian Forest, The* 146, 152
Hibbard, G.R. 88–90
Hoccleve, Thomas 164–65
Hotson, Leslie 101, 103, 114, 117
Howard, Henry, Earl of Northampton 158–59, 163, 167–68, 172
Hudson, Hoyt 4, 70, 146, 152n.4

Jacob's-staff 50, 52, 60
James I, King of England, and James VI, King of Scotland 36, 120, 123–24, 145, 148–52, 168
   genealogy of 150–51
   praise of 8, 73, 141
   satire or criticism of 121, 138, 141, 157
Jonson, Ben 59, 123–24, 149

Kalender of Shepardes 39, 44, 45
Kernan, Alvin 4, 22, 85n.12
King, John N. 6n.6, 41, 81
Knollys, Lettice, Countess of Leicester 32, 90n.4, 96–99, 109

Leicester, Earl of *see* Dudley, Robert, First Earl of Leicester
Leyburn, Ellen Douglass 4, 7
Lucas, Scott 6, 11–12, 42n.2
Lydgate, John, *Churl and the Bird, The* 153–54, 156

McCabe, Richard 25–26, 36, 79, 81, 102, 130, 145, 150–51
McRae, Andrew 24–25, 81, 121, 135, 167
Marlowe, Christopher 83, 88, 116–17
Marston, John 4, 49, 63, 85n.12, 105, 129
   Pigmalions Image 105
Martin Marprelate tracts 5, 13, 24–25
Marvell, Andrew 90
Mary, Queen of Scots 2, 36, 150–51
metaphor 54–57, 74, 114, 122, 153, 159
   cognitive metaphor theory 14, 27–28
Middleton, Thomas 9, 63, 86, 119–44
   Blacke Booke, The 119n.1
   Caesar's Fall; or, Two Shapes 123
   Father Hubburds Tales 9, 119, 122–23, 135–42, 146, 152
   Game at Chess, A 119, 121
   Ghost of Lucrece, The 123
   Marriage of the Old and New Testament, or God's Parliament House, The 124
   Micro-Cynicon 9, 49–50, 84, 119, 126–36, 142, 152, 158–59
   News from Gravesend: Sent to Nobody 123
   political and religious sympathies 118, 119–26, 135, 142, 145, 148
   Triumphs of Truth, The 122, 124–26
   Wisdom of Solomon, Paraphrased, The 121, 126, 129–30, 132
Miller, David Lee 46, 48, 49

Milton, John 3, 72
monster symbols, metaphors, and
    allegories 74, 77, 80, 134,
    158–59, 162–63, 168,
    170–71
Moulton, Ian Frederick 93–94, 99n.10,
    106

Nashe–Harvey controversy 24–25,
    35, 142
Nashe, Thomas 8, 35, 67, 69, 86–87,
    116, 118, 175, 119n.1, 123,
    126, 131n.8, 142, 146,
    174–75
  Choise of Valentines 8–9, 86, 87–
    100
  *Pierce Penilesse His Svpplication to
    the Diuell* 89, 145
  political sympathies 89, 118,
    119n.1
  Unfortunate Traveler, The 116n.21
Niccols, Richard 146
  The Beggers Ape 146, 152
  The Cuckow 146
Nicholl, Charles 88, 97n.9, 98, 99n.11,
    116n.21
Norbrook, David 6n.6, 18, 124, 142,
    147–48, 158–59, 164, 166
Northampton, Earl of *see* Howard,
    Henry, Earl of Northampton

O'Callaghan, Michelle 120n.2, 123n.5,
    127, 147, 159, 163–64,
    166–67
Oram, William 48, 51n.9, 52n.10,
    57–59, 63
Ovid 50, 88, 106, 116, 136–37, 141
  Metamorphoses 48, 50, 139–40

Parliament of Birds 153–54, 156
pastoral 12–14, 51, 58–60, 73–74,
    76, 80, 91, 147, 159, 164,
    168–69, 171, 174
Patterson, Annabel 5, 10–12, 17,
    24, 26, 30–31, 40n.1, 110,
    121n.3, 126, 154
Penry, John 5, 24
personification 29, 51–53, 57–60, 63
Peter, John 4, 22, 26, 68n.2, 81, 102,
    129
Peterson, Richard L. 6n.7, 14, 25–26,
    30, 34, 108, 115
Petrarchanism 98, 114, 117
  satirized as "Calthanism" 104, 111,
    113–14
plant symbols, metaphors, and
    allegories 55–56
  apple 142–43
  box tree 91–94
  flower 55
  fruit 55
  hawthorn 140–41
  ivy 91–92, 156
  laurel 153, 156
  mandrake 143
  marigold 104, 111
  primrose 55
  oak 140–41
  seeds 122
Ponsonby, William 26, 42
Prescott, Anne Lake 40n.1, 91n.5,
    116, 118, 121n.3, 122–23,
    130n.7
Puttenham, George 51, 85, 173–74

Quilligan, Maureen 24, 38–39

Raleigh, Sir Walter 36, 48, 99, 102
Rambuss, Richard 32–33, 97
Reynard the Fox 14, 15–17
Roman Catholicism 103–5, 148
  Catholic imagery 101, 105–6, 110,
    112–15
  English recusants 105, 112
  satire of 74–75, 77–78, 121
Ronsard, Pierre de, "L'amour oyseau"
    91–96, 100, 116

Index

satire 4–5, 13, 22
  allegorical 7, 8, 12, 101
  animal satire 10, 21
  of the court 20–21
  direct 12, 24, 173–75
  estates satire 11, 136–37, 141
  general 12, 15–17, 173–74
  Horatian 3, 23
  indirect 2–3, 7–8, 11–12, 14, 16, 22, 27–31, 118, 126, 155, 165, 173–75
  Juvenalian 3, 4, 23, 26, 79, 82, 128, 136, 142
  Menippean 3, 7, 23, 136, 142
  pastoral 19, 20, 87
  satirical pretexts 23, 38–39, 46, 57, 64
  "satiric personality" 4, 22
  "social turn" in 23–24, 26–27, 173, 175–76
  taxonomies of 3, 22–24
Shakespeare, William 66, 85n.11, 87, 131n.8
  Rape of Lucrece, The 116n.21
  "Sonnet 130" 54, 94
  Venus and Adonis 9, 115–18
Sidney, Sir Philip 40, 51, 88, 97, 102, 109, 148, 156–57, 173–74
  Astrophil and Stella 93, 98–99
Silberman, Lauren 11–12, 19, 20
Singleton, Hugh 5, 6n.6, 33
Skelton, John 6, 8, 32, 34, 38–43, 45–46, 49, 152–55, 175
  Agenst Garnesche 43
  as "British Catullus" 42–44
  Collyn Cloute 38, 40, 49
  Garland of Laurel 42–43
  as "new poet" 42–43
  Replycacion, A 43
  Speke Parott 5, 152–56
Spenser, Edmund
  annuity 6, 67
  career 8, 31–32, 39, 122
  as Colin Clout 32, 34, 38–42, 45, 73, 82, 152, 155
  as idea 10, 64–65, 69, 70–71, 78, 80, 82, 86, 159, 175–76
  as Immerito 39, 41, 42
  as "New Poet" 8, 39, 41–42, 45–46, 152
  reputation of 2, 106, 119
  as target of satire 89
Spenser, Edmund, *Amoretti* 40, 93, 128
Spenser, Edmund, *Astrophel and The Doleful Lay of Clorinda* 49, 63, 98, 157
Spenser, Edmund, *Colin Clouts Come Home Againe* 36, 40, 47, 75, 109, 128, 148
Spenser, Edmund, *Complaints* 36, 64, 68, 79, 117, 128, 135, 153
  calling in 6, 9, 14, 25, 35, 67, 69, 108, 115, 127, 160
  Muiopotmos 2, 8, 35, 87, 92, 100–3, 105–10, 115–18, 126, 136, 139
  Prosopopoia; or, Mother Hubberds Tale 2, 4, 7, 9, 11, 13–14, 19–22, 30, 34–35, 38, 49, 68n.2, 76, 79, 85n.12, 108–9, 117, 123, 127–28, 131–32, 134, 136–39, 142, 147–48, 160, 174–75
  publication details 6, 14, 34–35
  Ruines of Rome: By Bellay 117
  Ruines of Time 19, 34, 40, 60, 122, 161
  Teares of the Muses 82, 85, 122
  Virgils Gnat 60, 136–39, 156
Spenser, Edmund, *Daphnaïda* 8, 31, 35, 39, 46–63, 75
Spenser, Edmund, *Epithalamion* 128, 168
Spenser, Edmund, *Faerie Queene* 29, 34, 51–53, 59, 62–63, 65, 67–68, 79, 106, 128, 148, 161

Book 1
  Archimago 52, 105
  Despair 52–53, 59
  Duessa 35, 60
  House of Pride episode 59
Book 2 118
  Acrasia 94
  blazon of Belphoebe 103, 114
  House of Alma 84
  Occasion 29, 53
  Palmer 52, 94
Book 3 118
  Argante 118
  Chrysogone 83
  Malbecco 59
Book 4
  Thames–Medway marriage 83, 125
Book 5
  Belge episode 29
  Burbon episode 29
  Radigund 2
  trial of Duessa 29, 36, 60, 150–51
Book 6
  Calidore's pursuit of the Blatant Beast 170
  Mount Acidale 84, 165–66
Dedicatory sonnets 89
James VI's reaction to 36, 150
satire in 6, 29, 35–36, 60, 64
Spenser, Edmund, *Prothalamion* 75, 122
Spenser, Edmund, *Shepheardes Calender* 8, 11–12, 19, 29, 31, 33–34, 36, 38–41, 44–46, 64, 68, 76, 127, 152, 155, 163–66
  "August" 75, 84, 165
  "December" 93
  "Februarie" 60
  "Januarye" 88
  "Julye" 90
  "June" 93
  "March" 8, 32, 35, 87–97, 99, 126
  "Maye" 14, 18, 76
  "November" 49
  "October" 166, 171
  publication 5–6, 33, 97
  "September" 18, 32–33, 60, 74–75
Spenser, Edmund, *Theatre for Worldlings, A* (translator) 82
Stanley, Ferdinando, Lord Strange 89, 96–97, 99
Stapleton, M.L. 88n.2, 89
Stubbs, John 5–6, 33, 126

Test, George A. 7, 23–24, 173
Topsell, Edward 16, 19, 21, 161
Tresham, Sir Thomas 6n.7, 14, 25, 30, 34, 108
Turner, William 18–19

Van den Berg, Kent T. 11, 20
Verstegan, Richard 21, 24–25, 115n.19, 132, 134

Wadsworth, James 71–72, 77
Walsingham, Frances, Countess of Essex 9, 87–88, 97–99
  incorrectly identified as Sidney's "Stella" 98
Wandering Jew, legend of 60–63
Webbe, William 33, 42, 67
Weiss, Adrian 35, 51n.9, 123
Wither, George 9, 145, 158–72
  Abuses, Stript and Whipt 9–10, 158–64, 167–72
  Satyre Dedicated to His Most Excellent Majestie, A 158–59, 163, 167–69, 170n.7, 172
  Shepheards Hunting, The 9–10, 158–59, 163, 168–72
  Shepherds Pipe, The see entry under Browne, William
  Wither's Motto 163
Woodhouse, Peter, *Democritus His Dreame* 146

EU authorised representative for GPSR:
Easy Access System Europe, Mustamäe tee 50,
10621 Tallinn, Estonia
gpsr.requests@easproject.com